Canadian Foreign Policy Since 1945: Middle Power or Satellite?

ISSUES IN CANADIAN HISTORY

General Editor
J. L. GRANATSTEIN

ISSUES
IN
CANADIAN
HISTORY

Canadian Foreign Policy Since 1945: Middle Power or Satellite?

Edited by
J. L. GRANATSTEIN

THE COPP CLARK PUBLISHING COMPANY
TORONTO

To Michael

THIRD EDITION 1973

ISBN 0-7730-3103-0

Contents

Introduction

Those who regard the course of Canadian foreign policy since 1945 with admiration usually characterize Canada as a middle power. Less satisfied observers demur and say that Canadian policy exhibits more of the characteristics of a satellite than of an independent nation. The United States, these critics claim, is the planet around which the Canadian moon revolves with heavenly regularity.

More significant even than the rights and wrongs of this situation is that today it is possible to argue on both sides with the backing of some historical evidence and with the support of commentators and a wide cross-section of journalistic accounts. This is new for Canada. In the past Canadian foreign policy was virtually non-existent, and aside from the small but influential Canadian Institute of International Affairs, there were few men interested in current policy outside the ranks of the Department of External Affairs.

The Second World War changed all this. Canada had entered the war from the "low dishonest decade" of the 1930's weakened by depression, isolationist by preference, and still caught up in the struggle to "free" itself from the tyranny of Downing Street's control of policy. Mackenzie King had shaped Canadian external policy, and like the master it was dull, cautious and safe. Nonetheless, for all his protestations about "Parliament will decide" and for all his genuine and deep-seated resentment against the British, King followed the British lead unhesitatingly in 1939 and brought Canada into the war. In some respects this was ironic. King had struggled to preserve his freedom of action and he had refused adamantly to be consulted by the British or to advise them lest this freedom be lost. But when the war started, King was "ready, aye ready," and Canada was as committed to the slaughter as if she had shared in the decisions and stratagems of the pre-war years.

Nonetheless the war provided certain opportunities for Canada to expand its role. Between the fall of France in June, 1940 and the entry of the Soviet Union into the war in June, 1941, Canada was the second ranking Allied power. And even after the complexion of the war had changed, Canada exercised a power disproportionate to her pre-war status. The nation was unquestionably one of the great producing states on the Allied side. Wheat, meat, iron and steel, minerals and munitions, trucks, tanks and planes—all poured from the factories and fields of Canada. The Canadian Army, with over 600,000 men in its ranks, was a formidable and well-equipped formation; the Royal Canadian Air Force was probably the third most powerful striking force in Allied ranks; and the Royal Canadian Navy was large enough by 1943 to take on the major share of convoy duties in the North Atlantic. Canada had emerged as a key nation, and this was reflected in the way Canada was treated. In some respects. The Combined Food Board granted Canada membership in its ranks, but the Combined Chiefs of Staff, the strategic directors of the war, paid no attention to Canadian representations.

In sum, Canada was necessary but not necessary enough. To Mackenzie King and to the status-conscious officers of External Affairs, this would not do, and in July, 1943 King ventured into the delicate area of policy in a major way. "The functional principle," King called it. In effect, King said that in areas where Canada and other middle-sized powers had the capability to play the part of a major power, they should be so treated.

King's statement was really the first enunciation of the "middle power" concept. Canada was not a great power, but it was more powerful than the Dominican Republic and Haiti, and it should be treated differently. This was only reasonable, but the doctrine did not win the hearing it deserved. The Great Powers continued to act like great powers usually do, settling major questions among themselves, and paying scant attention to the lesser states in the back rows.

Not even the creation of the United Nations had much effect on this attitude. The Great Powers granted themselves veto powers in the Security Council of the new organization, and it was only with some difficulty that the small and middle powers won the right to consultation on questions involving the use of their military forces to control aggression. But all this soon turned to mere words, as the Cold War began to destroy the war time alliance between the Soviet Union and the western allies. The unprincipled use of the veto paralyzed the United Nations, and the dangers from Soviet military force were all too apparent.

The problems were clear to Canada. The nation had put its security eggs in the UN basket in 1945, and the armed forces had been demobilized. Now the UN had proven a weak reed. It was at this stage that Canadians, first among the officers of the Department of External Affairs and later in the Liberal Cabinet of 1947 and 1948, began to consider an alliance for security among the nations of the North Atlantic. The process of negotiation was long but the North Atlantic Treaty was signed in April, 1949. An all too brief era of reliance on the UN had ended, and regional collective security became the new Canadian gospel. Under the terms of NATO, Canadian forces were sent to Europe in 1951, and for the first time Canadians were serving overseas in peace time. The Korean War, nominally under the aegis of the UN but in fact an American-run operation, also saw Canadians in some numbers serving abroad. Canadian isolationism was dead, or so it seemed.

The Soviet threat also impelled Canada into arrangements for the defence of North America. In August, 1940 Mackenzie King had signed the Ogdensburg Agreement with President Franklin Roosevelt, thus tying Canada into the American defensive system for the first time. After the war against Hitler, cooperation continued with staff talks, joint equipment development, and specialized training. The culmination of the trend to defence integration came in 1958 when the North American Air Defence Command Agreement, negotiated by the St. Laurent government, was agreed to by the Conservatives under Prime Minister John Diefenbaker. The air defence of North America was henceforth to be considered as a joint problem, administered by Americans and Canadians both. Later agreements found Canada committed to accepting nuclear-tipped air to air missiles for Canadian fighter aircraft and nuclear BOMARC surface to air missiles for defensive purposes.

Curiously, by the time that NORAD was signed, Canada had found a new metier—peacekeeping. Canadians had participated in a minor way in the truce supervision efforts of the UN in Palestine and Kashmir, and Canada was one of three nations selected by the Geneva Conference of 1954 to police the truce in the three successor states to French Indochina. But this had been done without the glare of publicity, and it was not until the Suez Crisis of 1956 that peacekeeping captured the popular imagination.

Lester Pearson, then Secretary of State for External Affairs, was the key figure. In Ottawa he persuaded his Cabinet colleagues to give him something approaching a free hand, and at the UN in New York he was amazingly successful in securing great power agreement for his concept of a peacekeeping force to move into the battle area of Suez. By putting UN forces between the British, French and Israeli invaders and the Egyptians, Pearson hoped to win time for a permanent settlement to be reached. His plan was not successful, and no settlement was found. Peace was secured, however, for more than a decade. For Pearson, the Suez affair brought a Nobel Prize for Peace and the leadership of the Liberal Party as rewards. For Canadians generally, the crisis brought the attention and praise of the world, and thereafter peacekeeping became one of the key planks in Canadian policy.

For the next decade, Canada played a leading part in UN peacekeeping. Operations in Lebanon, the Congo, Yemen, New Guinea, Cyprus and India-Pakistan found Canadian servicemen in key positions. And always there was popular support in Canada—at least until the Cyprus affair, the expulsion of UNEF by President Nasser of Egypt in 1967, and the very real doubts as to whether Canada should participate in the new International Commission of Control and Supervision designed to cover the American withdrawal from Vietnam in 1973.

The concern about peacekeeping paralleled a rise in dissatisfaction with the formal alliances with which Canada was involved. NATO was an obsolete alliance, some Canadians claimed, and by remaining in it Canada was demonstrating her subservience to American interests, wasting defence dollars, and increasing the drain of Canadian money overseas. NORAD was even worse. By 1962 the United States was vigorously pressing Canada to take the nuclear weapons she had earlier agreed to receive, but the Diefenbaker government was dubious. In the election of 1963, the American Embassy in Ottawa briefed reporters on the rights and wrongs of the nuclear arms issue and there were partisan suggestions that other kinds of American aid were given the Liberals in the course of the election campaign. Certainly when the Pearson Liberals won the election, the BOMARC missiles were equipped with nuclear warheads, as were the Canadian aircraft in Canada and Europe. But, charged the critics, NORAD was no longer necessary in the day of the ICBM. The BOMARCS were obsolete.

The defenders of the alliance position, however, claimed all through the 1960s and into the 1970s that both NATO and NORAD were vital. The Russians were still potential aggressors in Europe, although the growing detente between east and west made this claim harder to support. And even if no one believed any longer in a Soviet bomber attack on North America, NORAD was still useful as a radar net, and as an excuse to keep the air element of the Canadian Forces flying. More important to the defenders of the Government's posture was the belief that Canadian and American interests were basically the same and that Canada should follow the lead of its most important ally.

This was, of course, the fundamental question. Were Canadian and American interests the same? There were many economic and resource conflicts between the two countries, and the growing nationalist movement in Canada kept opinion focussed on these differences. But were there any real options for a small country in a world of ICBMs, MIRV, and ABMs? Was there any possibility that Canada could develop a truly independent foreign policy that served distinct national needs? There were some tentative signs that the Department of External Affairs was interested in moving in this direction, but at the beginning of the second Trudeau government in late 1972 these stirrings were more rhetorical than actual. A beginning had been made, however, and that was more than most critics a few years earlier believed possible.

Clash of Opinion

There are, accordingly, reasons firmly based upon a consideration of Canadian national interests which lead to the conclusion that Canada must make some more than token contribution to Western defence. . . . she must be willing to enter into systems of collective security. . . . Canada's natural role is to form part of the strategic reserve of the Free World, and it is only in this role that she can make a significant contribution.

R. J. Sutherland

Clear-cut non-alliance objectives would thus be in the Canadian national interest in two senses: they would be our only possible contribution to the kind of world in which alone it is possible for a country such as ours to exist, and they would in themselves strengthen our national experiment by extending to our foreign policy the principles of tolerance, compromise and equality which we endeavour to establish at home.

Kenneth McNaught

Canada played an active and strategic part in the creation of NATO in 1949. . . . For a generation Canadian external policy had been wracked by a conflict between the advocates of continental and trans-Atlantic attachments. Now leaders of all parties, having cast off the tradition of Canadian helplessness, saw in the military alliance of Britain and France with the United States the opportunity to be part of a team in which Canada's international interests and its domestic emotions could both be satisfied.

John Holmes

. . . one ends with mingled doubt and hope that political leaders in Canada and the United States will be able to work as closely and effectively together . . . as the people of both countries wish them to. . . . If it is to be achieved, Americans must not take Canadians for granted. But something more is needed. Canadians must not take Americans for granted, either.

Dean Acheson

If, however, an act of aggression is committed against any of us, it will constitute an aggression against all the nations that have signed the pact. Then each will be bound on its national honour, to take in accordance with its own constitutional practice, such measures as the nation itself, its parliament and its government, consider best calculated to fulfil the obligations it has assumed in order to repel the aggression and restore peace.

Louis St. Laurent

The frequently expressed view . . . that Canada should maintain her silence on sensitive issues lest she inflame the emotions of the calculating policy-makers at the Department of State is almost certainly invalid.

Denis Stairs

Many problems between our two governments are susceptible of solution only through the quiet, private and patient ex-

5

amination of facts in the search for accommodation. It should be regarded as incumbent on both parties during this time-consuming process to avoid, so far as possible, the adoption of public positions which can contribute unnecessarily to public division and difference.

Canada and the United States
Principles for Partnership

Canada is physically joined to the United States just like the Siamese twins. If one of the twins gets hurt the other one suffers. It is just as impossible to separate the defence of Canada from that of the United States as it would be to separate the Siamese twins and expect them to survive.

Charles Foulkes

. . . the danger of anything deserving the name retaliation is minimal. "Pressure," yes; "retaliation," no.

A. F. W. Plumptre

. . . I do recall very well the use of the word "retaliation" on many occasions, within my own party and in Parliament, while I was a Liberal MP. It was used chiefly in the context of Canadian-American relations. . . .

Pauline Jewett

As a leading middle power, with a well-known record of support for United Nations peace-keeping operations in widely spread theatres, Canada is in a unique position to take the initiative. It is prepared to do so.

L. B. Pearson

If we are going to send off our best diplomats and our best soldiers and our best equipment on various peace-keeping ventures, we have got to bear in mind the kind of price that we are going to have to pay domestically. . . . For political reasons alone we should reassess our easy propositions about peace-keeping. . . .

Donald Gordon

Vive Montréal, vive le Québec, vive le Québec libre, vive le Canada français, vive la France!

Charles de Gaulle

Why draw the conclusion that France is pursuing here, under the veil of France-Quebec cooperation, the promotion of separatism or the undermining of the American Anglo-Saxon empire, and making more difficult the already difficult goal of world peace? Why not admit that Franco-Quebec cooperation is first and foremost a fact of life . . . ?

Le Devoir

The two great problems of the last third of the twentieth century are the economic development of poor countries and the relations between China and the rest of the world. . . . Canada can by its actions and its example make a substantial contribution to the solution of these two problems. . . .

Escott Reid

. . . I would hope that ten years from now this nation would be without the encumbrance of any nuclear association. . . . That our commitment to foreign aid would be maximum, and our obligations to military alliances and a military establishment would be minimal.

Dalton Camp

Part I

Canadian Foreign Policy Before 1945

For all practical purposes the foreign policy of Canada from the 1920s to 1945 was the policy of Mackenzie King. Unquestionably one of the nation's greatest prime ministers, King dominated Canada and Canadian politics for three decades, imposing his particular and peculiar stamp on the nation's affairs. Nowhere was this brand more evident than in foreign policy.

King had watched horrified while Canada tore itself apart in 1917, and he had resolved as Prime Minister never to permit such a cleavage to occur again. His whole policy was centered on this unshakeable rock, and it was for this reason that he deliberately made external policy as bland as milk in the 1920s and 1930s. His guideline was "no commitments," and his sacred words were that "Parliament would decide." If there were no commitments, King reasoned, then Parliament would never have to decide. And if there were no decisions, there would be no wars, and hence no internal difficulties between French Canadians and English Canadians. As late as March 30, 1939, after the Nazis had gobbled up Czechoslovakia, the Prime Minister could tell Parliament that his policy was unchanged. There was no reason, he stated, for Canada to go forth once a generation to rescue Europe from itself.

Mackenzie King was not entirely incorrect in his appraisal of this "nightmare and sheer madness," but when Britain went to war a bare five months later Canada was only one week behind. So much for the policy of no commitments. It had led only to Canada's being committed to war without any participation in the diplomatic efforts to prevent war. Unlike many Canadian politicians, however, King was capable of learning from his mistakes, and he soon came to recognize the folly of isolationism. As the war progressed, he first solidified Canada's relations with the United States, reaching an agreement in August, 1940 with President Franklin Roosevelt. The Ogdensburg Agreement associated the still neutral United States with a belligerent Commonwealth—an important fact in itself—and proclaimed that the defence of North America was a permanent and common problem for the Republic and the Dominion. This was a step away from isolationism of enormous significance for the future, and a fulfilment of King's life-long desire to foster Canadian-American relations.

After the United States entered the war in December, 1941, however, King soon found that Canada had hardly any say about the direction of the war. Canada was supplying men and munitions in huge quantities, but the Dominion was having precious little to say about their ultimate disposition. This situation soon began to produce a feeling of resentment that had to be repressed for the sake of Allied solidarity. In the prewar years resentment would have remained the solitary product of the Prime Minister's hurt pride. Wartime Canada was aggressive and cocky, however, and the result of King's *hubris* was his enunciation of the functional principle in 1943. King said in essence that where Canada had the muscle it was going to demand the right to be heard.

The Prime Minister's speech marked Canada's coming of age, and it would be pleasant to record that the Great Powers leaped smartly to attention at the word from Ottawa. Unfortunately this was not to be the case. Worse yet from King's point of view, the British even chose the beginning of 1944 as the time to resurrect the old doctrine of Imperial unity. Lord Halifax, the British Ambassador to Washington, was the culprit. In a speech that was delivered in Tory Toronto—without even the courtesy of clearance from Ottawa—Halifax called for the creation of a centralized empire so that Britain could compete in a post-war world with the "Titans"—Russia, China, and the United States.

Halifax's address was in the best traditions of power politics, but it was more than Mackenzie King could stomach. In his diary he raged against the British, seeing them in deep plots with the Canadian Tories. But King need not have feared. Very few Canadians rose to the bait, and even in Toronto there was scant support for Halifax's vision of the postwar Empire. Mackenzie King had shaped his nation's policy well. The war had brought an awareness of strength, a feeling of youthful power, and a desire to test out a more independent policy. While still a member of the Commonwealth, an ally of the United States, and a charter member of the United Nations Organization, Canada after 1945 was on its own.

House of Commons *Debates*, March 30, 1939, pp. 2418-9.

Isolationism 1939

[MR. MACKENZIE KING]: . . . Canada's attitude as to automatic commitments involving possible or actual participation in war has been asserted time and again both in this parliament and at Geneva. Whether it has been in reference to the application of sanctions under Article 16 of the covenant of the league or to participation in wars apart altogether from the league, Canada's position has been the same, namely, that in either case the approval of parliament will be required.

At the seventeenth session of the Assembly of the League of Nations, in September, 1936, in the presence of British ministers and representatives of other nations of the British commonwealth, and of other member countries of the league, I stated the position as I then understood it, very clearly. No exception so far as I am aware was taken at Geneva, at the time, to that statement nor has exception been taken to it since, by any political party at Ottawa, though the statement of Canada's position as therein set forth has been drawn to the attention of parliament at each subsequent session.

I feel I cannot do better at this time than to quote once more essential paragraphs of the statement making clear that they define, as accurately as I believe it is possible to define it, the position of the present government in the matter of Canada's participation in war whether it arises out of our membership in the league of nations or our membership in the British commonwealth of nations.

The paragraphs I regard as pertinent are the following:

There is another factor which inevitably influences Canadian opinion on many league policies, and particularly on the question of automatic obligations to the use of force in international disputes. I have in mind our experience as a member of the British commonwealth of nations. The nations of the British commonwealth are held together by ties of friendship, by similar political institutions, and by common attachment to democratic ideals, rather than by commitments to join together in war. The Canadian parliament reserves to itself the right to declare, in the light of the circumstances existing at the time, to what extent, if at all, Canada will participate in conflicts in which other members of the commonwealth may be engaged.

There is a general unwillingness of peoples to incur obligations which they realize they may not be able in time of crisis to fulfil, obligations to use force and to use it at any place, any time, in circumstances unforeseen, and in disputes over whose origin or whose development they have had little or no control. This difficulty of automatic intervention increases rather than decreases when conflicts tend to become struggles between classes, between economic systems, between social philosophies and, in some instances between religious faiths, as well as between states.

The Canadian House of Commons by unanimous resolution has made the adoption of undertakings to apply either military or economic sanctions subject to the approval of parliament.

What I have said and quoted does not mean that in no circumstances would the Canadian people be prepared to share in action against an aggressor; there have been no absolute commitments either for or against participation in war or other forms of force. It does mean that any decision on the part of Canada to participate in war will have to be taken by the parliament or people of Canada in the light of all existing circumstances; circumstances of the day as they exist in Canada, as well as in the areas involved.

I cannot accept the view which is being urged in some quarters to-day, that regardless of what government or party may be in office, regardless of what its policy may be, regardless of what the issue itself may come to be, this country should say here and now that Canada is prepared to support whatever may be proposed by the government at Westminster.

The international situation changes from year to year, sometimes from week to week; governments change, their personnel changes, policies change. Absolute statements of policy, absolute undertakings to follow other governments, whatever the situation, are out of the question. At the same time the decisions that would be made by our government and parliament, like those of other governments and other parliaments, are not incalculable, not matters of chance and whim. Much of course would depend on the special circumstances of the day. But equally important in determining our attitude are certain permanent factors of interest, of sentiment, of opinion, which set the limits within [which] any feasible and united policy must be determined.

May I refer to some of these known, in fact, obvious factors.

The first factor is the one that is present and dominant in the policy of every other country, from Britain and Sweden to Argentina and the United States. I mean the existence of a national feeling and the assumption that first place will be given to the interests, immediate, or long range, of the country itself. . . .

In many, but certainly not in all cases, this growth of national feeling has strengthened the desire for a policy which its defenders call minding one's own business and which its critics call isolationism. Assuming, it is urged, that Canadians like other people will put their own interests first, what do our interests demand, what amount of knight errantry abroad do our resources permit? Canada, it is contended is not a country of unlimited powers; it has not the capacity to stand indefinite strains. We have tremendous tasks to do at home, in housing the people, in caring for the aged and helpless, in relieving drought and unemployment, in building roads, in meeting our heavy burden of debt, in making provision for Canada's defence, and in bringing our standards of living and civilization to the levels our knowledge now makes possible. There is no great margin of realizable wealth for this purpose; we must, to a greater or less extent, choose between keeping our own house in order, and trying to save Europe and Asia. The idea that every twenty years this country should automatically and as a matter of course take part in a war overseas for democracy or self-determination of other small nations, that a country which has all it can do to run itself should feel called upon to save, periodically, a continent that cannot run itself, and to these ends risk the lives of its people, risk bankruptcy and political disunion, seems to many a nightmare and sheer madness.

J. S. B. Pemberton, ed., "Ogdensburg, Hyde Park—and After," *Behind the Headlines* (April, 1941), p. 3.

North American Alliance

The Ogdensburg Agreement,

August 17, 1940

On August 17, 1940, Mr. Mackenzie King arrived at Ogdensburg, N.Y., to meet President Roosevelt. He had gone at the President's invitation to discuss "mutual problems of defence in relation to the safety of Canada and the United States". On the next day the following joint statement was issued:

> "The Prime Minister and the President have discussed the mutual problems of defence in relation to the safety of Canada and the United States.
>
> "It has been agreed that a permanent joint board on defence shall be set up at once by the two countries.
>
> "This permanent joint board on defence shall commence immediate studies relating to sea, land and air problems including personnel and material.
>
> "It will consider in the broad sense the defence of the north half of the western hemisphere.
>
> "The permanent joint board on defence will consist of four or five members from each country, most of them from the services. It will meet shortly."

House of Commons *Debates*, July 9, 1943, p. 4558.

The Functional Principle

of Representation

[MR. MACKENZIE KING]: ... It is too early for me to attempt even a shadowy outline of the form of the international settlement, political and economic, which may follow the ending of hostilities. It may be useful, however, to say a word about one of its aspects. The strong bonds which have linked the united nations into a working model of cooperation must be strengthened and developed for even greater use in the years of peace. It is perhaps an axiom of war that during actual hostilities methods must be improvised, secrecy must be observed, attention must be concentrated on victory. The time is approaching, however, when even before victory is won the concept of the united nations will have to be embodied in some form of inter-national organization. On the one hand, authority in international affairs must not be concentrated exclusively in the largest powers. On the other, authority cannot be divided equally among all the thirty or more sovereign states that comprise the united nations, or all effective authority will disappear. A number of new international institutions are likely to be set up as a result of the war. In the view of the government, effective representations on these bodies should neither be restricted to the largest states nor necessarily extended to all states. Representation should be determined on a functional basis which will admit to full membership those countries, large or small, which have the greatest contribution to make to the particular object in question. In the world there are over sixty sovereign states. If they all have a nominally equal voice in international decisions, no effective decisions are likely to be taken. Some compromise must be found between the theoretical equality of states and the practical necessity of limiting representation on international bodies to workable number. That compromise can be discovered, especially in economic matters, by the adoption of the functional principle of representation. That principle, in turn, is likely to find many new expressions in the gigantic task of liberation, restoration and reconstruction.

Lord Halifax's Speech in Toronto, January 24, 1944, *in* Nicholas Mansergh, *Documents and Speeches on British Commonwealth Affairs, 1931-1952*, Vol. I (London: Oxford University Press, 1953), pp. 576-9. Reprinted by permission of Oxford University Press.

A Centralized Empire?

. . . between the Durham Report and the Statute of Westminster, the whole trend of development in the Dominions was towards equality of status. But there was hardly an equivalent effort towards securing what I would call equality of function. By that I mean that while the Statute of Westminster assured to each and every Dominion complete self-government, it perforce left unsolved the more obstinate problems arising in the fields of foreign policy and defence. . . .

But when this has been said, it remains a fact that, much as the unity of the commonwealth owed to a common Head and a common thought upon the things that matter most, it found little expression in outward form.

The right of each member to determine its own external affairs may mean a gain or it may mean a loss. It is plainly a loss if, with our essential unity of ideal, the responsibility for action which represents that unity is not visibly shared by all. It is an immeasurable gain if on vital issues we can achieve a common foreign policy expressed not by a single voice but by the unison of many.

So, too, in the field of defense, while there must be individual responsibility, there must also be a unity of policy. . . .

I speak frankly, as I know you would have me speak. On 3 September 1939, the Dominions were faced with a dilemma of which the whole world was aware. Either they must confirm a policy which they had had only partial share in framing, or they must stand aside and see the unity of the Commonwealth broken, perhaps fatally and for ever. It did not take them long to choose, and with one exception they chose war.

But the dilemma was there, and having occurred twice in twenty-five years, it may occur again. That is the point at which equality of function lags behind equality of status. The Dominions are free —absolutely free—to choose their path; but every time there is a crisis in international affairs, they are faced with the same inexorable dilemma from which there is no escape.

What then is the solution? Well, there are, broadly speaking, two roads which the Dominions may take. There is the road of national isolation. They can choose in peace, and, after full deliberation, the course that they rejected in 1939. They can say—and who should attempt to gainsay them?—that their foreign policy will be unconcerned with any but their own immediate national interests; that it will not reflect an underlying unity of ideal or strive towards unity in action; that they will neither defend others, nor expect others to defend them. . . .

But for most of us there is a stronger and more compelling argument towards choosing the second road. We believe that the British Empire has proved, not once or twice but many times, a powerful and beneficent world-force. We believe that without it the cause we uphold today would have been lost long ago; and therefore that the remedy for the difficulties which I have tried to describe is not that we and you should draw apart, but that we should try to fortify our partnership.

By that I do not mean that we should attempt to retrace our steps along the path that led from the Durham Report to the Statute of Westminster. To do so would be to run counter to the whole course of development in the Commonwealth. But what is, I believe, both desirable and necessary is that in all the common fields—Foreign Policy, Defense, Economic Affairs, Colonial Questions, and Communications—we should leave nothing undone to bring our people into closer unity of thought and action.

It may be that we shall find it desirable to maintain and extend our present wartime procedure of planning, and consultation, which itself adapted and extended the methods we practised in time of peace. The question admits of no easy answer. It should be constantly in our minds, and I have no doubt that it will be among the first problems to be considered, whenever the responsible ministers of the Crown from every part of the Commonwealth are able once more to meet together. . . .

. . . Today we begin to look beyond the war to the reordering of the world which must follow. We see three great Powers, the United States, Russia and China, great in numbers, areas, and natural resources. Side by side with them is the United Kingdom, with a population of less than 50,000,000, with a territory which could easily be contained in one of the larger States of the American Union, and with natural resources which, though great in proportion to her size, are by themselves scarcely comparable with those of her companions.

In the company of these Titans, Britain, apart from the rest of the Commonwealth and Empire, could hardly claim equal partnership. It is none the less likely that, when the war is ended, Western Europe, as never before, will look to her for leadership and guidance. She has been the one inviolate fortress of freedom in the West. Once again her people have shown their ancient virtue. They have disclosed unsuspected reserves of strength. Much will be asked of them.

Yet, while they will assuredly emerge from this war with a new self-confidence and feel rightly proud of their achievement, they will certainly be poorer. They will have drawn heavily upon their manpower and resources. They will have spent their accumulated capital without stint. If, in the future, Britain is to play her part without assuming burdens greater than she can support, she must have with her in peace the same strength that has sustained her in this war. Not Great Britain only, but the British Commonwealth and Empire must be the fourth power in that group upon which, under Providence, the peace of the world will henceforth depend. There, summed up in a sentence, is the need as I see it.

J. W. Pickersgill, *The Mackenzie King Record*, Vol. I: *1939-44* (Toronto: University of Toronto Press, 1960), 636-41. Reprinted by permission of the University of Toronto Press and the Literary Executors of Mackenzie King.

No Centralized Empire!

The new post-war programme was threatened with eclipse and the whole character of the opening of the Parliamentary session seemed about to change as a consequence of a speech given by Lord Halifax, the British Ambassador to the United States, in Toronto. On January 24, when Mackenzie King came out of the Cabinet, one of his secretaries told him that "Halifax was making a perfectly terrible speech in Toronto." . . .

The next morning (January 25), when he "read something of what Lord Halifax had said at Toronto last night," Mackenzie King "was simply dumbfounded. It seemed such a complete bolt out of the blue, like a conspiracy on the part of Imperialists to win their own victory in the middle of the war. I could not but feel that Halifax's work was all part of a plan which had been worked out with Churchill to take advantage of the war to try and bring about this development of centralization, of makings of policies in London, etc. As Englishmen, of course, they seek to recover for Britain and the United Kingdom and the Empire the prestige which they are losing as a nation. In a moment, I saw that again it has fallen to my lot to have to make the most difficult of all the fights. This perpetual struggle to save the Empire despite all that Tories' policies will do—by fighting the Tories, save the British Empire from its dismemberment through their own policies. There is nothing truer than that, from the days of Lord North to the present, English Tories have learned nothing." He felt that Halifax's speech "marks the beginning of the real political campaign of this year. I should not complain about what Halifax has done, for he has handed me, as someone said in Council this afternoon, an issue which ensures or should ensure the return of the Liberal party just as completely as Lord Byng, when he refused to grant a dissolution. I am perfectly sure that Canada will not tolerate any centralized Imperialism on foreign policy." As a precaution he telephoned Leighton McCarthy at the Canadian Embassy in Washington to find out if he had seen Halifax's speech and learned that "Halifax never mentioned a line of what he had in his mind or intended to say." He later told the Cabinet "I had never been more surprised. That it was what I had said many times would happen as soon as the war was over. I had not thought it would happen while it was on. I found all Members of Government thoroughly incensed. . . . I did not discuss the matter at length but said I would speak in Parliament on Monday. . . . There was mention that I would have to speak as Coldwell* had taken a very strong stand [in the press], and it would not do to let him steal our whole position."

*Leader of the Cooperative Commonwealth Federation.

Later in the day Mackenzie King told the Governor-General that, "if it were not for the war, I would this evening be asking him for a dissolution of Parliament to appeal to the people on this issue. I then said I could not understand Halifax having never said a word to me about what he intended to say, and coming to Canada to make a speech which raised the most controversial issue we had, with the possible exception of conscription. . . . However I said I would have to speak in Parliament on Monday, but would be as careful as I could; to avoid anything that would prejudice a position of the kind. I said if Hitler himself wanted to divide the Empire—get one part against the other, he could not have chosen a more effective way, or a better instrument. I said that politically, as far as I was concerned, I had no doubt it would help to defeat the Tories. He could see how Coldwell had spoken, and also that Bracken* did not wish to touch the question."

The next day (January 26) Mackenzie King felt "more relieved about Halifax's speech in that I had not had to make any pronouncement yesterday and had time to consider how it may best be dealt with in Parliament. Feel that Halifax has done the damage. I must seek to repair it so far as its effect on the war effort is concerned. Do what I can in what I say not to widen the division between different parts of the Empire which his provocative speech, made at this time, has already occasioned, but make a common statement that will make my own position clear and leave matters at that for the present." During the day, he saw Malcolm MacDonald** who had just returned from

*Leader of the Progressive Conservative party.

**British High Commissioner to Canada.

Britain and told him he "had never had a blow like it in my life, and could not understand with all I had done to help in this war, how Halifax could have made the speech he did, without ever consulting me about it either directly or through our Ambassador at Washington. . . . I said to him the extraordinary thing was that the speech seems to have been circulated well in advance. Was in full in *The Times*. Had been sent to Conservative papers here last week, but that no copy had come to me nor to any Members of the Government or to our legation at Washington, or any officials in External Affairs." He noted that "Malcolm felt sure Halifax would not have done anything of the kind intentionally so far as I was concerned. That he had the highest regard for me; affection as well, and what he had said about me at Toronto in the beginning of his speech about what I had done for the war, my leadership, etc., was evidence of it. That he could not have had any desire to work an injury politically. I, of course, could not accuse him of that, but as I said to Malcolm, it looked to me as if the whole business was part of a Tory attitude of mind, feeling they must force their views regardless of consequences to others." Mackenzie King also "told Malcolm I was speaking only personally to him. I had thought of sending a cable to Churchill to say that Halifax's speech had been most embarrassing to the Government, but thought it well to just keep quiet and say nothing. That I was determined not to make any situation more difficult while the war was on, but that once again I had had to allow myself to be put in a false position in appearing either to let a great issue of the kind pass and go into the hands of Coldwell and others, to the discrimination of my own party, or be placed in the position of helping to divide the Empire, working up separation, etc., while the war was still on. It was all very trying, but I would seek above all else to keep the war in mind."

On January 27, Mackenzie King "was immensely relieved in seeing in the evening paper that Attlee today had said in the British House that the Government felt no useful purpose would be served by a debate on Empire policy at the present time. That is precisely the view I have taken all along with respect to Prime Ministers' Conferences, Imperial Conferences, and the like. Our foreign policy is the winning of the war. We had better leave all controversial questions to the side until the war is won." Mackenzie King added that was the line he had pretty well decided to take in the House on Monday, the 31st. On January 29, two days after Parliament opened, he received from Malcolm Macdonald "a communication from Halifax regretting that he should have been causing me embarrassment, and pointing out how unconscious he had been that his speech would cause any concern. Malcolm seemed most anxious to know how far I would be going on Monday. I told him I intended to try to avoid controversy. To say as little about the speech as possible beyond making it clear that I favoured consultation, co-operation and co-ordination of policies within the Empire for the same reason that I favoured it among nations, but not for the purpose of having the British Empire line up against the rest of the world. That I would dwell on the perspective in keeping till after the war for discussion, matters related to constitutional changes."

Halifax's speech was Mackenzie King's main concern when he spoke in Parliament on the Address in Reply to the Speech from the Throne on January 31. . . .

In his speech, Mackenzie King had stated that "the question that has come very much to the fore in the last few days is whether there is to be a common policy for all parts of the Empire or Commonwealth on foreign relations, defence and other matters—a single or common policy as distinct from each nation of the British Commonwealth having its own policy on foreign affairs, on defence and on other matters." After stating his belief that there could not be "too close consultation and co-operation," he gave a fairly lengthy description of all the existing methods of consultation with their historical background. He next pointed out the difficulty of making decisions at an Imperial Conference in London where the Prime Ministers of the overseas members of the Commonwealth were necessarily separated from many of their colleagues and advisers, and the advantages of achieving co-operation between cabinets through existing means without attempting centralization of Imperial institutions. In reply to a question, Mackenzie King emphasized the fact that Halifax had spoken for himself and not for the Government of the United Kingdom. He concluded by reading a carefully worded statement which took direct issue with the conception of a world dominated by four great powers and urged that all peace-loving nations, great and small, should join together, after the war, to preserve the peace. He spoke throughout with great moderation and restraint. . . .

The next day (February 2) Mackenzie King concluded his diary entry with these words: "I begin . . . to see more clearly that Monday's speech may prove to be one of the most significant I have made in my life. It opens up the great broad division between centralized and decentralized organization, not only of Empire activities but the larger question of power politics by a few great nations leading inevitably to war against the conception of international world co-operation of nations great and small. In other words, a future world organization. Matter of preserving peace and preventing war. The largest subject that it is possible to deal with in politics."

Part II

Overviews of Canadian Foreign Policy Since 1945

The best place to begin an examination of Canada's post-war foreign policy is to permit several experts to present their positions. By sketching out their broad interpretations of Canada's record and importance they can delineate for us the boundaries of the discussion. What is the worth of the Canadian contribution since the Second World War? Has Canada demonstrated independence? or lost it? What are the options before us? These are the questions that are raised here.

Certainly the suggested answers differ. The first selection is by R. J. Sutherland, who until his death was the chief of the Operations Research Group of the Defence Research Board in Ottawa. Sutherland brought a tough, disciplined mind to bear on the problems facing Canada, and he carefully weighed reality and dream in his brilliant article. The options were few to Sutherland, and Canada had only scant room for manoeuvre. This view is rejected by Kenneth McNaught, a Professor of History at the University of Toronto and the author of the best biography of J. S. Woodsworth, the first leader of the C.C.F. McNaught feels that Canada has gone from colonial status directly to satellite without any intervening period of independence. Canadian policy, he states, is virtually indistinguishable from American, and this is tragic. The only course that could redeem Canadian independence is to opt out of alliance politics and find new roles.

McNaught's stand is rejected by John Holmes. Now the Director-General of the Canadian Institute of International Affairs, Holmes was a very senior officer in the Department of External Affairs and one of the makers of Canadian foreign policy since 1945. While not entirely satisfied with everything that Canada has done (and not done), Holmes continues to feel that on balance the record is a creditable one. Not so Dean

Acheson, the United States Secretary of State during the Truman administration. To Acheson, a perceptive and hard-hitting critic, Canada has been a moralizing and preachy neighbour readier with unasked advice than with aid. To read his article is a chastening experience, and perhaps it is well to remember that however great Canada's problems may seem they are rather insignificant when compared with those of the United States. And thank God for that.

R. J. Sutherland, "Canada's Long Term Strategic Situation," *International Journal*, XVII (Summer, 1962), pp. 199-223. Reprinted by permission of The Canadian Institute of International Affairs.

A Defence Strategist Examines the Realities

Since the end of Hitler's war the world has changed almost beyond recognition. The increasing power of weaponry has played a conspicuous role, but developments of a political nature have been equally revolutionary, and are, in the long run, almost certainly more important. This sequence of rapid and dramatic change has led to two results: traditional conceptions of national security and national defence have been called into question, but visibility has been reduced. Nevertheless, security and the protection of vital national interests remain for every nation a constant preoccupation of policy. It is also true that the very concept of national security implies a consistency of purpose and major policy extending over decades and even generations.

The search for stable foundations of policy in the face of drastic and revolutionary change poses a problem of almost excruciating difficulty for all nations, including the two super-powers. We should not be surprised that Canadians find these problems intractable and in some respects insoluble. However, in our case there is a special consideration. Canada has no particular tradition of strategic calculation. Such tradition as we possess seems to be that strategy is a suitable diversion for retired generals who need not be taken very seriously. Yet the increasing attention which is being given to the problems of security and survival by Canadians of the most diverse opinions and backgrounds shows that we too are caught up in the fortunes of a dynamic and dangerous world. We have discovered, as Leon Trotsky once observed, that anyone who desires a quiet life should not have been born in the twentieth century. . . .

To borrow a term from mathematics, there are certain invariants of Canadian strategy. It is worth examining these rather carefully because they shed a great deal of light upon the foundations of Canada's national existence and her place in the world community. They determine, to some very considerable extent, the agenda of Canadian national policy—that is, those major questions with regard to which there is some genuine choice. And they also reveal important areas where there is no choice, however much we as Canadians might like to believe that there is.

Geography

The most important of these invariants is geography. It is a safe prediction that at the end of this century, Canada will occupy the north half of the North American continent and the United States will occupy the south half. This geographical fact has a vitally important strategic consequence. It means that the United States is bound to defend Canada from external aggression almost regardless of whether or not Canadians wish to be defended. We may call this the involuntary American guarantee. For as far ahead as one can possibly foresee, this will be the central fact of Canadian strategy and the basis of Canada's external security.

The involuntary U.S. guarantee to Canada is subject to certain conditions. In 1938, speaking of Canada's relationship with the United States, Prime Minister Mackenzie King had this to say:

We, too, as a good friendly neighbour, have our responsibilities. One of them is to see that our country is made as immune from possible invasion as we can reasonably be expected to make it, and, that should the occasion ever arise, enemy forces should not be able to make their way, either by land, sea or air, to the United States across Canadian territory.

These are not idle words. What Mackenzie King said was that Canada must not become through military weakness or otherwise a direct threat to American security. If this were to happen, Canada's right to existence as an independent nation would be placed in jeopardy.

When Mackenzie King made this statement, the threat of military operations against the United States via Canadian territory was rather far-fetched. However, the principle was not novel even in 1938. One need only think back to the part played by Canada in the abrogation of the Anglo-Japanese Alliance in 1921. But the principle goes back even further to the Rush-Bagot Treaty in 1817 and the Monroe Doctrine of 1823. One may suggest that in combination these amounted to an outline non-aggression treaty between the United States and Great Britain in right of her American possessions. In the course of almost a century the terms of this treaty were worked out in detail to produce the famous undefended frontier. Mackenzie King was therefore drawing attention to a basic condition of Canada's national existence. If this condition had not been understood and adhered to in the past,

there would be, very probably, no British North America and no Canada.

In the final analysis, a Great Power will take whatever action it finds necessary to the maintenance of its security. It must do this or cease to be a Great Power, and the United States is no exception. However, at least for the past half century, relations between Canada and the United States have never approached this brutal basis. It is difficult to believe that they ever will. This is owing to the fundamental community of interests between the two nations. If the United States is bound to defend Canada, it is also true that Canada can never, consistent with her own interests, ignore the requirements of American security; because, in the final analysis, the security of the United States is the security of Canada.

Economic Strength

Now let us turn to economic strength and the raw materials of national power. Canadians are prone to measure themselves against the United States, and by this standard Canada is a rather minor country. By any other standard she is a very powerful nation. The best index of national potential is probably a combination of Gross National Product and technological competence. This is a good measure of the ability of a nation to produce modern military hardware—and military power is still the gold coin of diplomacy. It is equally a good index of a nation's ability to produce the silver coin of diplomacy: to participate in aid programmes, to supply technical assistance, and— most important of all—to engage in old-fashioned international trade. According to these criteria, Canada is somewhere between the seventh and ninth most powerful nation in the world today. This in a field of about 130 political entities which can be regarded as sovereign, and the number is going up from day to day.

In 1945, Canada was, very probably, the fourth most powerful nation in the world. She had a sizable military establishment backed up by a fully intact economy. She was one of four nations which possessed an on-going programme of military research and development, and she had played a subordinate but significant role in the development of the atomic bomb. In the immediate post-war period, Canada's international prestige owed much to the brilliance of her diplomats, but it may be well to remember that in those years Canadian diplomacy could draw upon reserves accumulated during the Second World War. These were in the hardest kind of diplomatic currency— demonstrated military power.

By the year 2000, it is likely that Canada will have slipped a few places as more populous nations gain mastery over modern technology. Nevertheless, Canada will still be at the high end of the international batting order. Of course, Canada is not a super-power in the same category with the United States and Russia. And, unlike such countries as China and India, she cannot reasonably aspire to become a super-power. But she is in the next category along with such nations as Britain, France, Germany, Italy and Japan.

One further point. Owing to the close integration of the American and Canadian economies, an attempt to destroy the productive capacity of the United States would almost certainly result in some Canadian targets being attacked. The two countries constitute a single target system: it would not make sense to attack the United States and leave Canada alone. This has nothing to do with Canada's participation in NATO or NORAD; it is a fact which no treaty can change one way or the other. The same principle applies to any kind of attack aimed at the North American economic system, such as the cutting of sea communications. It is also true of economic warfare pursued by non-violent means, with the reservation that in this respect Canada is substantially more vulnerable than the United States. It is therefore clear that the community of interests between Canada and the United States is much more than a matter of geography. Geography has been the predisposing factor; but economics has forged an even more powerful bond.

Natural Alliances and Alignments

Now let us turn to the subject of alliances and alignments. Friendships between nations are based upon interests in common and enmities are based upon interests in opposition. Among nations, both friendship and enmity are relative. No two nations have precisely the same interests and hence there is no such thing as perfect friendship. Neither is there any such thing as absolute enmity. But there are certain natural alignments based upon a natural community of interests.

In Canada's case, her strongest natural alignment is with the United States. This is based upon close economic ties and the fact that Canada relies upon the United States for her security. But there is also a cultural affinity, a basic compatibility of social institutions and attitudes which goes beyond any ordinary conception of common interests. Canada and the United States are joint participants in the much criticized and greatly envied North American civilization of the twentieth century. As this civilization is their common property, its survival is their common concern.

Canada's second natural affinity is towards Western Europe and especially towards Britain and France. However, it is worth noticing that a sizable proportion of our population comes from such countries as Germany, Italy, Scandinavia and even Central Europe. We share with the nations of Europe a common historical tradition, as well as ties of language, religion and culture. There is also a racial compatibility, and, in spite of what one might wish, race is likely to be a powerful political motive during the next half century.

Canada is also a Pacific power. Her interests in the Pacific area have led her to take part in two wars: the war against Japan and the war in Korea. And, although the Organization of American States is somewhat out of fashion, Canada has a potential role within the Western hemispheric system. We also bear, rather more conscientiously than most, the responsibilities of membership in the United Nations, and participate with conviction in the fraternal association of the Commonwealth.

It is an article of faith with many Canadians that they have some special affinity with the new nations of Africa and Asia based upon the fact that we are a "non-colonial" power. If this were true, a great historic role would be mapped out for Canada: to serve as the link and the interpreter between Western civilization and the cultures of Africa, Asia and Latin America. Unfortunately, it is simply not the case. So far as the Afro-Asians are concerned, Canadians are members of the well-fed white minority. One may hope that Canadians will continue to view the problems of the new nations with sympathy and understanding. However, in the long run our relations with these nations will be governed by interests rather than sentiment; and their interests must figure as prominently as our own.

We should recognize that the new nations are engaged in establishing their historic identity, and they cannot afford to be too choosy about the means. For the moment they are weak. Since they can barely afford penny ante, they naturally disapprove of high stake poker. But one should make no mistake, their aspirations include the full panoply of national power. As they acquire this power they will use it to advance their interests as they see them. Unfortunately, these interests will in some cases not be our interests.

By recognizing this fact now we can at least spare ourselves from severe disillusionment. Well before the end of this century, the problem of accommodating within a genuine world community a number of powerful nations which do not share the traditions and values of European civilization (even in the perverted version of Russian Bolshevism) may well supersede the East-West conflict as the prime problem of international policy.

This point seems to be worth making because there is a persistent idea that aid programmes and similar activities are an alternative to defence. This is simply not true. These programmes are defensible on their merits; but they do not necessarily lead to stability and security. They are all too likely to lay the basis for revolution and turmoil.

The Policy of the Opening Towards Europe

Traditionally, Canada has aimed to off-set excessive influence on the part of the United States by maintaining a close tie with Britain. This was the strategy pursued by Sir John A. Macdonald in creating a single state in the vast expanse of British North America. For the first fifty years of our existence, the "British connection", backed up by the power of the Royal Navy, was the basis of such national security policy as Canada possessed. The tie with Britain was the legal basis and the principal political justification for Canada's participation in the First World War. Between the wars, Canada achieved constitutional independence, but in 1939, it was the historic tie with Britain, more than any other factor, which accounted for Canada's prompt declaration of war.

During the war, there emerged a new conception of Canada's role which was rather flattering to Canada, namely that Canada is the bridge which unites the two great English-speaking democracies and forms with them the North Atlantic Triangle. This idea was given an eloquent formulation by Sir Winston Churchill in a speech in Ottawa in 1943. At that time, it was, beyond doubt, the British belief that after the war the Americans would revert to their traditional isolationism. In this event, a major role would be marked out for Canada—to serve as the vanguard of North American policy and power. It was, it seems clear, the British expectation that Canada would play this role in close association with Britain and to some extent under British tutelage. However, the Americans have not reverted to isolationism; the bridge theory and the concept of the North Atlantic triangle have therefore fallen into some disrepute.

The concept of the North Atlantic Triangle nevertheless plays a certain role in Canadian defence. In 1947, arrangements were entered into between the United States, Britain and Canada in the field of research and development and in certain other important areas. These arrangements have functioned ever since to the very great advantage of Canada. As a result Canada is one of the half dozen nations in the world which possesses a com-

prehensive and up-to-the-minute understanding of contemporary military technology.

The idea of an opening towards Europe as an off-set to excessive American influence was a powerful factor in Canada's enthusiastic support for NATO. A Canadian statesman might have cribbed from Canning: "I have called into existence the Old World in order to restore the balance of the New." A former Minister of National Defence put it a little differently: with fifteen people in the bed you are less likely to get raped!

Britain's approach to the Common Market has come as a shock to many Canadians, and has tended to call into question the strategy of the opening towards Europe. A clearer reading of Canadian history might at any rate have spared us some surprise. The various fisheries disputes and the Alaska Boundary dispute showed that even in the hey-day of her power Britain had at some point to subordinate Canadian interests to her own. It is not necessarily true that in a bed which contains fifteen other nations Canada is less likely to get raped. One must inquire into motives, and, since all nations have something to gain from the United States, they might possibly be prepared to assist and applaud. It is not necessarily in Canada's interest to involve NATO in the entire agenda of Canadian-American relations.

Does this mean that Canada's membership in NATO is a source of weakness rather than of strength? It depends upon what we expect to gain. If we expect to gather allies against the United States we are going to be disappointed. And this is true of any other forum including the United Nations. However, by participating in NATO, and conceivably other collective defence systems, Canada can achieve two things. Firstly, by being present at the table we can serve as the spokesman for our own interests. If we are not present, our voice will not be heard. Secondly, to the extent that Canada plays a significant role in Western security, she can maintain real influence in Washington. It seems evident that this principle of independent representation is the key to a vigorous Canadian national existence. And although a certain amount can be achieved outside the area of security, in a world as dangerous and dynamic as our own the forum which deals with security will be many times more important than any other. . . .

The Guidelines of Canadian Security Policy

For the present, at any rate, Canadian geography is of direct and immediate concern to the United States mainly in relation to defence against the bomber. However, the need for defence against the bomber must be expected to continue for the more or less indefinite future. For reasons already discussed, the broad conception of Canadian national security policy is primarily a matter of Canada's relationship with the United States. What can we say about this relationship? One way of approaching this problem is to consider the range of feasible alternatives. In theory, at least, a wide spectrum of possible policies is available: one extreme is a policy of unrestricted global alliance; the other extreme is a policy of complete and rigorous neutrality under all circumstances. There are also intermediate possibilities.

In fact, neither of these extremes is remotely feasible. If Canada were to attempt to share in all United States global undertakings this would involve burdens and responsibilities which are far beyond our capacity to bear. We should, more-

over, become involved in a great many commitments which correspond to no clearly recognizable Canadian interest. It is also true that no military programme which is remotely within the realm of feasibility could effect a divorce between our fortunes and those of the United States. Indeed, the United States with its immensely greater capabilities could not achieve this. Thus, the extremes of policy, which have exercised some Canadians, are essentially fictional.

What are the feasible alternatives? One possibility might be called a policy of minimum defence. Under such a policy Canada would undertake to provide those North American defences which must be sited on Canadian territory and nothing else. Such a policy might be described as neutralist but it could more accurately be called isolationist. It would not reduce Canada's strategic dependence upon the United States or provide the basis of an "independent" foreign policy. It would, however, provide reasonable assurance with respect to the preservation of Canadian sovereignty.

What would such a policy require? We should have to keep the Canadian radar systems going and make radar information available to the United States. We would also need some active air defences. If we were to withdraw from NORAD, sacrificing operational co-ordination with the Americans, this would make necessary larger forces than we have now, but not impossibly large. We would need a coastal type navy and some ability to carry out land/air operations in the Far North. With such a programme Canada would make essentially no contribution to Western security. It would not add anything, but it would not detract. Any lesser defence effort would infringe a basic principle of Canada's national existence, namely that

Canada must not become a threat to American security.

A policy of minimum defence involves, almost by definition, the smallest possible defence budget. This is a desirable aim of Canadian policy and no one need apologize for saying so. Indeed, one can go further and say that any alternative policy which involves greater defence expenditures must be justified on the basis of major Canadian interests. However, according to this thoroughly hard-boiled calculus, a policy of minimum defence is subject to severe disadvantages.

Such a policy would require the abandonment of the principle of collective security which has been the cornerstone of Canadian foreign policy. In so doing we would give our effective support to the concept of a world dominated wholly by the super-powers. More specifically, such a policy would greatly reduce Canada's influence in Washington, and would deny to us the opening towards Europe. Furthermore, such a policy would involve our effective withdrawal from NATO. This would lead to repercussions within the Western group of nations, including the United States, of which, in our own interests, we are bound to take account.

It has been argued that such a policy would increase Canada's acceptability to the neutrals and would lay the basis for a larger role within the United Nations. Analogies have been rather freely drawn with Sweden, Switzerland, Yugoslavia and India. These overlook one central and compelling fact: Canada's geographical location and the extent to which our interests are bound up with those of the United States. Contrary to what is often said, Canada's influence vis-à-vis the neutrals depends precisely upon the fact that Canada is a paid-up member of the Western Club and is on terms of special intimacy with the United States.

There are, accordingly, reasons firmly based upon a consideration of Canadian national interests which lead to the conclusion that Canada must make some more than token contribution to Western defence. A very important point is that if Canada is to make such a contribution she must be willing to enter into systems of collective security and/or collective defence. In this respect our position is quite different from that of nations such as Germany, Italy, Greece or Turkey. The best contribution these nations can make to the security of the West is to defend themselves. Canada's natural role is to form part of the strategic reserve of the Free World, and it is only in this role that she can make a significant contribution. . . .

Canada's Place in the U.S. Alliance System

Now let us turn to the U.S. alliance system and Canada's place within this system. The United States has formal alliances with some forty odd countries and unwritten alliances with a number of others including such "neutrals" as Yugoslavia, Sweden, Austria and India. At the apex of the hierarchy there are three arrangements involving the U.S.A., Britain and Canada—the North Atlantic Triangle. These are:

(a) The North American defence system which dates from the Ogdensburg agreement of 1940;

(b) The tripartite ABC agreements which operate in the field of research and development and in certain other areas. These were entered into in 1947, but are really a continuation of the war-time partnership;

(c) The U.S.-U.K. system which operates in the area of strategic weapons systems and again goes back to the war-time arrangements.

The Canada-U.S. system is the senior American alliance—the first departure from splendid isolationism. The principal instrument of this alliance is the Permanent Joint Board on Defence which is a "political" body. The role of NORAD has often been misunderstood. The purpose of NORAD is to achieve operational co-ordination of North American air defences and to provide machinery for joint planning. NORAD replaced less formal machinery which had existed for this purpose since 1945. The C.-in-C. NORAD does not exercise "command" over Canadian forces in peace or war. In an emergency he carries out operational co-ordination in accordance with a directive approved by both Governments. Command of Canadian components is exercised by the Air Officer Commanding Air Defence Command, R.C.A.F., who is responsible to the Government of Canada through the Minister of National Defence.

The U.S. global alliance system includes five regional systems: NATO in Western and Southern Europe; CENTO in the Near East and Middle East; ANZUS in the South-west Pacific; SEATO in South East Asia; OAS in South America. The United States is not formally a member of CENTO, although the alliance depends upon U.S. support. In addition, there is an informal Central Pacific system including Japan, Formosa, South Korea and the Phillipines.

Canada is a member only of NATO. Her role as a Pacific power is to some extent in abeyance. The same is true of OAS. OAS is a good illustration of the dilemma of Canadian policy. Since Punte del Este there has been some tendency for Canadians to congratulate themselves that they are not members of OAS. The fact remains that if one believes that South America is of growing importance to Canada, then Canada's absence from OAS represents a real restriction upon the effectiveness of Canadian diplomacy in South America. This illustrates the principle of the presence at the table. Unless a nation possesses overwhelming power, it cannot play a significant role if it isn't there. In the future, Canada may be faced with a similar dilemma in the Pacific.

Summing Up

There is a fairly common belief in Canada that power politics is a nasty business which we should stay out of. Unfortunately, we have no such option. Calculations of national interest and relative power have figured in Canadian statecraft since the beginning of our history. Barring some total and presently unforseeable transformation in the international order this will continue to be the case.

A few years ago Mr. James M. Minifie wrote a book with the provocative title *Canada, Peacemaker or Powder-Monkey?* The defect in Mr. Minifie's thesis is that these are not real options. Canada does not possess the ability to transform the present system of international politics; nor, indeed, does any other nation. It is also true that prime responsibility for major decisions involving peace and war will not rest with Canada regardless of what we may or may not do.

What are the real alternatives? It seems evident that in the future as at present Canada will remain an American ally. This is the result of our geography; but in an even more compelling sense it is dictated by our interests. The question is whether we will be a powerful and effective ally or a weak and reluctant one. There is a parallel choice: whether our role in world affairs will be one of dependence upon the United States or whether we will be effective members of a larger community. This is a genuine choice and one, indeed, which we cannot avoid.

Does this mean that Canada is necessarily a U.S. satellite? No doubt many Canadians will continue to torture themselves with this thought; but the answer is that it is beside the point. In the second half of the twentieth century, no nation, including the United States, can pursue a truly independent policy. By recognizing and acting in accordance with our interests we do not become a U.S. satellite merely because our interests coincide with those of the United States. Instead of lamenting the consequences of our geography we should reflect that it is largely owing to our geography and our uniquely close relationship with the United States that a nation of eighteen millions has been able to achieve so large a share of wealth, power, and constructive influence.

Kenneth McNaught, "From Colony to Satellite," In Stephen Clarkson, ed., *An Independent Foreign Policy for Canada?* (Toronto: McClelland and Stewart, 1968) pp. 177-183. Reprinted by permission of The Canadian Publishers, McClelland and Stewart Limited, Toronto.

From Colony to Satellite?

Satellite Status Confessed

The most recent version of King-St. Laurent functionalism goes under the name of "quiet diplomacy." The doctrine that only quiet, behind-the-scenes, confidential methods should be applied by Canada-size powers was succinctly stated by Prime Minister Pearson in March, 1967. In a public letter replying to an appeal by 360 University of Toronto professors to dissociate Canada from the American war in Vietnam, he wrote:

Confidential and quiet arguments by a responsible government are usually more effective than public ones. . . . Too many public declarations and disclosures run the risk of complicating matters for those concerned. . . . The more complex and dangerous the problem, the greater is the need for calm and deliberate diplomacy.

But Mr. Pearson in the same letter went behind the reasons of diplomatic method to other, more profound reasons for his unwillingness to rock the North American boat. He . . . pointed to the World War II origins of our entanglement in continental defense. He reviewed the extent to which defence production has been integrated, the technological and mass production advantages we receive and then declared that because of these developments we could not, in fact, refuse to contribute to the American war effort in Vietnam:

For a broad range of reasons, therefore, it is clear that the imposition of an embargo on the export of military equipment to the USA, and concomitant termination of the Production Sharing Agreements, would have far-reaching consequences which no Canadian government could contemplate with equanimity. It would be interpreted as a notice of withdrawal on our part from continental defence and even from the collective defence arrangements of the Atlantic Alliance.

No more concise or authoritative statement has been made on the subject. After his letter no one can maintain that acceptance of continental integration in defence production and planning leaves us free in general foreign policy—leaves us free to accept one part of the American alliance structure while rejecting other parts of it. Nor can anyone seriously doubt that it is this integration that has produced, as James Eayrs has put it, the smooth Canadians who haunt the corridors of Washington with their confidential, ineffective briefs.

The process by which we accepted the bipolarization of the world was both curious and facile. During the second half of 1947 and through 1948 Canada did appear to define an external objective. It was the objective described by Senator Vandenburg, George Kennan and Harry S Truman—the objective of crippling communist power by encirclement of Russia. For the Canadian government this essentially American objective was overwhelmingly attractive and Canada leapt with agility to its support. The concept of a deeply divided world within which the West was imminently threatened by aggressive communist imperialism and which required a unified military response was attractive because it settled the Canadian foreign policy question automatically. Moreover, it settled that question along lines which could and did eliminate any serious internal political division.

But, most people say, it is all very well after the crisis is past to discourse upon the other side of the case; in fact the real danger was so great that we only saved Europe and ourselves from having to cower under the Kremlin's knout by building the Nato shield. While one may agree that a genuine dilemma existed in 1949, one should be quite equally aware that a crucial commitment was made to an increasingly military assessment of the situation—and that this emphasis remained while any justification for it grew steadily less credible as the Communist military threat declined. While the original case for Nato may or may not be convincing, the case for maintaining the alliance as the centre of our foreign policy is entirely without substance.

From the Canadian point of view the case for disbanding Nato (or for simply withdrawing from it) seems virtually unanswerable—except from the abashedly continentalist premises put forward by the Prime Minister and which imply acquiescence in Washington's ideological anti-communism. The case for leaving Nato depends upon one's interpretation of its present and likely future role as well as upon an assessment of its impact upon Canadian foreign policy.

The impact of Canada's membership in Nato has determined our other external policies. The basic premises of the alliance's dominant member have governed our position on all major questions—recognition of China, disengagement in Europe, nuclear disarmament, the creation of a genuine UN police force. While it can be argued that we have been able to play honest broker on occasion (e.g. Suez) the initiatives of this sort that we have taken have always been either in conformity with US policy or they have been such as to cause the US minimum discomfort. Whenever basic questions affecting the US position arise, our commitment to "nuclear security" and production agreements has been decisive. The effects of total loyalty are sometimes veiled, as in the case of Cuba—where we do not formally toe the line but where we are excruciatingly careful not to mount any trade campaign or to facilitate Russian-Cuban air communications. Loyalty is unveiled in hotter situations such as Vietnam where the government defends openly the legal and moral position of the United States and concedes that our position on the ICC is not that of an independent but that of a representative of "the West." One does not envy Mr. Chester Ronning, [special Canadian envoy to North Vietnam] who no doubt found it difficult explaining in Hanoi why we send aid only to Saigon—an aid policy which enabled General Westmoreland [U.S. Commander in Vietnam] and the State Department to list Canada as one of the "supporting" allies in Vietnam. Indeed this automatic loyalty in situations deemed crucial by Washington is taken absolutely for granted.

But it is not just by choice that we forego within the alliance system the rights and opportunities of independent initiative in major matters. Despite the rhetoric of equal partnership and consultation, Nato remains a military alliance dependent upon United States decisions and it is now abundantly clear that real influence will not be shared by the power that controls the essential nuclear component of the system. As long as Canada accepts the alliance basis of security she will accept the shackles of nuclear loyalty and the stigma of total commitment. Thus we violate our liberal traditions by refusing entry to deserters from the US army under a "Nato commitment." As Melvin Conant put it somewhat harshly a few years ago: "Fifteen years of effort to meet the security requirements of the air age have concluded with the prospect that the Canadian role from now on will be marginal and certainly not consequential."

Even apart from the question of hobbling ourselves by accepting the nuclear measuring rod, there is the question of the general effect of Nato upon the most dangerous of the world's outstanding problems. Clearly, Nato stands as the principal obstacle in the path to a German settlement. . . . Nato stands also as the symbol, in an image-minded age, of western commitment to a cold-war interpretation of international affairs. On these grounds alone Canada should withdraw her Nato contributions and should give notice that she will exercise her right under Article 13 of the Treaty to withdraw from the alliance in 1969. Just as our acceptance of Nato was an implicit definition of external objectives, so our withdrawal from it should be the occasion for redefinition of such objectives.

A Return to "Balance"?

If we cannot return to the simple formulae of earlier times, we *can* define from the frustrations of our alliance experience a more fruitful set of policies.

What we lost in the Nato period should be our chief guide in the future. We abandoned any serious concern for our national independence and based policy upon considerations that are wholly archaic—especially in the light of American predominance, nuclear weaponry and the rise of Afro-Asia from imperialist control; and we have almost wholly ignored the glaring inequality of welfare and opportunities amongst the world's peoples. In "defence" matters we have ignored the obvious reality that the only serious threat to our own territory stems from our proximity to the centres of US nuclear power—and the presence of Bomarcs which have been described by Mr. McNamara [U.S. Secretary of Defense] as bait for Russian missiles. The "nuclear umbrella" is for us a nuclear lightning rod. New definitions of foreign policy should aim at rectifying such crippling inadequacies of assessment and they should take into account changes within Canada as well as changes abroad.

Since Canada's security, prosperity and any hope she may have of exercising a beneficent influence abroad all depend upon the maintenance of peace and are hindered by continuance of cold war divisions it should follow that her principal external objectives should be to achieve: 1) enhancement of the United Nations at the expense of regional alliances; 2) absolute priority for nuclear disarmament; and 3) top spending priority for foreign aid.

These three objectives are obviously interrelated and rest upon certain assumptions about the post-1945 world which are implicit in the foregoing discussion, but which deserve explanation.

The most important assumption is that after the nuclear revolution in the nature of military power Canada can no longer seek to measure her influence in terms of the dominant military weaponry. She cannot hope to build a nuclear weapons system and therefore cannot be completely Gaullist; she is therefore, if she continues as a committed party to the arms race, completely dependent upon American decisions. Moreover, the evidence of the past twenty-two years leads irresistibly to the conclusion that no one can help to moderate the arms-race tensions simply by pious participation in disarmament conferences while wearing prominently the US arm-band. Yet, while nuclear disarmament is already a subject to produce yawns it is, nevertheless, one which must lie at the heart of our international objectives. Few people now doubt that the *gravest* danger facing the world is unlimited nuclear war and that limited nuclear war is, at the very least, unlikely. While we remain committed to Nato we are also committed to the use of nuclear weapons on our behalf, and in some cases by our own forces—that is, committed to risking the destruction of civilization. Although we have learned to live with the bomb, we do not have to love it. If our foreign and defence policies are to be founded on morality and realism they must exclude membership in alliances which depend upon nuclear power. Even in terms of seeking to persuade others to deny themselves the bomb (i.e. the limited goal of non-proliferation) our present position is hypocritical.

A military non-aligned Canada could do more than a committed Canada to mobilize a growing pressure within the United Nations for acceptance of the most advanced disarmament offers that have been made by both the United States and Russia during the ebb and flow of past disarmament talks. While the history of the arms race is not such as to encourage ill-considered optimism neither is the present instability of terror something to induce lethargy and a failure of nerve. Surely the most striking facts ignored by advocates of cautious debate, quiet diplomacy and iron-clad guarantees is that twenty-two years of such methods have succeeded only in producing the most dangerous arms-race in history—whose most recent peak is the edgy debate about anti-missile systems and the development of Chinese nuclear capacity. It is clear that in this field words are no substitute for actions. Our most significant action would be immediate renunciation of nuclear weapons and withdrawal from nuclear alliances. The cries of hypocrisy that would be raised in some quarters would have much less base than those which can now be *legitimately* raised.

Much of what I have been suggesting by way of redefining our international objectives has already been canvassed by our government. But in each case the extent of the tentative moves has been minimized by the facts and psychology of commitment to the American military alliance. We do not, for example, really wish to keep any military force in Germany and it is evident that in terms of power our presence there is ridiculous. Thus we have elected a kind of equipment-erosion method of withdrawing from the scene—a method that impresses no one, but which is required in order not to offend American political-strategists openly. We have expanded our aid to the West Indies and Afro-Asian states but on a scale that should make us blush. Many people hope that Norad will be phased out in the face of new air-screen devices developed in the US, but we retain in Canada the useless and dangerous Bomarc missiles. We are rearranging our own military forces so that their essential role will be that of mobile emergency forces for peace-keeping operations. But we have made no real progress toward the establishment of a full-fledged UN police force.

The concept of do-it-yourself stand-by forces clearly falls far short of the police project proposed by Tryggvi Lie as early as 1949. Since it is not possible, save in the case of individual or collective mania, to use nuclear power, the roles of economics, diplomacy and minor specialist military force have been remarkably enhanced. Our role in peace-keeping must be complemented by a serious commitment to the concept of international equality. In our own country we have decided that, on grounds both of justice and utility, we must establish basic minimum standards of welfare and that we must work for the realization of equality of opportunity. The same grounds should be the basis of our approach to international affairs. Utilitarian reasons also require the effort to establish international equality of opportunity—for the seeds of conflict and of extremist nationalism find favourable ground in the desperate inequalities that divide the affluent from the underprivileged world. Without entering the debate about the most efficacious methods of raising welfare and opportunity levels in Latin America and Afro-Asia it is more than apparent that we now devote to the problem only a tiny proportion of the manpower and resources that we consider appropriate in other fields. Here again, as in the area of nuclearism, our intentions and policies will be convincing and have influence to the extent that they are wholehearted and unambiguous.

Clear-cut, non-alliance objectives would thus be in the Canadian national interest in two senses: they would be our only possible contribution to the kind of world in which alone it is possible for a country such as ours to exist, and they would in themselves strengthen our national experiment by extending to our foreign policy the principles of tolerance, compromise and equality which we endeavour to establish at home. While to some the detailed implications of the policy basis I have suggested will appear to be merely anti-American, in fact this bogey is now an irrelevant, timorous excuse for inaction. Imperial Washington's loyalty requirements are tougher than were those of Imperial London. But the conditions of the present require, just because this is so, a vigorous response and return to a concept of survival and balance in our external relations.

John W. Holmes, "Canadian External Policies Since 1945," *International Journal*, XVIII (Spring, 1963), pp. 137-47. Reprinted by permission of The Canadian Institute of International Affairs and the Author.

A Diplomatic Assessment

Until the Second World War, Canada's external relations were tentative and circumscribed, limited in later years not so much by colonial status as by a lingering colonial mentality—a mentality even more characteristic of Liberal nationalists like Mackenzie King than of the traditionally imperialist Conservative Party. Mr. King, having secured with disconcerting ease recognition of Canada's right to an independent role in the world, was left with undeveloped convictions about what to do next. He cherished the view that Canada was a remote and uniquely peace-loving area, too much burdened with domestic problems to be drawn into the struggles of an obstreperous world. Because his primary impulse was to keep out of trouble, he preferred that Canada's role in the world be a modest one. To satisfy a modest sense of mission the illusion was nourished that Canada was a linchpin which kept the United States and Britain in harmony, and Canadians lectured the League of Nations without pain or cost on the virtuous example of North America.

This attitude was swept away at the end of the War. Self-doubt, an innate suspicion of great powers, and a quality of self-righteousness lingered. Nevertheless, Canada went through a remarkably swift transition from the status of a wartime junior partner in 1945 to that of a sure-footed middle power with an acknowledged and applauded role in world affairs ten years later. The change was accentuated by the passing from the political scene of Mr. King in 1948 and his replacement by Mr. Louis St. Laurent, a Prime Minister less inhibited by the phobias which had prevented both nationalists and imperialists in the past from seeing Canada's place in the world clearly and confidently. Mr. St. Laurent, furthermore, worked in close harmony with his new Secretary of State for External Affairs, Mr. Pearson, who had been trained as a professional diplomat. Mr. Pearson became a major architect of the United Nations and of NATO, and the rapid growth of Canada's stature was inextricably associated with his position as one of the most respected foreign ministers of the post-war era. The new approach was encouraged also by the national pride of a country in the course of unparallelled economic expansion, capable even of assisting the ruined great powers of the pre-war world. The rise of the United Nations, which acknowledged the formal equality of states regardless of size, set the stage for accomplishments by lesser powers with will and skill to play the new kind of diplomatic game.

It can be said of Canadians as of Americans, however, that their new international activity was the result more of responding to a need than of thrusting themselves forward as world salvationists in accordance with preconceived notions of national mission. The precarious state of the world after 1945 required the forceful intervention in far corners of a benevolent great power like the United States. It turned out also that the preservation of order often enough required the services of middle powers whose principal value was their very incapacity to threaten or command. Canada was no longer reluctant to be useful. Canadians coveted responsibilities, and Canadian diplomatic missions multiplied from seven in 1939 to sixty-five in 1962.

At the conclusion of the War, Canada was faced with the problem of finding for itself, along with Australia, Sweden, Brazil and other countries of middle stature, a place in international councils appropriate to their position as something less than major and something more than minor powers. In the case of Canada and Australia, this was a continuation of the frustrated struggle to acquire some influence on the direction of the Allied war effort. It was not surprising, therefore, that at San Francisco in 1945 it was directed most often towards reducing the pretensions of the great powers and prescribing as much international 'democracy' as possible in the United Nations. Canadian demands were, however, tempered by some understanding of the relation between function and power, and the more rabid campaign against the great powers was left to the Australians and New Zealanders. Canada did accept the special position of the great powers and the inevitability of the veto, even while seeking to place restraints on it.

Contrary to habit, Canadian officials even evolved a theory which determined their attitude on the composition of the new international bodies being established in the late 1940's. They called it the "functional theory", and although the term has dropped out of use, it is perhaps worth mentioning to illustrate the nature of Canadian pragmatism in foreign policy —a characteristic endeavour to find theories to fit the facts of international life and at the same time justify a Canadian role rather than to impose moral abstractions on an untidy world. The essence of the "functional theory" was that each nation should have responsibility appropriate to its particular capacities. Great powers, by reason of their extraordinary military capacity, were entitled to special positions in matters of security. For the nonpermanent seats of the Security Council, however, preference would be given to middle powers able to make some military contribution, over smaller powers which might act irresponsibly because they had no forces of their own. Important trading nations would be accorded special influence in international commercial organizations whether or not they happened to be great military powers. Those concerned with colonial questions would have places on the Trusteeship Council, and the privileged places in bodies dealing with health or communications or immigration would go to those countries which had special interests or special qualifications in those specific subjects. To each according to his capacities seemed to be the best rule of thumb to encourage a maximum sense of responsibility in world councils, and also to avoid a permanent hegemony of the great powers on all subjects and see that middle and lesser powers had reasonable parts to play.

On the whole, this conception of function and responsibility in international organization was subdued by the pressure of regional and group representation, although it still conditions the attitudes of member states, especially middle powers, on such matters as disarmament negotiations and the direction of U.N. operations in the Middle East or Congo. The theory was, of course, never intended to be applied rigidly—rigid theories are very un-Canadian. Its application did at the beginning provide one triumph for Canada when, as one of the three powers which had worked to create nuclear energy, it became a permanent member, along with the great powers, of the U.N. Atomic Energy Commission. This priority position for Canada on an important security organ was maintained in successor bodies dealing with disarmament until 1957, and contributed considerably to Canada's prestige as a middle power which kept influential company. Canada's anxiety to limit the functions and privileges of great powers were replaced by a conception of special functions for great powers and special functions for middle powers—and even for small powers as well. Each nation was seen as unique, its history and geography as well as its size giving it some special part to play ad hoc in world affairs. The world did not consist merely of great powers on the one hand and small powers on the other. Nor should it be divided arbitrarily into blocs, Western, Communist, and Uncommitted. Or into good guys and bad guys, black and white. The international scene would be more manageable if relationships remained flexible, if we were not driven into rigid blocs and regions. Canada became the persistent advocate of flexibility in international associations, constantly worried about what seemed a too categorical approach in Washington.

Having staked out a claim for the powers of middle strength, Canada worked throughout the 1950's to put meaning into the concept—along with other comparable countries, nations of the Commonwealth and Scandinavia in particular. If the San Francisco concept of world

order maintained by the great powers in unity had been maintained, the middle powers would probably have continued to see their mission in banding together to mitigate the rule of the great. When the great powers fell apart, however, their smaller associates soberly recognized that the first priority was to maintain the strength of their large friends. The polarization of the blocs produced a situation in which middle powers found themselves with functions unlike those they had conceived for themselves in 1945. When crises developed in the Middle East, in Indo-China or the Congo, for instance, middle powers were required to fill diplomatic and even para-military roles from which the great powers excluded each other. Whereas Canada in the past had kept free of entanglements in Asia because it had no direct interests there, now it found that its very lack of interests was the reason it was involved. For this reason and because Canadians had developed a reputation for objectivity and independence, if not neutrality, in international affairs, Canada was chosen in 1954, along with India and Poland, to man the International Supervisory Commissions to patrol the truces in Indo-China. In 1956 Canada took the lead in proposing and also in staffing the first United Nations Emergency Force. Canadians participated in similar operations in Kashmir and Palestine, Lebanon and Congo. The performance of these essential tasks gave a certain style to Canadian diplomacy. The reputation for independence and objectivity had to be reflected in endeavours to establish bridges between the blocs, to find compromise solutions. Because this independence was more natural in colonial questions than in cold war questions, the mediatory role was, of course, more assiduously cultivated in relations with the uncommitted than with the Communists.

There were those in Canada who began to argue that Canada would be a more useful force in the world if it could move to a position of neutrality in the Cold War and concentrate on mediatory functions. This was not necessarily a rejection of nuclear diplomacy for the great powers but rather a pushing to extremes of the theory of a functional distinction between the roles in the world of great and middle powers. For Canada, however, it was not possible because Canadians felt too directly committed in the struggle against communism.

Canada played an active and strategic part in the creation of NATO in 1949. Canadian spokesmen were, in fact, among the first to enunciate the North Atlantic idea. In doing so they were moved by fear of the Soviet threat to Western Europe and also by the opportunity perceived to end their historic schizophrenia. For a generation Canadian external policy had been wracked by a conflict between the advocates of continental and trans-Atlantic attachments. Now leaders of all parties, having cast off the tradition of Canadian helplessness, saw in the military alliance of Britain and France with the United States the opportunity to be part of a team in which Canada's international interests and its domestic emotions could both be satisfied.

Although differences between the major allies were by no means extinguished in NATO, Canada's mutual alliance with them all did have a soothing effect on the considerations which determine external relations. The Canadian hand in diplomacy was strengthened by an unprecedented unity among parties and races within the country on the basic directions of foreign policy. Within NATO, however, Canada found itself

aligned not with one large friend against another so much as with the other smaller members against the domination of the great powers. A persistent but not very successful campaign was waged to persuade the larger powers to consult their allies. Another Canadian prejudice, a traditional uneasiness about the morality of military alliances, was reflected in the continuing effort to emphasize the economic, cultural and spiritual aspects of the North Atlantic association. Whatever success this worthy endeavour achieved was largely rhetorical. Canada contributed forces to NATO in Europe and never doubted the need to resist the Soviet Union with military power, but Canada usually joined the Scandinavians in NATO to oppose the rigidities of the great powers in their attitudes both to the Communist states and the neutralists. This approach was attributable not to neutralism or to softness on communism but, rightly or wrongly, to a somewhat less ideological concept of the forces in conflict. It frequently brought Canadians into sharp difference with Americans and French but less often with the British with whose intellectual traditions of foreign policy they had more in common.

One way in which Canada maintained its independence was by keeping its feet in two camps. To balance its close continental and Atlantic associations with the major Western powers were the unique associations through the Commonwealth with the leading states of Asia and Africa. The footwork was tricky; Washington often thought Canadian policy too much swayed by Mr. Nehru; and Paris and Lisbon were offended by Canadian association with the anti-colonialists. These ambivalent loyalties did, however, encourage the Canadian inclination for compromise and trouble-shooting and fortify its diplomatic strength for this purpose.

The Commonwealth played a significant role in shaping Canadian external policy after 1945. Although the impact of the Commonwealth on Canadians was more diffuse than in imperial days, the institution roused a new and in some ways more positive kind of enthusiasm, an enthusiasm which reflected the new self-confidence of a nation which saw in the ancient ties not a limitation upon but an instrument for Canadian policy. As it was transformed from an unfashionable empire into a more fashionable association among peoples of different races, the Commonwealth caught the imagination of young and progressive elements in the country, the very elements which traditionally had looked askance on the imperial tie as nostalgic, reactionary, and racialist. Canadian nationalists, no longer afraid the British were restricting their freedom, saw in the Commonwealth a counterforce to the threat to Canadian independence posed by the increasing dominance of the United States in world affairs.

The Commonwealth, futhermore, was being reshaped in the Canadian image. The British and the Australians until the late 1940's had hankered after a more unified Commonwealth, speaking in unison in international councils. Canada had insisted that the effort to impose a rigid framework on scattered peoples would induce friction rather than harmony. India, Pakistan, and the other new countries were disposed to continue membership only if the Canadian concept prevailed, and Canada's obvious preference for the new over the old Commonwealth inspired a special bond with the non-European members. In the United Nations especially, Canada found that the Commonwealth association, including as it did the major nations of Asia and Africa, extended its own diplomatic resources. Canada was canny, nevertheless, about sharing Britain's responsibilities for dependent territories. It did participate wholeheartedly, although with restrained generosity, in the Colombo Plan, a scheme for mutual economic aid of Commonwealth origin. The British proceeded to transform their empire into the kind of Commonwealth Canada preferred, and the end product, not surprisingly, now seems to appeal more to Canada than to Britain itself. It is by no means for commercial reasons only that the Canadian Government has sought of late to rally other Commonwealth countries to question the advisability of Britain's inclination to align itself with the Europeans.

Canada strove after 1945 to play an active role in the United Nations for sound and conscientious reasons. In the foreign policies of democracies, however, there is always an element of calculation as well as conscience, and neither the cynic nor the idealist is ever right in an absolute judgement on motives. Trust in the possibilities of the United Nations is more necessary to a weak power than a strong power. The United Nations, furthermore, provides a middle power with a stage on which to perform, and an arena in which skill counts for more than muscle. Thanks to its racial homogeneity and brief history, Canada escaped censure in the United Nations and was inevitably disposed, therefore, to look upon its activities with more enthusiasm than were, say, France or South Africa. The Commonwealth, NATO, GATT, and dozens of other international associations likewise gave Canada scope to exercise its national capability. The zeal with which a distinct and forceful foreign policy was pursued was not unrelated to the constant compulsion Canadians felt to preserve and assert their identity.

It is significant that the international associations which Canada favoured were trans-oceanic rather than regional. The very existence of Canada is a defiance against regionalism, and Canadians instinctively have clung to overseas associations for balance. An international association for which they were presumably eligible but which they did not embrace was the Organization of American States. The practical reason for this aloofness was that a country, one-tenth the size of the United States, had limited diplomatic resources for playing a responsible hand in international bodies. This was compounded by wariness about extending the areas of trouble in which to become involved. The "Western Hemisphere", furthermore, is not a geographical reality but a historical tradition. Canadians, never having shared the Washington-Bolivar mystique and the revolutionary republican tradition, have not taken very seriously the idea that they have special links with peoples of vastly different political traditions merely because they happen to be linked by an almost untraversible neck of land. History has bound Canada across traversible oceans to the Northern Hemisphere.

In recent years, however, there has been increasing interest in the O.A.S. The continuous brain-washing from the United States to which Canadians are subjected has led many to accept the assumption that the Western Hemisphere is a region. More significant perhaps has been the escalation of Latin America from the status of backwater to that of crisis zone, and some Canadians have sniffed another useful role to play in the world. They have been brain-washed also by the new dogma of regionalism inspired by the Western

Europeans. Goaded by economists crying doom, many Canadians, against all their political instincts, have been troubled that they too will have to find a region to cling to. The fear that their traditional associates across the Atlantic will draw in on themselves, taking Britain along, threatens, although it has by no means triumphed over, the deep historical instinct to brace against a southward pull. In any regional reorientation that might take place, however, the Continent is likely to be taken more seriously than the Hemisphere.

Relations with the United States since 1945 illustrated the validity of the statement in 1950 of the Secretary of State for External Affairs, Mr. Pearson, that the days of easy and automatic relations were over. Relations were more complex and more irritable not because the two nations were drifting apart but because they were impinging more. Bilateral disputes, the problems of water power and canals and tariffs, continued as they presumably always will continue between neighbours. Although they inspire regional passions, they have come to be taken for granted, and in the past decade and a half they disturbed official harmony less than in earlier years when there were fewer world issues to think about. However, since the United States and Canada moved actively into the international arena, their policies on international issues clashed more frequently. Harmonious relations were threatened more by differences over defence or disarmament, over Cuba or trade with China, than over the St. Lawrence Seaway or the Columbia River. The distinct identities of the two countries have been more readily discernible in their approaches to international problems than their common social and economic habits would suggest—differences reflecting diverse political institutions, histories, overseas associations, temperament, and the inevitable variations between the approach of a nation of decisive power and that of a nation of modest influence in the world. Canada was, in fact, less docile than more distant allies, Australia and Turkey, for example. These differences reflected on the Canadian side honest convictions, tempered with a strain of perversity perhaps and the assurance of a country which was never dependent on economic aid from the United States and which, unlike overseas friends and clients, knew that the United States could not disinterest itself from its defence. In its defence policy, however, Canada was stimulated at all times by sober recognition of the fact that Canadian defences must not fall below a certain minimum lest the United States be tempted in its own interest to intervene.

These strains, however, should not obscure the profound change that took place in the formal relationship between the two countries in the period under consideration. The United States and Canada became peacetime military allies, a fact so taken for granted now that its revolutionary nature is perhaps grasped only by historians. Contrary to the view recently repeated in the highest circles, history did not make the United States and Canada friends; it made them natural antagonists —and they remained antagonists from the eighteenth to the twentieth centuries. It took the Germans and then the Russians to make them allies. And even at that, Canada was prepared in 1949 to enter into such an alliance only in partnership with others, including its two mother countries. Having grown accustomed to this association and having grown more conscious of present perils than past anxieties, Canada was ready in 1957 to

enter into a more specific bilateral commitment in the North Atlantic Air Defence Command, NORAD. The surrender of independent action involved in this agreement continued to disturb many people in Canada, even though few doubted the practicality of integrated continental defence. Canadians have shown an inclination, therefore, to see NORAD not as an isolated bilateral arrangement but as a regional but integral part of the NATO Alliance—thereby, as is their custom, seeking to bring in the Old World to redress the overwhelming imbalance of the New.

The process of rise and decline which affects good and evil states alike is normally spread over centuries, or at least generations. Canada, however, experienced a cycle of unnatural expansion and subsequent diminution of its international influence in considerably less than one generation. The phenomenon has been disconcerting. At the end of the Second War, Canada emerged as the third strongest of the Western powers and assumed in international organizations a position of influence not far behind that of the minor great powers. During the decade and a half since that time Canada's population and resources continued to grow, but its relative position in the world fell off considerably. The reasons were natural and not discreditable. Canada's position in 1945 had been temporarily inflated because of the exhaustion of countries such as France, Germany and Japan. Then, the appearance of new independent states and the multiplication of the membership of the United Nations gradually reduced the relative importance of the founding members. Canada, for instance, had two active terms on the Security Council in the first fifteen years, but is unlikely to have another for decades. Canada in no time at all became one of the older nations of the world, and the appeal of youth and chastity which a new country enjoys is a waning asset. As it lurches through a decade of active diplomacy, even a lesser power steps on toes and injures feelings.

Many people are inclined to attribute the decline of the Canadian position in the world to the end of the long period of Liberal government in the election of 1957. There was, however, little detectable difference in the basic external policies of the Liberal and Conservative régimes. It was inevitable, of course, that a new government whose members had had little experience of diplomacy would find difficulty sustaining a position of influence which, in the case of middle powers, is peculiarly dependent upon the authority of personality and experience. The change of government did, however, tend to obscure certain inexorable factors.

Others would say that the influence of all powers other than the two largest declined because the role of nuclear weapons throughout the 1950's became more and more decisive. There is force in this argument. Paradoxically, however, it was the nuclear stalemate that paralyzed the initiatives of great powers in fear of each other's intervention and enabled militarily weak but diplomatically influential lesser states to act effectively, particularly in those areas where there was no direct confrontation of the major powers.

During this swift period the theory of Canadian foreign policy never caught up with the reality. By the time theorists had begun to define a middle power role for Canada, based on a record of diplomatic honest brokerage culminating in a leading role in the Suez Crisis of 1956, the continuing effectiveness of this role was already being challenged by new alignments of the powers and shifting patterns in the United Nations. The patterns of middle power diplomacy can never be set for long periods if it is to retain its vitality and its relevance. Finding themselves a role appropriate to the circumstances of the 1960's is the present preoccupation of Canadians, and it is complex. The foreign policies of middle powers are inevitably directed not only at the substance of an issue but also at the means by which they can affect the resolution of that issue. The machinery of world politics is their special concern. The more responsible of them want to be of some serious consequence in the world. Since Canada first recognized its power to influence events, Canadians have been groping for a justification of their existence. What might have been a sordid pursuit of international recognition was redeemed by a puritan conscience. It was not enough to possess sovereignty, Canada must justify its independence by being somehow good for humanity. In the record since 1945 there are some grounds at least for satisfaction and encouragement for those who believe that powers of middle size have the capacity, if they wish to use it wisely, to contribute to the international community as sovereign entities.

Dean Acheson, "Canada: 'Stern Daughter of the Voice of God'," in Livingston Merchant, ed., *Neighbours Taken for Granted* (Toronto: Burns and MacEachern, 1966), pp. 134-47. Reprinted by permission of Frederick A. Praeger, Inc.

A Tart American Comment

Americans take Canada for granted, and Canadians are forever saying so. By this they mean that Americans assume Canada to be bestowed as a right and accept this bounty, as they do air, without thought or appreciation. Perhaps they do; and perhaps they should. For, if it were not taken as a bounty of nature, America might not grasp Canada at all for sheer difficulty in figuring out what Canada is.

By Canada, one means Canadians. The land is clear enough on the map; the economy, in innumerable prospectuses; and both are much appreciated by visitors and investors. What Americans take as the bounty of nature is the people—not the politicians, not the press, not something called Canadian culture or cultures—but Canadians.

Americans—and, perhaps, Canadians, too—do not have much of an idea what this generic noun Canadian describes, if it describes anything. One who has relatives in Canada is the most bemused of all, for he confidently believes that his relatives are "typical" Canadians.

Yet the one sure thing about this belief is that it must be wrong. If his relatives are British Canadians they throw no light on French Canadians, and vice versa. If they live in the Maritimes, they are quite different from the inhabitants of the Prairie Provinces or British Columbia. And if they are what is left of the United Empire Loyalists of Upper Canada, they are unique. When Prime Minister Lester Pearson tells us that despite regionalism the people of Canada are "essentially Canadian," he unhappily does not enlighten us further.

Americans, then, are uninformed about Canadians, but infinitely well disposed, and, too often, infuriatingly patronizing. A poll taken in the United States would bring out the unanimous opinion that Canadians are fine, straightforward, hard-working, intelligent, courageous, great hockey players, and—God forgive us!—the highest encomium, "just like Americans." They are ideal neighbors. We would rather they lived in Canada than live there ourselves, or have our dear friends, the Vietnamese, do so. For the knight of romance, a wise man has written, it was not enough to say that his lady was a very fine girl. You must agree that she was the finest that God ever had made or would make, or you must fight. So it is with Mr. Pearson. He writes in *Foreign Affairs*:

A few Americans know Canada well, but many do not know it even a little. This irks us. Indeed a major irritant in our relations with the United States is the tendency of some Americans simply to take Canadians for granted.

The remedy for this deplorable situation is, of course, greater knowledge. But is greater knowledge wise? Another, and, perhaps, more percipient Canadian,

Robert Fulford, considering the same problem in the *Toronto Star*, concludes:

Americans, we have argued for years, don't show enough interest in Canada.

But now this is changing. American magazines are developing a persistent as opposed to a fitful appetite for material about Canada. Perhaps this means that in the future the Americans will begin to understand us.

When that happens, we may well find ourselves looking back on the days of their ignorance with acute nostalgia. For surely those Americans who study Canada will sooner or later discover both our assumed moral superiority and the pitiful reality that lies behind it. When they do their laughter may be hard to bear.

What does he mean by Canadian "assumed moral superiority," and what is its relevance? It begins with the fact that Canadians of all regions suffer from the common failing of all people everywhere, not excepting the United States—parochialism. Its virulence, until recently, at least, was pre-eminent in Quebec. In the light of this parochialism we must examine something about which one has heard a good deal from Ottawa; that is, from politicians and publicists rather than one's Canadian friends. Canadians, we are told, have in the culture of their "two founding peoples" something which must be safeguarded from engulfing vulgarity from south of the border. The French Canadians, writes Mr. Pearson, possess a "culture which is French both in its source and in its quality. Yet they are completely Canadian. After the original Indians and Eskimos, they were the first Canadians."

What he says about the culture of the "first" Canadians after the "original" Canadians is doubtless justified by what we might call political license. Undoubtedly the French *voyageurs* brought with them to Canada the French ideas and Catholicism of the sixteenth and seventeenth centuries. Their descendants still speak a form of French related to that currently used in literate France, as the language of the less-penetrated portions of the southern Appalachian Mountains is related to that spoken today in literate England. But if there have been French Canadian contributions to French culture they have had scant recognition in French scientific or literary journals, in French music, or in French galleries.

The story is different on the English-speaking side. Though not comparable to the contributions of the Netherlands, Belgium, or Denmark, Canadian nuclear scientists have done notable work at Chalk River. Canadian writers have far surpassed Ralph Connor's once popular book *The Sky Pilot*. Canadian orchestras and ballet are good; and Riopelle is an important painter, even though, like Whistler and Picasso, he has found an atmosphere congenial to his art outside his own country. The Canadian "Seven" of an earlier day were also painters worthy of respect. Yet, when all is said, one cannot quarrel with Mr. Fulford's summing up: "In the arts and sciences we are so far behind them [the Americans] that no meaningful comparison can be made."

From this conclusion, he passes to another: ". . . but we at least see ourselves as morally superior to the Americans. We cling to this as the white trash cling to segregation. Heaven help us if it ever vanishes and we must see ourselves naked."

The origin of this bit of folklore lies, Mr. Fulford finds not surprisingly, in the minds of the believers: "The trouble is that the idea of Canadian moral superiority is hard to sustain if you take into account the facts of Canadian history and Canadian society. Most of us solve this problem in the most obvious way. We ignore the facts."

They are aided by scrupulously following a "policy of selective recall" and "know, for instance, that in the 1930's England practiced something called 'appeasement' and the Americans . . . 'isolationism.' " These two powers were responsible for World War II, even though "Canada's government was more appeasement-prone than England's in the 1930's, and Canadian statesmen as a whole made mid-western Americans look, by comparison, like internationalists." Indeed, the folklore about war goes further. "When the Americans have shown reluctance to enter a war in which we have been involved, we have regarded them as shirkers. When they have armed themselves carefully against their enemies and ours, we have helpfully pointed out that they are warmongers."

Selective recall operates equally well in the political field to sustain Canada's "moral pride":

Canadians have never mounted a foreign aid program that is better than niggardly, yet we have always felt it our duty to criticize the more generous Americans. . . . We have systems of public housing and social security which are sensationally inferior to those of the Americans, yet we believe we are more open to liberal ways than they are. . . .

Our federal Parliament has for several years found it all but impossible to pass the simplest measures. In the last 18 months the United States Congress has passed bold new legislation. Yet every schoolboy knows (because his history teacher tells him) that the British parliamentary system as practised in Canada is vastly superior to the unwieldy and backward system of the Americans.

We English-speaking and French-speaking Canadians have rarely if ever shown any genuine interest in understanding each other, yet we have for generations told the Americans exactly how to settle their monumentally challenging race issue.

Canadians feel about their moral superiority as the authors of the American Declaration of Independence did almost two hundred years ago: "We hold these truths to be self-evident!"

And yet, one doubts. Has not Mr. Fulford been too harsh? Surely these views are familiar. One hears and reads them often. But from the mouth or pen of a professional or political Canadian. Not from one's friends.

Fortunately, there is something approaching evidence—proof would be too strong a word—that this is true. Last year, in *Maclean's* magazine, a leading Canadian publication, Blair Fraser analyzed a remarkable survey by the Canadian Peace Research Institute, a private Canadian corporation supported by 25,000 contributors. Mr. Fraser, who enjoys a wide reputation in Canada as an experienced, perceptive, and fair-minded political commentator, discussed the Institute's conclusion that on matters of foreign policy "a majority of Canadians differ sharply from the majority of politicians, regardless of party.". . .

Let us start with five related questions, the answers to which were reported both by totals and by national origin and other groupings. First, the bare outlines:

Policy	National Opinion for	Politicians' Opinion for
	(in per cent)	
Hard line against Communist bloc	41	4
Peaceful coexistence	33	73
Nuclear arms for Canada	45	27
More foreign aid now	12	73
Strengthening the United Nations	46	55

Equally significant is the fact that the answers of neither the "informed" group nor the two national origin groups differ substantially on most questions from opinion as a whole. Perhaps the most startling revelation of this survey is the radical difference it portrays from earlier single, general question polls. In 1961, 86 per cent of Canadians thought that the United Nations did a "good" or "fair" job. Now only 46 per cent are in favor of "strengthening" it. Conclusions from these data are tricky to make and can be deceptive. But they do not bear out the view which Mr. Fraser believes some Canadians have had of themselves as "leading the march toward peace, stalwart and loyal supporters of the United Nations, conscientious objectors to nuclear weapons, generous donors of aid to less-favored nations, standard bearers in any movement toward disarmament and peaceful coexistence.". . .

In "the vast external realm," however, the Canadian politician can and does appear with more panache. At first, his role was seen as a loving reconciler of common mother and long lost son. But as the consequences of World War II extended the Statute of Westminster and the British Empire faded into the Commonwealth, the role changed radically. It became more ambitious; its purposes and medium more adapted to Canada's potentialities and position in the postwar world. A leading Canadian politician has remarked that a representative of a middle-sized power has advantages. He is listened to, but not held responsible for results; thus, he can acquire reputation and honors, while blame for failure goes to those possessed of power and means. What role, then, beckons him? It has not been a smooth or altogether satisfactory one.

Canada, writes Mr. Pearson, "in the troubled years since the last great war . . . has developed a special interest in international peace-keeping in many of the world's trouble spots and has played a leading part—with men, equipment, money and ideas—in the effort to make peace-keeping activities effective." At the same time, "Canada played a leading part in the formation of the NATO alliance and from the outset has been a strong advocate of the development of an Atlantic community embracing North America and the European nations from which came the forebears of most Canadians and Americans. We believed in this concept, but we would lose interest if it degenerated into merely an old-fashioned military alliance directed by three or four of its most powerful members." To hold Canadian interest, NATO must be "genuinely collective." General de Gaulle, the head of one of Canada's "forebears," would not express his interest in NATO in just the same way, nor has he, like Mr. Pearson, "developed a special interest in international peace-keeping." This illustrates one of the many difficulties of combining Canada's "leading role" and her "special interest."

There are others, too. Some of them, perhaps, lie behind the warning that Canadians would lose interest in NATO should it become "an old-fashioned military alliance." The plain fact, of course, is that NATO is a military alliance. Its purpose was and is to deter and, if necessary, to meet the use of Russian military power or the fear of its use in Europe. This purpose is pretty old-fashioned. Perhaps to avoid this stigma, Canadian draftsmen had Article 2 inserted in the Treaty. That article calls for joint action by the signatories in economic and cultural fields as well as in the military; but despite studies by two groups of "wisemen" guided by Canadians, no promising areas were discovered. Effective economic and cultural cooperation requires a more broadly based group. So Mr. Pearson concludes on a note of doubt: Canadians as members of NATO will "continue to bear our share of the burden of collective defense, so long as it is genuinely collective.". . .

Unhappily, the prospect for her "special interest in international peace-keeping" does not seem much brighter to Mr. Pearson:

Next there is the United Nations, full support of which, as I have been saying for 20 years, is a basic foundation of our foreign policy.

I still believe this, but I think the time has come—especially in the light of the current crisis in the Assembly—to have a long, hard look at the organization.

One may suggest that the "long, hard look" should be directed not only at the organization but at the problems which international peace-keeping will increasingly pose for Canada in her own integrity, her political alignment, and her ultimate purposes.

First, the country must be clear on the relative importance of the sort of international peace-keeping which has been the "special interest" of Canadian politicians. These measures are peripheral and ancillary to the policies, organization, and power which have been created by and under the leadership of the United States to maintain security for free societies in a divided world. No responsible Canadian politician would for a moment question this directly. But the essential, fundamental power and purpose is not strengthened by deprecating NATO as a "defense coalition," by questioning Canada's continued contribution to it, by relying upon Europe as "strong," and by believing that "the Communists are less obstreperous."

Furthermore, "action to contain local or regional disputes" (Mr. Pearson's phrase for U.N. peace-keeping) can only succeed if the forces instigating the dispute are weak enough to be contained by such forces as the U.N. can raise and finance over Communist opposition and (often) neutral debilitating conditions. In Korea and Vietnam, the power and finance had and has to be supplied by the victim and the United States.

Success, it is true, came at the time of Suez, and was crowned with the laurel of a Nobel Peace Prize. The falling out of allies in the most inept diplomatic episode since Munich furnished the opportunity. But when, through a series of moves bizarre on all sides, the United States found itself separated from Britain and France and joined with the Soviet Union in demanding that military action cease, the major act of "peace-keeping" had been done. The U.N.'s function was to tidy up the mess—a useful job, but one which left a disagreeable impression that the troublemakers had ended up on top and been sprinkled with holy water.

Finally, a Canadian politician anxious to lead in international peace-keeping must in fairness to his fellow citizens face up to the questions: Who will control these operations and what will their purposes be? Mr. Pearson has been frank about this: "Of course, any policy decisions with respect to the U.N.'s peace-keeping capacity can be taken only in and by the United Nations itself. I hope that progress may be made here, but it will be difficult in an atmosphere of cold-war and neocolonial suspicion.". . .

Local or regional disputes are what the Communist and neutralist members of the United Nations describe by the euphemism "wars of national liberation." The Soviet- and Chinese-mounted attack on Korea was a "war of national liberation," and the attempted *coup d'état* in

Lebanon in 1958 would doubtless have been called the same thing if U.S. Marines had not landed and scotched it. This is what Sukarno calls his aggression against Malaysia; Nasser and Nkrumah, the Communist-subsidized vendetta in the Congo. Most recently, it is the name given by Chou En-lai and Ho Chi Minh to their decade of subversive and guerrilla war against Vietnam.

Canadian officials in pursuit of their peace-keeping functions on the International Control Commission have recently been made brutally aware of this last. To their great credit, they have said so with complete candor. Thus Paul Martin, Canadian Secretary of State for External Affairs, on February 18, 1965:

In its special report of June 1962, the International Commission in Vietnam, after careful analysis of a large number of South Vietnamese complaints, came to the conclusion that armed and unarmed personnel, arms, munitions and other supplies, had been sent from North Vietnam into South Vietnam with the object of supporting, organizing and carrying out hostile activities, including armed attack directed against the armed forces and administration of South Vietnam. This same report also concluded that the North Vietnamese authorities had allowed their territories to be used for inciting, encouraging and supporting hostile activities in South Vietnam aimed at the overthrow of the South Vietnamese administration.

It is against the background of these established facts that recent events must be judged. . . .

The United States Government has made it clear that it seeks no wider war. In responding to provocation, its military action was limited and specific, in being confined to military targets forming an integral part of the network by which the North steers and supplies the rebel military forces in the South. As proof of its intentions, the United States has taken prompt action in informing the Security Council of what had happened.

In some quarters, a new Geneva conference has been urged. . . . The machinery for such a conference exists within the framework of the 1954 agreements. As far as Canada is concerned, I have stated on many occasions that we are prepared to participate in such a conference provided it is held in the right conditions. But so long as the North Vietnamese authorities persist in their policy of intervention in the South, it is difficult to see what useful contribution could be made to the peace and stability of Vietnam by a new conference.

This is an admirable recognition of reality in a current and critical situation; but it could well lead to further and profound consideration of the entire prospect of Afro-Asian-controlled international peace-keeping policy.

For a long time, Soviet leaders have been most explicit that military aggression, when called a war of national liberation, is wholly compatible with their conception of peaceful coexistence. Hence, instigation and supplying of attempts to overthrow non-Communist governments by force is always proper, while help to the victim is a violation of the U.N. Charter, an interference in the internal affairs of another country, and warmongering. Hence, also, the Soviet-Sukarno-Nasser interpretation of a solution to such a dispute "negotiated at the political level" is pretty obvious. One does not require an overly suspicious nature to foresee such action in the present composition of the United Nations developing into a "die easy" policy, in which non-Communist regimes will be succeeded by Communist or Communist-front controls. Can anyone doubt that U.N. containment of the "local or regional disputes" in Malaysia and Vietnam would have instantaneous and adverse effect on the governments of both countries? Can one have much doubt of conflict between such a policy and the more basic and rugged peace-keeping and freedom-keeping responsibilities which fall so heavily on the United States? Finally, can one doubt that ambition to lead in U.N. peace-keeping, as the U.N. is presently constituted, and still maintain a "leading role" in "a genuinely collective" NATO could create ambivalence and ambiguity in attitude and performance?

So one ends with mingled doubt and hope that political leaders in Canada and the United States will be able to work as closely and effectively together in their relations with the world outside their continent as the people of both countries wish them to. One hopes that they can "show understanding and respect for each other's views," and still retain fidelity to their own. But this is not a mere matter of goodwill; nor is it foreordained. If it is to be achieved, Americans must not take Canadians for granted. But something more is needed. Canadians must not take Americans for granted, either.

Part III

A Responsible Member of the International Community: Canada as Middle Power

The heyday of Canadian foreign policy occurred in the dozen or so years after the end of the war. The Department of External Affairs, while still small, was staffed with a dazzling array of talent, and more than one historian has remarked that the Department archives will contain diplomatic correspondence of great worth. Canada was the greatest of the middle powers, rich, strong, and sure of its mission, and Canadian diplomats were treated with respect in the corridors of power.

The times were not easy after the war. The heady taste of victory in 1945 was soon transformed into the bitter dregs of frustrated hope. The Cold War replaced the peace, and phrases like the "Iron Curtain" became commonplace. To many in the West it seemed that Hitler had been defeated only to be replaced by a new and greater tyranny in the Soviet Russia of Josef Stalin. By 1947 it was evident that the United Nations was frozen into futility by the chilling tensions between the Russians and the Atlantic nations, and after the Soviet coup in Czechoslovakia in 1948, it was apparent that the Western nations would have to take defensive measures outside the orbit of the United Nations.

Canada was involved in these security discussions from the beginning. Escott Reid, in 1947-48 a senior official of the Department of External Affairs, was one of the architects of the North Atlantic Treaty. In a speech at the Couchiching conference in 1947, he spoke out clearly on Canada's disillusionment with the United Nations and its lack of faith in the world body's ability to respond effectively to crises. As the Principal of York University's Glendon College twenty years later, Reid for the first time divulged some of the behind-the-scenes activities that accompanied NATO's birth pangs in Canada.

Over the years NATO did accomplish the effective stabilization of the European situation, but there were still other trouble spots. Korea was one. The Asian peninsular state had been divided into two spheres of influence after the defeat of Japan: one American, one Russian. Efforts to re-unite the country were quickly bound up in the Cold War, and not even the presence on the scene of a United Nations Commission could resolve matters. The Korean Commission also had the effect of involving Canada in diplomatic difficulties with the United States, as Denis Stairs, a young and able professor at Dalhousie University, effectively demonstrates in his article. Stairs suggests that there are lessons to be found in this Korean experience, and he clearly believes that Canadians could be more adventurous in their diplomacy, even if it differs from Washington's, without gravely angering the United States.

Korea was soon the source of more serious difficulty. On June 25, 1950 the North Koreans invaded the South, and because the Soviet Union fortuitously happened to be boycotting the Security Council, the United Nations was able to move to stop aggression. Under the lead of the United States, the UN was mobilized and troops from many nations were involved in the fighting. Curiously, perhaps, Ottawa's initial response was cool. The army was in a weak condition, and there seemed to be little official disposition to get involved in a shooting war only five years after V-E and V-J Days. Public opinion, however, said different. The Opposition press and some government papers, too, demanded that Canada demonstrate its support for the UN's anti-communism in tangible fashion. This meant the commitment of ground forces, and early in August—fully six weeks after the outbreak of the war—Ottawa agreed to recruit a special force for UN service. In the House of Commons, members of all parties were agreed that Canada should contribute troops to the UN Command, and it seemed as if the isolationism of 1939 might have belonged to another country in another time.

New commitments were to be filled shortly. The termination of the Indochinese war in 1954 led to a request for Canadians to serve as the Western representatives on tripartite control commissions set up in the three successor states of French Indochina— Laos, Cambodia, and Vietnam. This task and its frustrating development over the years is discussed by John Holmes of the Canadian Institute of International Affairs, previously one of the government officials responsible for Canada's Indochina policy. His memoir of Geneva in 1954 sheds new light on Canada's commitment to the International Commissions for Supervision and Control, and he argues powerfully in support of the Canadian (and the American) positions.

Canada was again asked to supply troops in 1956, this time for the United Nations Emergency Force created to secure and maintain peace along the Israeli-Egyptian border. In fact, the force was virtually a Canadian creation, largely attributable to the formidable diplomatic talents of Lester Pearson whose role is brought out in the excerpts and documents assembled here. Pearson figures prominently in the account by Dale Thomson, University of Montreal political scientist and the biographer of Louis St. Laurent. His role in the Suez crisis clearly was not one that met with universal approval, and there were many in the country and in Parliament who bitterly resented the Canadian minister's attitude. Some hot-tempered remarks by Prime Minister St. Laurent about the days of the "supermen of Europe" being numbered did not ease the consciences of the Opposition. Pearson's speech at the General Assembly on November 2, 1956, however, provided the way out of the crisis for all concerned, and it was this address that led to Pearson's being awarded the Nobel Prize for Peace in 1957. On balance, Suez marked the high water mark of Canadian diplomatic influence. The recessional was yet to come.

Escott Reid, "Canada's Role in the United Nations," Address, August 13, 1947. Department of External Affairs, Statements and Speeches, No. 47/12.

The Failure of the United

Nations, 1947

. . . The Canadian Government, in the name of the Canadian people, undertook serious commitments when Canada joined the United Nations. . . .

It is not, of course, merely a matter of the Canadian people realizing the extent of the international commitments which Canada has undertaken by joining the United Nations. It is also necessary for the Canadian people to realize the limitations of the United Nations, some of which are found in the provisions of the Charter, and some of which result from the present strained relations between the great powers.

Most of us had hoped before San Francisco that the Charter would be less imperfect than it is. The most that can be said for it is that it represents the greatest possible measure of agreement which could be reached at the time between the great powers and that probably they were able to reach a greater measure of agreement at San Francisco than they would be able to reach today. The Charter sets up a Security Council to maintain peace but makes it possible for any great power

to paralyze most of the operations of that Council. The International Court of Justice has no jurisdiction over legal disputes between two states unless both states have formally accepted its jurisdiction. The Trusteeship Council has no jurisdiction over any territory until the states concerned have put that territory under its jurisdiction. The Assembly can make no binding decisions except on such matters as the internal organization of the Secretariat. It can merely make recommendations. . . .

Most of the things which I have referred to hitherto in discussing the role of Canada in the United Nations have had to do with Canadian actions at the Assemblies of the United Nations. But that is only part of the story. In the formative period of the United Nations it is the main part of the story but in the long run the vastly more important part of the story will be the actions which Member governments take as the result of the obligations they have entered into under the Charter, and of the studies, recommendations and decisions of the various organs of the United Nations. Will we frame our internal and external policy in the light of our obligations under the Charter, and of the studies and recommendations of the United Nations? Will we obey loyally the decisions of the United Nations?

Up to the present there have not been many opportunities for Canada to demonstrate by actions its good faith as a Member of the United Nations. There are, however, already a few indications of Canadian policy. I shall cite four of them.

Under the Charter, each Member is obliged to impose economic sanctions when so directed by the Security Council. Sanctions, to be effective, must be swift and certain. A government would, therefore, be failing to carry out its obligation if it had to wait for parliamentary approval before imposing economic sanctions against an aggressor. Therefore the Canadian Government secured legislation from Parliament last session giving the government power to implement immediately any decision of the Security Council on economic sanctions. Canada is one of a relatively few Members of the United Nations which have taken this step.

We would like to do the same sort of thing for military sanctions but we could not reasonably be expected to do so until we have negotiated a special military agreement with the Security Council placing Canadian armed forces, assistance and facilities at the disposal of the Council. Under the Charter such agreements are to be negotiated "on the initiative of the Security Council". The Security Council is, unfortunately, not yet in a position to take this initiative. All we have been able to do, therefore, is to express at the last regular Assembly our concern over the failure of the Security Council and of the Military Staff Committee to make substantial progress towards concluding the special military agreements, to state that Canada is anxious to conclude its agreement, and to urge the Security Council and the Military Staff Committee to go ahead with all possible speed in the constructive work of negotiating the special agreements and of organizing military and economic sanctions. . . .

Towards the beginning of my talk I said that, in view of the deficiencies in the Charter, it would have been possible for Canada after San Francisco to have taken the line that the Charter needs radical amendments, but that the Canadian Government, like the governments of almost all the other Members of the United Nations, had considered that to press for radical amendments at the present time

would be a sterile task since amendments can come into force only when they are approved by all the great powers and there is today no possibility of all the great powers approving amendments of any importance. The government had therefore concentrated on the practical though undramatic task of making the best of what we have in the United Nations. In my talk I have outlined some of the things which Canada has tried to do in order to make the best of what we have in the United Nations.

The question which some people ask is whether such a policy ought to be continued much longer. Should we not, they ask, press for far-reaching changes in the Charter of the United Nations in order to make it a more effective instrument for maintaining peace? Some advocates of changes would be content with the abolition of the great power veto. Others go a good deal further; they advocate proposals, the adoption of which would mean the creation of a world government in a limited sphere.

The supporters of all the proposals for far-reaching changes in the Charter realize that, under present circumstances, their proposals could not be adopted except at the expense of the secession from the United Nations of the Soviet Union and the Eastern European states. . . .

A rejection of proposals for immediate, drastic revision of the Charter does not necessarily mean that those states of the Western world which are willing to commit themselves to a much closer degree of union than that embodied in the Charter should not, if they so desire, work out such arrangements. Indeed, they have already done so. The mere fact that the Soviet Union has not so far been willing to cooperate in international organizations charged with dealing with food and agriculture, aviation, refugees, international lending, monetary questions, education, science and culture has not prevented the other nations of the world from establishing F.A.O., I.C.A.O., the I.R.O., the Bank, the Fund and U.N.E.S.C.O. . . .

Since the Soviet Union is by its own choice not a member of most of the international economic and social organizations, it would have no voice in the adoption of amendments of this character to the constitutions of these organizations. Thus the states of the Western world are not debarred by a Soviet veto or by Soviet membership in the United Nations from the creation of international federal institutions to deal with international economic and social questions if they decide that such institutions are required.

Nor are they debarred by the Charter of the United Nations or by Soviet membership in the United Nations from creating new international political institutions to maintain peace, if the time should come when it was generally agreed by them that this was necessary. Nothing in the Charter precludes the existence of regional political arrangements or agencies provided that they are consistent with the Purposes and Principles of the United Nations and these regional agencies are entitled to take measures of collective self-defence against armed attack until the Security Council has acted. The world is now so small that the whole of the Western world is in itself a mere region. If the peoples of the Western world want an international security organization with teeth, even though the Soviet Union is at present unwilling to be a member of such an organization, they do not need to amend the United Nations Charter in order to create such an organization; they can create it consistently with the United Nations Charter. They can create a regional security organization to which any state willing to accept the obligations of membership could belong. In such an organization there need be no veto right possessed by any great power. In such an organization each member state could accept a binding obligation to pool the whole of its economic and military resources with those of the other members if *any* power should be found to have committed aggression against any one of the members.

I am not saying that the time has come when these things ought to be done What I do say is that it is not necessary to amend the Charter of the United Nations in order to do these things and that it would perhaps be better to do these things than to try to turn the United Nations itself into something which the Soviet Union is not at present prepared to accept. . . .

Escott Reid, "The Birth of the North Atlantic Alliance," *International Journal*,
XXII (Summer 1967), 426-40. Reprinted
by permission of The Canadian Institute
of International Affairs and the Author.

The Birth of NATO

In November 1947, United States,
British, and Canadian politicians and civil
servants started talking with each other,
very privately and confidentially, informal-
ly and tentatively, about these matters in
groups of two or three in Washington and
in New York. There seemed to emerge
a general feeling that we should explore
what might be done under Article 51 of
the U.N. Charter which refers to the inherent right of individual or collective
self-defence. These talks were reported to
Ottawa (to which I had by then returned)
by Gerry Riddell, the permanent Canadian representative to the U.N.

I hoped that these informal discussions would start things moving quickly.
I was disappointed when nothing happened in December and when I could not get
support for Canada taking some kind of
initiative. I was, therefore, greatly hearten-
ed when a top-secret, "prime minister to
prime minister" telegram from Clement
Attlee to Mackenzie King arrived in mid-
January 1948, in which Mr. Attlee spoke
eloquently of the urgent necessity of rally-
ing the forces of Western civilization to
stem further encroachment of the Soviet
tide in Europe.

This telegram was an opening gun
of the successful British campaign led by
Mr. Attlee and Ernest Bevin which finally
resulted in the creation of the Western
European Union by the Brussels Treaty
of March 17, 1948. The telegram also
sparked the discussions which resulted in
the North Atlantic Treaty of April 4,
1949.

Mr. Pearson was delighted that the
British had made this opening move. If
the campaign for a security pact was to
gather momentum, it was clearly essential
that Canada should welcome the British
initiative. But there was one unfortunate
phrase in Mr. Attlee's telegram which was
capable of arousing Mr. King's suspicions
that the British had still not reconciled
themselves to the existence of the new
Commonwealth of independent nations.
Mr. Pearson prepared for Mr. King's consideration a favourable reply to Mr. Attlee's telegram and girded himself for a
struggle.

King Gordon was in Ottawa towards
the end of January. Mr. and Mrs. Pearson
and my wife and I arranged that he should
have dinner with us in the grill room of
the Chateau Laurier. Mr. Pearson was late
in arriving. He looked drawn and tired.
He whispered to me: "I got the reply
through. But it was the worst struggle
I've ever had. I had no support from any
one in my arguments with King."

Mackenzie King had by this time become incalculable on major issues of foreign policy. During the war he had urged
the creation of an effective collective security system but as soon as the war was
over he began to retreat to his pre-war
isolationism. We, in the External Affairs
Department, never knew which way he
would jump. Because of this, we, of
course, did our best to take advantage of
opportunities to get him to put himself on

record against a retreat to isolationism.

Thus, in October 1947, I was asked to prepare a reply for him to a letter from Sir Alfred Zimmern. I thought I might as well try to get him to endorse the idea of a security pact which would supplement the U.N. Charter. I prepared for his signature a letter in which he would say:

It is vital to ensure that there is an overwhelming preponderance of power on the side of those who wish to see peace maintained. . . . If the United Nations is to be kept in existence as a meeting ground between the two worlds and if, at the same time, a more effective system of international security is desired, are we not forced to the conclusion that we shall have to get that security in some other way than by amendment of the Charter? Perhaps those members of the United Nations who are willing to accept more specific international obligations in return for greater national security will have to consider whether they should not be prepared to agree to a treaty of mutual defence against any aggressor.

I thought that this letter would come back to me from Mr. King drastically amended. To my surprise he signed it without changing a word.

Having committed himself thus far to the idea of a mutual defence treaty, he should logically not have balked at the first hurdle in January 1948, the reply to Mr. Attlee's telegram. But he did; and it was only with great difficulty that Mr. Pearson persuaded him to take the jump.

Two months later, following the rape of Czechoslovakia, Mr. St. Laurent and Mr. Pearson persuaded him to give a public blessing to the treaty of alliance between Great Britain, France and the three Benelux countries—the Brussels Treaty.

At the beginning of June 1948, Mr. Pearson went off on a speaking tour of the United States. I was left in charge of the Department of External Affairs. Mr. Pearson's final words to me were that if while he was away the crucial issue arose of whether Canada would send an observer to the military committee of the Brussels Treaty powers, I was to get Mr. St. Laurent to speak to the Prime Minister. If Mr. King were to refuse to take this jump there would be no hope of persuading him to support Canada's entry into a North Atlantic treaty.

We were very much afraid that he would refuse to take this jump. He disliked participation by Canada in military committees of any kind. He disliked any kind of committee in London. This was to be not only a military committee but a military committee in London. It was the symbol of everything he had fought against in the period from 1921 to 1939.

The invitation came in while Mr. Pearson was away. I drew up a very careful memorandum to the Prime Minister. I remember it just ran over to a second page. It ended with the recommendation that we accept the invitation.

I took it to Mr. St. Laurent in his office in the Parliament Buildings late one June evening. Mr. St. Laurent changed the last sentence to read that we should join the committee because this "would enable us to make our position clear from the outset". This was the kind of ambiguous phrase calculated to soothe Mr. King's suspicions.

In those days the Under-Secretary of State for External Affairs still used to send memoranda direct to the prime minister. This was a carry-over from the time less than two years distant when the prime minister was also foreign minister. Mr. St. Laurent said to me: "You will be initialing the memorandum." I demurred. I thought it would be better if he initialed it. He agreed.

I wanted Mr. St. Laurent to go to Mr. King with the memorandum and not just send it to him. I was afraid that if the memorandum was sent to Mr. King it might be returned with a curt "no" in the margin. Then it would be extremely difficult to get Mr. King to change his mind. If Mr. St. Laurent would only take the memorandum to Mr. King he would have a chance to argue the points.

Mr. St. Laurent said it was not possible to see Mr. King. Mr. King was not in Ottawa. He was at his country place, Kingsmere. Mr. St. Laurent said that he was not prepared to take the memorandum to Kingsmere. The memorandum would have to be sent out to Mr. King.

I went way from Mr. St. Laurent's office dejected. I thought the chances were that Mr. King would reject the invitation to send a Canadian observer to the military committee of the Brussels powers. If he rejected that invitation it was scarcely conceivable that he could later be persuaded to agree to Canada joining in peace-time in a military alliance. I passionately believed that the only way of holding the line in Europe against further Russian expansion was a North Atlantic treaty. I also believed that such a treaty could be the basis for the building of a federation of North Atlantic countries—a real North Atlantic Community.

I went from St. Laurent's office to Mr. King's office in the House of Commons just behind the Speaker's chair so that I could make sure that the memorandum would go to Mr. King by the next messenger to Kingsmere. Mr. King's secretary said: "But you don't need to send the memorandum to Kingsmere. Mr. King is here in his office". I immediately telephoned Mr. St. Laurent. I said, "Mr. King is not at Kingsmere, as we thought. He is in his office here and would be happy to see us immediately".

Mr. St. Laurent arrived in a few minutes. We went in together. I could see that Mr. St. Laurent had nerved himself for a battle with Mr. King. He said: "You know, Mr. Prime Minister, that we have been expecting an invitation from the Brussels Treaty powers to send an observer to their military committee in London. We have now received the invitation." He paused before going on to marshal the arguments in favour of our accepting the invitation.

But he had no opportunity to advance the arguments. Mr. King interrupted him: "And about time too. Now as to the visit of the Prince Regent of Belgium." And we spent an hour talking over every detail of the forthcoming visit of the Prince Regent.

It was in this manner that Mackenzie King gave his approval to Canada being associated with the Brussels Treaty organization. Some years later I told this story to a leading Canadian civil servant who had worked closely with Mr. King over many years. His comment was: "And he might just as probably have said, 'No', and refused to listen to any argument."

That was the prime difficulty in dealing with Mr. King in that final sad year of his prime ministership when it was clear that he was lingering on the stage too long. He was incalculable.

Shortly after this episode the estimates of the Department of External Affairs were being debated in the House of Commons. It was on June 19, 1948. In accordance with custom, I, as Acting Head of the Department, sat on the floor of the House in front of Mr. St. Laurent.

A question was asked about what had "been done toward completing any relationship between Canada and the countries of Western Europe, and, in particular, with the other members of the Commonwealth with regard to resisting any possible breach of the peace from any quarter whatsoever". In his reply Mr. St. Laurent began by referring to a statement in the *Ottawa Journal* that Canada had been conducting a crusade for a North Atlantic pact. "That title of crusade", he said,

perhaps justly describes the attitude we have adopted. We feel that, should war break out that affected the United Kingdom and the United States, we would inevitably be involved and that there might be great value in having consummated a regional pact . . . whereby these Western European democracies, the United Kingdom, the United States and ourselves agreed to stand together, to pool for defence purposes our respective potentials and coordinate right away our forces, so that it would appear to any possible aggressor that he would have to be prepared to overcome us all if he attempted any aggression.

That was strong medicine for June 1948. It went beyond anything which had been said in public by the United States Government or any Western European Government. But, warming to his subject, carried away by the fervour of his crusade, Mr. St. Laurent went further. He said that if the United States were willing to join in an alliance with Great Britain, France,

and the three Benelux countries, "we think the people of Canada would wish that we also be associated with it." This was the first unambiguous public statement of Canada's willingness to enter a North Atlantic military alliance.

He sat down. He leaned across to me and said, "I wonder how that will go down." I said, "I think it will go down very well in the country." Mr. St. Laurent said: "I wasn't thinking of the country. I was thinking of Laurier House"—Mr. King's residence in Ottawa.

Mr. St. Laurent had made his decision in favour of a North Atlantic treaty by the end of March of 1948. Once he made up his mind he became the leader of a crusade for the treaty, with L. B. Pearson as his senior partner and Brooke Claxton as his junior partner. The task was not easy. It meant for Canada a complete break with the past. Up to then we had resolutely rejected any proposal from any source that we enter into any kind of military treaty, even with our mother country, Great Britain. Opposition to such proposals was nation-wide but it was especially strong in French Canada. It was, therefore, especially difficult for a French Canadian to lead a crusade for a North Atlantic treaty. Yet Mr. St. Laurent did.

Denis Stairs, "Confronting Uncle Sam: Cuba and Korea," In Stephen Clarkson, ed., *An Independent Foreign Policy for Canada?* (Toronto: McClelland and Stewart, 1968), pp. 57-83. Reprinted by permission of The Canadian Publishers, McClelland and Stewart Limited, Toronto.

Confronting Uncle Sam,

Korea 1948

. . . After the end of the war with Japan, the United States and the Soviet Union divided the Korean peninsula for occupation purposes at the 38th parallel, with the Americans in control of the South and the Soviets in charge of the North. Originally it was planned that a united and independent Korea would be established "in due course," but as the cold war grew more bitter cooperation between the two occupation administrations proved impossible. This unfortunate development was embarrassing for the American government, partly because it was under pressure by the South Koreans to make good the wartime promise of genuine independence, and partly because it wanted to withdraw its troops from what had become an expensive and vulnerable theatre. In September 1947, therefore, the Americans took the matter before the United Nations. There, in spite of Soviet opposition, they succeeded in having the General Assembly pass a resolution creating a UN Temporary Commission on

Korea (UNTCOK) which would supervise an election throughout the peninsula. The elected candidates would then form an administration and take over the governmental functions of both occupation authorities. Korea would thus become united and independent, the Department of State would be relieved of a distressing political dilemma and the American army could happily withdraw its troops without leaving an inviting vacuum of power in their wake.

What was significant from the Canadian point of view was that the United States without prior consultation had included Canada among its nominations for UNTCOK membership. The principal historian of the Commission has suggested not only that the Canadians were startled and surprised when the American list of nominations was read out to the Assembly but also that their decision to accept it was governed by a desire "to save the United States from embarrassment." This may or may not be true. What is certain is that the Americans made the nomination because they felt that Canadian membership would strengthen their hand. Indeed almost all the Commission members appear to have been selected with this purpose in mind. Most were closely tied with the United States, and those that were not were firmly committed to the principle of national self-determination and could be expected to support proposals for a united and independent Korea.

But if the Americans really thought UNTCOK would give them little trouble, they were shortly to suffer a rude surprise. The Commission assembled at Seoul in January 1948 only to discover that the Soviets would not allow it to function north of the 38th parallel. In the light of this development the American Commander suggested on behalf of his government that the necessary elections should take place in South Korea alone. It was at this point that conflict appeared for, while the US position was supported by China, France and the Philippines, it was opposed by Canada, Australia, India and Syria (El Salvador remaining neutral). These four powers insisted that the Commission consult with the Interim Committee of the UN General Assembly in New York before making a decision, clearly expecting that the Committee would advise them not to proceed unless they could operate in both occupation zones.

At the Interim Committee Philip C. Jessup of the United States argued that UNTCOK should be advised "to implement its programme . . . in such parts of Korea as are accessible to the Commission," and he and other members of his delegation engaged in several days of corridor-to-lounge lobbying for the American position. Leon Gordenker has suggested that the Americans "were especially anxious to convince India, Australia and Canada" to support the US view but in the case of the two Dominions they met with little success. Australia and Canada were the only two countries to persevere in their opposition to the American resolution, and the final vote was 31 to 2 in favour, with 11 abstentions.

In presenting the Canadian case Lester Pearson argued that to hold elections in the South alone would involve changes in the Commission's terms of reference which were beyond the power of the Interim Committee to decide. He appeared to agree with the Australian view that the creation of a separate South Korean regime would tend to harden the 38th parallel into a permanent and therefore disruptive international boundary, and in

defence of the Canadian position he commented acidly that it "would at least have the advantage of proving the unwarranted nature of certain allegations to the effect that the Temporary Commission was in the service of the United States of America." More startling still, he warned the Committee that if the advice contained in the American resolution were accepted by the UNTCOK majority, "a new and serious situation would be created which would have to be taken into consideration by the governments who are members of the Commission and who feel that the advice from this committee is unwise and unconstitutional." If this was a threat that Canada would withdraw from UNTCOK if the Americans had their way, then in terms of the usual interpretation of Canadian subservience to Washington it was a bold stroke indeed.

It was also, however, a futile one. When news of the success of the American resolution reached UNTCOK headquarters in Korea, Dr. Patterson was occupied with other business in Tokyo, and on February 28 the seven remaining members met on an informal basis without him. By now the growing impatience of a number of political groups in South Korea had reached alarming proportions, and with a view to forestalling public demonstrations the seven representatives unanimously decided to announce on March 1 that elections would be held in the American zone not later than May 10. The American Commander promptly issued a declaration setting Sunday, May 9, as the precise date.

On instructions from Ottawa Dr. Patterson immediately journeyed to Korea to protest the Commission's decision. A procedural wrangle ensued with Dr. Patterson arguing that the election announcement was not binding and warning, as he had been authorized to do, that unless the Commission changed its mind he "would be compelled to abstain from further participation in the activities of the Commission until he received further instructions from his Government." Finally he withdrew, and when confronted with his departure the Commission decided by a vote of 4 to 3 to issue a press release stating that the Canadian delegation had questioned the March 1 declaration and that the Commissioners were therefore still considering whether it would be confirmed. For the time being Canada had scored a point: UNTCOK had to consider again the "advice" of the Interim Committee, and American plans for a May 9 election were once more placed in jeopardy.

The victory, however, was small and short. When discussions resumed, Dr. Patterson once again reiterated his position and added that he was haunted by "the terrible doubt that the one and only purpose for which the Commission is in Korea will not be furthered one step but rather perhaps disastrously set back if the advice of the Interim Committee is accepted. . . . If elections in South Korea alone contribute nothing to the unifying of Korea, then the United Nations Commission has no right to participate in them." But in spite of his efforts the final vote was 4-2-2 in favour of proceeding with elections in the South alone, with Australia and Canada opposed, and France and Syria abstaining. Dr. Patterson withdrew once more to await instructions from Ottawa but after an absence of 11 days he returned with orders to cooperate in the task of supervising the elections. Canada had at last capitulated.

Three observations can now be made with regard to this lamentable chronicle. The first is the obvious point that, in spite of the fact that Ottawa had used every

diplomatic technique at its disposal from simple persuasion to outright boycott, in the final analysis its policy failed in the face of American opposition. The second is that this failure was due almost entirely to the fact that, in a situation in which Canada and the United States were competing for the support of the same foreign powers, the Canadians were bound to lose; indeed while Dr. Patterson was at first supported by a majority of the UNTCOK membership, by the time the dispute had been debated in the General Assembly's Interim Committee his diplomatic allies had been reduced to one. The third is that there is no evidence anywhere that Canada's relations with the United States were seriously or even temporarily jeopardized by the Canadian role in the UNTCOK episode. It is true, of course, that in view of their ultimate success the Americans had no serious motivation for undertaking retaliatory measures. Nevertheless the Canadians had put up a good fight and Washington must have been irritated as well as surprised; yet so far as is publicly known there were no untoward effects on the Ottawa-Washington connection.

Conclusions

Not forgetting that generalizations drawn from specific cases must be regarded with caution and that a rigorous study would require a far greater number of tests and much more intensive analysis than has been provided here, the two instances of post-war Canadian foreign policy discussed seem to suggest four conclusions.

. . . as a matter of historical fact the Canadian government occasionally *has* executed foreign policies which have conflicted with those of the United States. A thorough review of Canada's external relations in the postwar period would probably reveal that these occasions have not been so rare as many Canadians assume. . . .

. . . when Canadian policies have in fact collided with those of the United States, they apparently have *not* produced serious or permanent ruptures in the important Washington connection. The threat of American retaliation therefore is probably not as effective a restraint upon the options of Canadian policy-makers as some commentators have alleged. Canadians would accordingly do well to view such excuses for governmental inaction with some degree of scepticism, at least in cases where the conflict with the United States is not vital to the American national interest. There are doubtless many theoretical policy options which would indeed invite severe American retaliatory action; the conclusion of a Canadian military alliance with the USSR provides an obvious hypothetical example. But the evidence suggests that within the range of realistic choices Canada enjoys a genuine freedom which she can exercise without fear that her fundamental interests will subsequently be mutilated by Uncle Sam.

Finally, it is probably true to say that the direct influence of Ottawa upon decision-makers in Washington is very slight, and certainly in cases like that of UNTCOK, where Canada and the United States are in competition for the support of other members of the international community, Canada seems destined for defeat. By the same token, however, it is true to say also that an independent Canadian position, as in Cuba, is unlikely to make the Americans more intractable than they already are. The frequently expressed view therefore that Canada should maintain her silence on sensitive issues lest she inflame the emotions of the calculating policy-makers at the Department of State is almost certainly invalid. Canada cannot single-handedly make the world a community of angels, but neither on the other hand is she likely to populate it with demons.

House of Commons *Debates*, August 31 and September 1, 1950, pp. 92-122.

Confronting the Communists, Korea 1950

[Mr. Pearson]: ... If the issue raised by the attack on the republic of Korea was clear, so was our obligation under the charter of the United Nations. That obligation, I should say at once, is to the United Nations alone, and to our own security. In the case I am talking about it concerns nothing beyond the restoration of peace and the defeat of aggression in Korea. The action of the United Nations covers that and nothing else. How were we to carry out those obligations?

It had been intended by the framers of the charter that member countries would make available to the United Nations, as a result of agreements to be concluded individually, certain of their national forces to assist in repelling aggression on orders of the security council. The detailed arrangements for those agreements were to be worked out by the military staff committee of the United Nations. Negotiations in the military staff committee were, however, completely frustrated by the Soviet representatives. In consequence the United Nations, in this crisis, was left unprovided with the forces which should have been at its disposal if the intention of those who drafted the

charter had been carried out. That omission did not relieve any of the members of the United Nations from their obligations, though it certainly affected the way in which the obligations could be carried out. When the security council determined, as it did determine on June 25, that an armed attack on the republic of Korea by the forces of North Korea constituted a breach of the peace, and when it had recommended, as it did on June 27, that the members of the United Nations should furnish such assistance to the republic of Korea as might be necessary to repel the armed attack and to restore international peace and security in the area, our obligation was clear.

Before the house adjourned on June 30, three days after the security council resolution, it was announced in this place that three Canadian destroyers would move at once into western Pacific waters where they would be closer to the area where they might be of assistance to the United Nations in Korea, if such assistance were required.

While they were moving towards the scene of United Nations operations, almost continuous discussions were held in New York and elsewhere as to the way in which the United Nations forces should be organized. The representatives of Canada participated actively in these discussions with a view to making sure that this was to be a genuine United Nations operation under a unified command which would receive authority from the United Nations. We considered this to be no academic matter, but to be a very important principle and one which should be established in a way which would be not only satisfactory for the present but a valuable precedent for the future. This was done when the security council passed an additional resolution on July 7 establishing a unified command and requesting the United States to designate a commander of such United Nations forces as might be made available. We welcomed this resolution because it established the United Nations character of the operations in Korea without limiting unduly the military authority which any commander must have if he is to be successful.

After that resolution was passed, the three Canadian destroyers, which by that time had reached Pearl Harbor, were made available on July 12 to the United Nations unified command for the restoration of peace in Korea. Then on July 14 came a request, not from the security council this time but from the Secretary General of the United Nations, for further assistance; and on July 19, a few days afterwards, the Prime Minister (Mr. St. Laurent) announced that a long-range R.C.A.F. squadron would be provided at once for service in the Pacific airlift. This kind of air assistance, and not the provision of fighter aircraft, was, we were told then by those concerned with operations, what was required at that time.

Then on August 7, after further discussions not only in Ottawa but also in Washington and Lake Success, and after I had made visits to both those places and talked with both the United States Secretary of State and the United Nations Secretary General, it was announced that a decision had been taken by the government to raise an additional brigade, to be known as the Canadian special force, which would be available—subject, of course, to parliamentary approval—for service in Korea as part of the United Nations forces there if it could be most effectively used in that way when it was ready for service; and I can assure the house—and my colleague, the Minister of National Defence (Mr. Claxton) can do

so with more authority than can I—that this brigade is being made ready with the greatest possible speed. . . .

I think it should also be remembered that ordinarily it is only great powers such as the United States or the United Kingdom which possess ground forces in being which can be moved rapidly to distant theatres without imperilling the security of their homelands or of other areas in which they may have urgent commitments, such as the commitments of the French in Indo-China and of the British in Malaya and Hong Kong. Smaller countries and middle countries like Canada, in any normal circumstances, would not have the effective ground forces for use in collective security situations such as that which has developed in Korea.

Futhermore, before June of this year it was reasonable, I suggest, for all members of the United Nations, and for the smaller countries in particular, to assume that the chances were fairly small that they would be called upon by the United Nations to contribute to collective military action against aggression occurring many thousands of miles away. The articles of the charter which had been specifically designed to provide for military sanctions had remained inoperative, and even now have not been invoked. The Russian use of the veto also seemed to make it impossible for the security council to invoke military sanctions against any communist aggression. What happened in June in the security council because of the rather fortuitous absence of the U.S.S.R., and because of the initiative and leadership of the United States of America, changed the whole character of the United Nations, at least for the time being, and changed it for the better. . . .

Canadian defence policy . . . until June of this year, had been based on the concept of providing a small, highly-skilled regular army, charged with responsibility of doing its immediate share of North American defence, especially in the Arctic, and designed to be capable of rapid expansion in the event of a general war which might require Canada to be defended outside of Canada. The furnishing to the United Nations on short notice of expeditionary forces capable of quick deployment in distant areas wherever acts of aggression might take place had not, I admit, entered into our planning as it had not entered into the planning of any other country. . . .

This special force is unique in one way among the offers of military forces which have been made to the United Nations as the result of the war in Korea; and provides, I think, a valuable example and precedent. If other countries were, in the same way, to earmark a portion of their forces which might be made available to the United Nations for collective defence, there would be ready throughout the free world national contingents for a United Nations force which could be quickly brought together in the face of a future emergency. In this way the United Nations would be equipped with that military strength which it was intended in the charter that it should have at its disposal but which, in fact, it never has had, largely because of the attitude of the U.S.S.R. . . .

[Mr. Drew]: . . . The vital question before us, and the question we must ask ourselves now, is not merely how much we can do, but how quickly we can do it. What we need now are not just plans the completion of which Canada is capable, but the quickest and most effective plans for building up defence. What we must do now is to make use of the resources we possess in the shortest time possible; and

in this we can learn from the communists. The pattern of communist logistics is something that has disturbed many of the people living in the free nations. Their armies move with much less in the way of supplies and equipment than our armies require. They have improvised more than we have felt it necessary to do. That applies not only to Russia but also to the forces of the satellite countries which have been engaged in military action, either in civil war or otherwise.

It seems to me that we must be ready to improvise to some extent and to build our forces with what we have now and with what is readily available. We have many trained units in this country; we have the equipment, and it seems that we must adjust our minds to the simplest means of effective employment of what we have, while at the same time making our longer plans as well. . . .

May I emphasize my belief that in carrying out our new tasks it is imperative that we make every cent in every dollar count. The people of Canada, when they learned to their amazement a short time ago something of what the state of our defence forces really was, were disturbed not only by the fact that they were inadequate, but also by the fact that we had spent so much to produce so little.

Let us remember that at no time has this government been restrained from spending what it has requested for the purposes of defence. No government of Canada has had such a free hand in time of peace to prepare whatever defences are necessary. No government of Canada has ever spent anything approaching the sum that this government has spent on defence in years of peace. Since the end of the last war, in the last five years, Canada has spent $1,500 million on defence. The people are asking themselves what has been done with that $1,500 million. It is the responsibility and duty of every hon. member to know what has been done and to make sure that we know a great deal more about the additional expenditures we are being asked to support than we have been permitted to know in the past. . . .

[Mr. Coldwell]: . . . We believe we must continue to support collective security because Canada is a small nation, with a population of fourteen million people inhabiting the northern half of a great continent. We cannot hope to remain at peace if we rely only upon ourselves for defence, so we must participate in measures of collective security to the fullest extent of our power and resources. I think, however, we can offer a criticism of the government on the manner in which it handled the Korean situation. If we look over the record we find that on July 12 Dean Acheson stated to the world that offers of ground troops would be very helpful. Two days later the Secretary General of the United Nations telegraphed all the member countries an urgent appeal for ground troops to assist in putting the aggressors in Korea back beyond the 38th parallel. Six nations did reply immediately. They were members, in part, of the commonwealth of nations with which we are associated: Australia, the United Kingdom, New Zealand. In addition, there were Turkey, Bolivia and Thailand.

The point I am making in criticism of the government is that when that occurred I thought and I said that parliament should have been called immediately to make provision for our participation in assisting the United Nations forces in driving back the aggressor in Korea. It was not until August 7, almost a month after the first call, that the Prime Minister announced that a special United Nations

brigade would be recruited and that parliament would meet in the course of the next six or seven weeks which would have brought us to the end of September. Parliament, because of another grave matter, met in the meantime, and we can now discuss the problem of assistance to the United Nations as well as the problem of our own defence.

I am certain that the vast majority of the Canadian people are ready and willing to assist the United Nations in bringing a speedy end to the aggression in Korea. May I add that I believe the bringing of this aggression to a speedy end is of vital importance to the whole world. If there is a prolonged fight in Korea I fear the United Nations Organization may lose the confidence of some of the smaller nations who may think of their own country being subjected to aggression, and only after devastation and a prolonged fight restored to independence and peace. Consequently I am of the opinion that the sooner effective help can be given to the United Nations forces in the present circumstances, the better it will be for the peace of the world and for the United Nations Organization.

The international crisis created by aggression in Korea enabled the people of Canada to show a large measure of unity. I believe that all parties in this house are now pledged to support the principle of collective action, collective security, and all that is implied in those terms. So far as we are concerned, as we said at the time, we welcome the prompt action of the security council in connection with this matter. We believe that the police action necessary must not be left to one nation, or even mainly to one nation. The danger is very great that if the whole campaign is dominated by, we will say, the United States, it does give an opportunity to the communist propagandists to present this police action to the nations of the world, and particularly to the nations of Asia, as American imperialism. Of course that statement is absurd on the face of it be-cause of the manner in which the present situation arose, and the manner in which all the non-communist nations of the world have co-operated in supporting police action to stop the aggression. . . .

John Holmes, "Geneva: 1954," *International Journal*, XXII (Summer, 1967), pp. 469-83. Reprinted by permission of The Canadian Institute for International Affairs and the Author.

Taking up Responsibilities:

Indo-China, 1954

My own recollections of Geneva may be coloured by some personal embarrassment over its conclusion. After the Korea conference had ended in stalemate, I remained on in Geneva as the Canadian observer of the Indo-China negotiations. Geneva in June is a pleasant place and I had no objection at all to lingering there. However, Geneva ceased to be the main centre of negotiation for a time and the centre of interest shifted to Paris and Berne. I decided that I could no longer justify my happy existence in the Hotel de la Paix. I persuaded my superiors in Ottawa that I should come home and embarked from Genoa early in July on a leisurely voyage for Halifax which would provide my summer holiday. I had argued that as Canada was not directly involved in the Geneva negotiations, however important they might be for world security, we could well leave what was only a watcher's brief in the able hands of the Canadian Permanent Representative to the U.N. in Geneva.

When I left, there was a good deal of arguing over the composition of the supervisory body to be set up. It was one of the major causes of dispute. Eden had been unable to secure agreement to his proposal for a genuinely neutral Asian commission, not only because the Americans didn't like it but because the Russians wanted some *bona fide* Communists involved. On the Western side there was absolute resistance to anything resembling the Commission set up in Korea a few years before in which two genuine neutrals, Sweden and Switzerland, were confronted by two not at all genuine neutrals, Poland and Czechoslovakia, with total stalemate as a result. The Western negotiators eventually assumed that there would have to be at least one Communist member of the Commission and therefore there would have to be an equal number of committed Western countries. Before I left Geneva, the Western country most prominently mentioned was Belgium, which seemed to be the likeliest spokesman for French interests, but the Communists rejected this suggestion because they considered the Belgians French agents. Canada's name had sometimes been mentioned jokingly, but there seemed no reason to take it seriously. Canada had already acquired, over Korea and other issues, the reputation of being the most objective of the NATO countries and it is believed that Krishna Menon persuaded Chou En-lai that Canada would be the best Western candidate. . . .

This historical background is of some importance because of the criticism occasionally voiced in Canada that Canadians on the Commission have acted not neutrally but on behalf of the United States. The question when the I.C.C. was set up was not whether a member was a spokesman for the United States but for France. The very composition of this troika, however, made clear that Poland and Canada were chosen as representatives of East and West, with India as the neutral arbitrator in the middle. What was required by Canada was not neutrality but a judicial approach—a willingness to look at evidence and if necessary agree with decisions which might be contrary to the wishes of the South Vietnamese, the French or the Americans. Consideration was given to this question in Ottawa before the I.C.C.'s were established and one reason why our first distinguished Commissioner in Vietnam was Mr. Sherwood (later Mr. Justice) Lett of Vancouver was that he was not only a soldier but also judicial by training and temperament. No one could have been more fair-minded. If Canada was driven to an increasing extent into being an advocate for the South or rather against the Communist side it was largely because the Poles, whose ideology did not permit impartiality, supported the other side 100 per cent. We had been appointed at Geneva to make sure that the other side of the case got a fair hearing. . . .

The invitation to Canada to be a member of the tripartite I.C.C. came as a shock to Ottawa. It is often stated that the Canadian Government was reluctant to take on this obligation. Of course it was. It was an arduous assignment which required the diversion immediately to Indo-China of capable Army and External Affairs officers whom we could ill-afford to spare from services both of which were undermanned. It meant taking on an important duty in a part of the world with which we had no direct acquaintance. Unlike the United Nations commissions to which we had previously contributed personnel, in this case there would be no United Nations direction of policy or responsibility for deployment or logistics. The three Governments themselves had to

supply all those things which the United Nations was accustomed to supply in such situations, except for transport, accommodation and commissariat which were to be provided largely by the French. What was worrying also was that we would be accepting the delicate task of upholding an agreement to which the Americans were not prepared to give their support. In the early stages the Americans offered us neither support nor understanding, going no farther than to say that if there was to be a Commission they would prefer to have us on it. On the other hand, the Government, or at least the Prime Minister and the Secretary of State for External Affairs, never doubted for a moment that it was an obligation we had to accept. To have embraced it with cheerful enthusiasm would have been much too light-hearted. To have rejected it, however, would have caused the whole settlement to become unstuck, for the composition of the I.C.C. was one of the most delicate and latest of the compromises reached.

The response of the Canadian Army to this challenge was highly creditable. They had not, as they have since, become accustomed to "peacekeeping" operations as a normal obligation. They were trying hard to meet the military requirements prescribed for NATO, at that time considered highly inadequate to meet a Soviet challenge. I recall some quite understandable tendency in military quarters to say that this was not a soldier's but a diplomat's job and they did not want to do the dirty work for the Department of External Affairs. There may have been some validity in this argument, but the Department of External Affairs could not possibly have fielded officers on the scale required. Furthermore, the Geneva Agreement itself made clear that the teams of the Commission were to be drawn from the armed forces of the three countries. The Canadian Army might have scrounged whatever officers were most easily expendable and sent them off to do this thankless task in the jungles. This they had too much pride to do. They rounded up on short notice the best staff-trained officers who could be taken away from their present duties and fielded within a few weeks teams for Vietnam, Laos and Cambodia which carried on their unaccustomed duties of soldier, diplomat and judge with remarkable success. The numbers involved seem small in the light of total commitments—never more than about two hundred Canadians at one time. Military personnel, however, were almost entirely officers and their assignment inevitably affected a much larger percentage of the armed forces. For the political tasks External Affairs officers and staff were assigned in numbers which considerably disrupted the Department.

The Army regarded this as a temporary assignment, as did the Government itself. We had no great illusions about the possibility of elections in two years, but there was a general expectation that in one way or another the job of supervision would be wound up within a year or so after the end of fighting. Within two years, however, we were still there. Then Canada took on another peacekeeping assignment —the United Nations Emergency Force in the Middle East. When still more assignments were added later, there came about a revised attitude towards such obligations. Most military planners, although in some cases reluctantly, recognized that this kind of work was likely to be permanent, that they would be well advised to plan for it, and that it gave armed forces variety in active service aboard which was by no means entirely a bad thing. . . .

It is difficult for any Canadian associated with the work of the I.C.C. to accept without protest the constant assertion that it was the United States which first violated the Geneva Agreements. Their attitude towards the Agreements was ambiguous and unhelpful, but the United States representative in Geneva did formally promise to respect them and this the Americans did in Vietnam (if not in Laos), albeit reluctantly. The attitude of the South Vietnamese towards the Geneva Agreements was entirely negative and they were most unco-operative towards the I.C.C. I recall the sharp hostility towards the Commission expressed to me by Diem and all his colleagues when I was in Saigon in 1955, although this was always accompanied by embarrassing professions of friendship towards the Canadians. Their attitude did improve later when the elections had been forestalled and even the Americans were beginning to revise their view of the Geneva Agreements. It was not, of course, up to the South Vietnamese alone whether to respect the terms of the Agreement which forbade the importation of arms or armed forces; they needed a friend to supply them. The French, who could have kept their military forces in Vietnam without violating the Geneva Agreements, pulled out. It was up to the Americans to fill the gap if anyone was to do so. The Americans were certainly tempted and they pressed hard against the Agreement. They embarrassed the Canadians from time to time by some of the proposals they thought up to strengthen the Vietnamese without technically violating the terms, but there is no doubt that their record was respectable. They made a habit of discussing their intentions with us in advance. Canadians made it clear to the Americans that they were prepared to look at proposals which, although they might seem to violate the exact terms of the Agreement, were nevertheless in accordance with its spirit, but they would never defend within the Commission what they honestly considered an American violation. For instance, a proposal to bring in American officers for the purpose of collecting and withdrawing American equipment which had been left in Vietnam during the fighting was acceptable to the Canadians and Indians because it would lead to a net reduction of arms in the country.

The record in the North was quite different. It was impossible to discover whether or not there had been any reprisals because no complaints could reach the Commission in that controlled society. The Commission could not reach any valid conclusions about the import of arms because by consistent ruses and deceptions they were never allowed to maintain a reliable inspection at those points where the traffic might flow. The Commission could never report that military supplies or forces were coming in from China or anywhere else, but it was never possible for them to say that this was not taking place. The tactics of the North Vietnamese were at times ludicrous; they were not concerned over the credibility gap. It is no wonder that the impartiality of Canadians involved in Indo-China has been severely strained.

When I visited Vietnam in the spring of 1955 just after the French had left Haiphong and the Communists had completed their occupation of North Vietnam, the solid work of the Commission was finished and the frustration was becoming more and more apparent. The morale and enthusiasm of the Canadians in that difficult country was quite remarkable, but I recall reporting on my return how difficult I thought it would be for them to sustain this over a long period when they could

see little success in what they were doing. The extraordinary thing is that although the frustration has got steadily worse, they have continued even with diminished personnel to do their job with integrity. It is pretty galling for them, therefore, to be told by fellow-citizens who do not trouble to study the record that the Commissions have been a farce and that they have been nothing but docile agents of the Americans. It is not true to say, for instance, that the Canadian members of the team have closed their eyes to the obvious violations of the Agreement by the Americans since they ceased observing the prohibition against arms on the grounds that it was operating one-sidedly. They could hardly be so stupid. They have simply said what should be obvious to any fair-minded person: that these violations must be considered in relation to the lack of respect for the terms of the Geneva Agreement shown by the other side. Whether or not the United States has been wise or justified in its policy of escalated military support of the South Vietnamese is a complex issue. They should not be charged, however, with unilateral or unprovoked violation of the terms of the Geneva Agreements.

Another aspect of the Geneva settlement upon which there is confusion, and understandably so, is the provision in the Final Declaration for general elections, which "shall be held in July 1956, under the supervision of an International Commission composed of representatives of the member states of the International Supervisory Commission". Neither the United States nor South Vietnam could be clearly considered parties to this Declaration, and they could argue that they had no obligation to see that elections took place. The Geneva settlement does, as mentioned earlier, make it possible to argue almost any legal position. I don't think any of us who watched the Geneva negotiations up close, however, had any doubt at the time that the whole settlement was a package deal. The Communists, who were winning the war, were persuaded to stop fighting in exchange for certain things most important of which was the promise of elections in two years. Who then was committed to seeing that the elections "*shall be held*"? There was certainly an obligation on the North Vietnamese and their Soviet and Chinese friends who fully subscribed to the Declaration to provide for *free* elections. The British and French were also morally committed, although one might wonder what right the British had to make such a promise for a sovereign country. Given the weakness of the State of Vietnam and the assumption held by most of those involved that France would continue to call the shot, the French were deemed to be in some position at the time to make the commitment, but they had neither authority nor influence in 1956. The French could be accused of having walked out on their obligations in the Geneva settlement, but they left because the South Vietnamese wanted them to go. They soon became so preoccupied with Algeria that they washed their hands of Indo-China and preferred to watch the Americans make mistakes.

Canada and the other members of the Commission, as I have said, were under no obligation to see that the elections took place. As members of the Commission on the spot we were inevitably involved in the pressures and politics of Vietnam (though to a much greater extent in Laos) and we had some unofficial opportunity to point out to the parties the advisability of preparing for elections. Insofar as this was possible, we did so. We assumed from the wording of the Agreement that it was not the responsibility of the I.C.C. as such to supervise the elec-

tions but that Indians, Poles and Canadians would man an independent body for this purpose. Although we were ready to do what might be required of us, the prospect was something of a nightmare. It was difficult to get enough people to man the I.C.C.s, but for anything like adequate supervision of elections in a country of this size and population we would have to recruit special teams. Although the prospect of elections at no time became imminent enough to force us to the definitive planning stage, we did do some preliminary thinking and in fact enlisted a political scientist to go to Indo-China in 1955 for the specific purpose of forecasting what might be involved. During my visit to Vietnam in 1955 the question of the elections was one of my major concerns. In Hanoi with the barbed wire still in the boulevards, the curfew and the iron discipline, free elections seemed about the last thing one could contemplate. In Saigon the regime was still taking a very cool view of the Geneva settlement and was not prepared to discuss elections. In Paris, London and Delhi, in discussion with people concerned with Vietnam, we were inclined to agree that the idea of uniting the country through free elections held little promise and that the only possibility was to encourage contact on a practical basis between the two zones, somewhat as it has developed between East and West Germany, and hope that eventually common services might grow into some kind of union. If there is to be another settlement for Vietnam, surely reunification should be sought in this way, and patiently. Thinking in terms of nation-wide free elections may seem in accordance with good democratic theory but it is irrelevant to the facts of life on the ground.

The South Vietnamese and the Americans made a great mistake at the time by refusing to take any steps in the direction of free elections. American officials did assure us at the time that they were advising the Saigon Government to make proposals for the elections, but the trouble was that louder American voices were saying that this was just a means of putting the Communists on the spot. They conceded a propaganda point to the adversary which has cost them dearly. Many of the most conscientious critics of American policy base their position on the view that the North had been promised free elections in the Geneva settlement and that the South Vietnamese, encouraged by the Americans, refused to hold these elections. For this reason, it is argued, the North Vietnamese were justified in seeking reunification by the renewal of guerilla activity. There is some validity in this logic, but it ignores the paradoxes involved. It was cynical of the Communists to agree at all to free elections when they don't believe in free elections. Free elections did not take place because there never was the slightest possibility that they could take place. North Vietnam was in 1956 a Communist state in its iron phase. The South could hardly have been called a free democracy although there have been elections in that country since that time which allowed for some of the elements of freedom. In 1956 the country was still in a state of chaos, with the sects barely subdued and large pockets where Communist agents had been left behind. I don't think it is true to say simply that Diem would not hold elections because he knew the Viet Minh would win. By 1956 the Diem Government, having had some success and the assurance of American support, was feeling much more confident than in 1954. I think he refused to put forward proposals for elections because he would not acknowledge the validity of the Geneva obligation and, what was more, he would not have any communication with what he considered a loathesome regime in Hanoi. He was afraid that once he put forward proposals he would come under pressure to compromise them and he felt that a willingness to talk would be interpreted as a sign of weakness in Hanoi and, more important, in the South. . . .

The failure to hold elections posed a serious dilemma for Canada, and for the other Commission powers as well. We had accepted a difficult assignment for a period unspecified but which we assumed to be related to the two year period before elections would be held. It was our view that international commissions ought not to linger on as a form of foreign intervention when their work was done. The job was done in a few months in Cambodia, and we wanted to withdraw the Commission. The other members insisted, however, on the link which must be observed between the settlements in the three countries and we reluctantly agreed to a token commission remaining in existence in Cambodia. Later, when a political settlement had been reached in Laos, precarious but what the Geneva Agreements had required, the Laotian Government insisted the Commission withdraw and we agreed with them. Again we were forced to accept a compromise, and some years later the Commission was reconstituted after a second Geneva Conference on Laos. With the prospect of reunification of Vietnam by elections fading, there seemed no hope of our ever getting out of this onerous responsibility.

It wasn't the onerousness that mattered; it was the apparent futility. When I returned from Indo-China to Ottawa in the summer of 1955 I was already convinced there would be no elections, and

I raised the question whether we should stay on or not. The Commission in Vietnam had by that time accomplished its principal work, the disengagement of forces. The period when the movement of refugees was allowed had come to an end, and although after a year's experience our teams were learning to operate more efficiently and comfortably, the chances of accomplishing anything either in the protection of human rights or the prevention of arms were dimming. There was only the endless attempt to cope with the chicanery of Northern officials. The French were preparing to withdraw, and there seemed little hope of getting the southern officials to do business with the Commission at all. The Commission could only note violations and report them to the two Co-Chairmen, Messrs. Eden and Molotov. To get agreement on a violation in that troika was nearly impossible, although a Canadian-Indian majority was by no means unusual. Needless to say, the Co-Chairmen's attitudes to the reports usually reflected the division within the Commissions. There is this to be said for the troika formula: it did reflect realistically the forces at play on the ground. A more harmonious or totally neutral commission could certainly have reached agreement more easily, but such agreement could have been without any influence at all on events. The Commission reflected stalemate; it didn't create it. Sometimes the Co-Chairmen could use their influence to prevent a situation from getting too hot, but they couldn't do much to see that the political provisions of the Geneva settlement were carried out. The Americans could not concentrate their power to this end because they were outside the Geneva understanding.

Canada did have one weapon it could

use: it could always threaten to walk out if the attitudes of the parties were too outrageous. Both we and the Indians did talk in these terms from time to time. Perhaps we should have used this form of blackmailmanship and packed up, thereby saving the country frustration and humiliation and criticism of the Commission for failing to do what it was never expected to do—enforce the peace in Indo-China. The trouble with threatening to walk out is that it is not a game you play often. Refusing on a matter of principle to continue would have been something different and not discreditable. We never walked out because we feared the vacuum that would be created if we did. Not that the teams would have been much missed, but if the I.C.C. went home it would seem as if the Geneva Agreement had lost a leg, and at that time the desire on all side to hold the truce seemed the only thing that prevented the area from lapsing into anarchy. Our only hope was that the tenuous peace could last long enough for the South and the two other states to acquire stability and the North to learn that the world forces against it were too strong to be defied. The Americans were beginning to see the value of Geneva and of the Commissions although they kept talking in 1955-6 about the desirability of calling in the U.N. to keep the peace or defend the South. No one would have been more delighted than the Canadians to hand over to the United Nations, but we knew it wasn't possible. Geneva had been held outside the U.N. because it had to involve the Peking Government, and the Peking Government would have nothing to do with the U.N. Nor would Hanoi. Perhaps it wouldn't have made much difference if we had pulled out, but I am sure we were right not to take the chance.

Dale Thomson, *Louis St. Laurent: Canadian* (Toronto: Macmillan, 1967), pp. 461-9. Reprinted by permission of the Macmillan Co. of Canada Ltd.

Suez 1956: Like Finding a Beloved Uncle Charged with Rape

Throughout the summer and autumn [of 1956], St. Laurent observed the gathering storm through the diplomatic dispatches, news reports, and briefings from Pearson and his staff. The 'users' conference was held in London in mid-August, and while several nations soon withdrew, eighteen others agreed on a proposal for international control of the Suez Canal. Dulles was asked to lead a delegation to Cairo to present the plan to Nasser, but he declined, and Prime Minister Menzies of Australia accepted the assignment. Shortly after the group arrived in the Egyptian capital, President Eisenhower declared in a press conference that the United States could not 'in any circumstances' support the use of force in settling the dispute. Encouraged by the statement, Nasser rejected the 'users' proposal.

Worried by the increasing tension, Norman Robertson, High Commissioner in London, called on Lord Home, British Secretary of State for Commonwealth Affairs, and asked him directly: 'Is it your intention to proceed with an attempt to humiliate and replace Nasser?' 'The possibility can't be washed out,' the other man replied circumspectly, and countered with a question of his own: 'If we have to use force, would we have the approval of Canada?' Robertson answered: 'In my opinion, no.' A short time later, he was more categorical. 'We sympathize with your predicament,' he told Sir Ivone Kirkpatrick, senior staff member of the Foreign Office; 'we even support your concern that the canal operations should be insulated against the political whims of any one nation. But we cannot support, nor even approve, any resort to force [for that purpose].' In London on September 3, Pearson discussed the situation with Foreign Secretary Selwyn Lloyd, and urged him not to resort to force except under the authorization of the United Nations; a few days later he repeated his argument before the NATO Council in Paris. During the NATO meeting Lloyd commented to Pearson almost casually that 'if things drag on, you know, Israel might take advantage of the situation to move against Egypt. . . . They'd probably win, Nasser would go, and most of our troubles would be solved for us.' 'Ingenious idea,' the Canadian minister replied, 'but it won't work. A few Arab leaders are sitting tight on the fence now. An Israeli attack would unite them all behind Nasser. I hope you won't do any urging in that direction. The repercussions would be terrible.'

Anxious to avoid a situation in which the British and French would appear to be taking the law into their own hands, and even using the Arab-Israeli conflict for their own purposes, Pearson sought to place the dispute before the United Nations. Even if the Soviet Union used its veto in the Security Council, he argued before members of the NATO Council in private session, the weight of a majority opinion would be valuable for subsequent negotiations; more important, it would align the British, French, and Americans on a common approach to the problem. He instructed Heeney to find out how the United States would regard an Anglo-French resolution to the Security Council; Dulles opposed the suggestion, accusing the British of trying to impose their will on Egypt and manoeuvre the Security Council into appearing to support them. The American Secretary of State had devised a new plan of his own, the creation of a new body called the Suez Canal Users' Association that would operate the canal, and he had just obtained the very reluctant agreement of the British and French to join it. The Canadians were convinced that it would never become operative, particularly since the United States had announced that it would not use force if Egypt refused to cooperate. On September 23, the first cracks in Anglo-American solidarity appeared when Eden ignored the American viewpoint and sent a letter to the President of the Security Council, asking that Egypt's seizure of the Canal be inscribed on the agenda: France joined in the request, but the United States refused to be associated with it. . . .

As was generally expected, the Security Council meeting proved abortive, the Soviet Union imposing its veto on a proposal to have shipping tolls on the Suez Canal paid to the Users' Association. Eden decided that the time had come for more forceful action; on October 16, he flew to Paris to arrange the co-ordinated Israeli-French-British military operation. According to the plan that was drawn up in the French capital, the Israelis were to attack first, and the other two countries were to appear to be reacting to an Israeli-Egyptian war by intervening to protect the canal. The D-day was set for November 1 for the Israelis, with the Anglo-French landings to take place five days later. On October 24 a document setting out the agreement was signed in Paris by Israeli Prime Minister Ben Gurion, Pineau, and Patrick Dean of the British Foreign Office. On October 29, Israeli paratroops were dropped twenty-five miles from the Suez Canal; at 4:15 p.m., London time, on October 30, Britain and France issued an ultimatum to both Israel and Egypt to cease fire and withdraw ten miles from the waterway.

The British-French-Israeli operation was prepared in the greatest possible secrecy, neither the United States nor the other Commonwealth countries being given a hint of it. The Commonwealth high commissioners in London were informed of the terms of the ultimatum at the same time as it was delivered, and messages were also dispatched by Sir Anthony Eden to the prime ministers; however, news reports, based on Eden's statement to the House of Commons at 4:30 p.m., reached North America first. St. Laurent learned of the sensational development first through an Ottawa newspaper. Still in an aggressively confident mood, the Canadian Prime Minister read the press report and reacted with indignation and alarm, realizing that all the time that he and Pearson had been working to maintain western unity, and to prevent Britain and France from being charged with violating international law, the two countries had been plotting in secret the very course of action against which Canada and other friendly countries had advised them. While he could understand their concern over Nasser's conduct, the decision to take matters into their own hands smacked, in his view, of old-style imperialism; worse still, the deliberate decision not to take their friends into their confidence made a mockery of the much-vaunted system of consultation among members of the Commonwealth. Even the timing of the military action seemed unfortunate. Since October 20, reports had been leaking out of Hungary of a popular uprising; the free world was observing with a mixture of anxiety and hope the first serious attempt to throw off the Communist yoke in eastern Europe, and the reported use of Soviet troops to suppress it was being widely condemned; an equally blatant aggression by the British and French in Egypt could only make a mockery of Western protests and seriously jeopardize the possibilities of assisting the Hungarian people to regain their freedom.

When Eden's message arrived a short time later, it did nothing to assuage the Canadian Prime Minister's feelings. It repeated Israel's claim that Egypt was the aggressor, and the fiction that Britain and France were merely concerned with stopping the fighting between Israeli and Egyptian troops, as well as ensuring the safety of the Suez Canal. Although Israeli troops had not yet reached the waterway, and the Canal Zone had been recognized as part of Egyptian territory, both sides were being ordered to cease hostilities and withdraw from its banks; otherwise, military action would be taken 'to compel the offender to conform'. If the British Prime Minister's argument was—to say the least—misleading, the conclusion of the message was bound to irritate. He knew, declared Eden, that he could count on Canadian understanding and support, and would continue to keep St. Laurent closely informed of developments.

St. Laurent had sent for Pearson as soon as the news report arrived, and delivered himself of a blast of indignation against the British and French. The Minister for External Affairs returned to his office to see what additional information he could find, but was summoned back shortly by his still more concerned leader, who tossed Eden's message across the desk at him, with the comment 'Tell me how I ought to answer this.' Pearson was equally disturbed by its contents, but remained calm. 'I agree he presumes a bit,' he conceded, 'but let's look at it from the British side. They couldn't very well tell us, the Americans, or anyone else in advance, because if they had we would have stopped them. And they're in no mood to be stopped.' The two men agreed that each should prepare a draft reply, and that they would compare them before raising the matter at a cabinet meeting later in the day.

Putting aside all other business, St. Laurent went to work, setting down in words his feeling of indignation and his sense of having been betrayed; Pearson suggested some changes to make the tone somewhat softer, expressing more regret than indignation over the turn of events, and looking ahead for a possible way out of the critical situation. To this end, he proposed to reject Canada's association with the British and French action and to work for a solution within the terms of the United Nations Charter. That was the proposal made in the Council Chamber at the end of the busy afternoon. . . .

On October 30, United States Ambassador Henry Cabot Lodge placed before the Security Council a resolution calling on Israel to withdraw behind the 1950 armistice line, and asking all members of the United Nations to refrain from giving her aid until she did so. The British delegate pleaded for a modification of the resolution in order that he and the French delegate could support it, but his request was brushed aside, and Lodge urged that a vote be taken as soon as possible. The Soviet Union and five other members supported the Americans; Australia and Belgium abstained; the British and French used their veto for the first time, and against the United States!* Later in the day, they used it a second time, on a somewhat similar Soviet resolution; on that occasion, the United States abstained. At the end of the Security Council meeting, the Yugoslav member called for an emergency session of the General Assembly under the terms of the 'Uniting for Peace' resolution that had been designed by the Western nations in 1950 to circumvent a Soviet veto relating to the Korean War.

The Canadian cabinet met on Wednesday morning, October 31, to approve the government's reply to Sir Anthony Eden. Since the previous meeting, the Security Council had met, Nasser had rejected the British and French ultimatum, the Royal Air Force had dropped leaflets over the Port Said area to warn the population of an imminent air attack, and British and French troops were reported to be moving towards Egypt from bases in the Mediterranean Sea. In London, opposition leader Hugh Gaitskell condemned the joint venture as 'an act of disastrous folly that we shall regret for years'. Jawaharlal Nehru denounced it in equally forceful terms. The British veto had not improved St. Laurent's humour, reminding him of the discussions at San Francisco in 1945, when Canada had opposed the rule of unanimity in the Security Council, and the Americans and British had given solemn assurances that they would use the veto only as a last resort to prevent abuses

*The United States, the United Kingdom, and France had all voted 'no' on numerous occasions, but only France, of the Western powers, had voted 'no' in isolation.

of the Charter. The votes against the United States resolution made a mockery of that assurance, for Britain and France were clearly acting to save the remnants of their prestige as world powers, and doing so in direct violation of the United Nations Charter.

In the circumstances, the final draft of St. Laurent's telegram to Eden was surprisingly mild and conciliatory, regretting that Britain should have acted without prior consultation, but expressing understanding of the reasons for doing so. At the same time, on the basis of available information, the Canadian government could not endorse the military actions of Israel, the United Kingdom, or France; it was, therefore, suspending all shipments of arms to Israel, and would shape its course in conformity with its obligations under the United Nations Charter. While he and his colleagues were 'never unmindful . . . of the very special relationship of close friendship and intimate association' of Canada with the United Kingdom, and 'the vital importance of the Suez Canal to the economic life of the United Kingdom', three aspects of the situation were causing them particular anxiety. The first was the effect of Eden's decisions upon the United Nations, of which the United Kingdom had been such a staunch and steady supporter; taking military action while the Security Council was seized of the matter was most regrettable, as was the vote itself on the American resolution. There was also a danger of a serious division within the Commonwealth over the British action that might 'prejudice the unity of our association'. And finally, there was the 'deplorable divergence of viewpoint and policy between the U.K. and the U.S.A.'. Anglo-American co-operation and friendship was the surest foundation for a peaceful world, St. Laurent remarked, and it would be a tragedy beyond repair if that basis were to disappear, or even be weakened; it was difficult for a Canadian to consider anything, except Canada's national survival itself, as more important. He concluded the message by saying that, while he had no desire to add to the heavy burdens already being borne by Sir Anthony, he felt he should explain frankly, and as a friend, the concern of the Canadian government over the tense situation. . . .

. . . When the message reached London the next morning, it created consternation; Sir Anthony Eden had really assumed that Canada would back him up in the hour of need, regardless of legal and political niceties. The assumption was another in the growing list of British miscalculations. Still, the shock and disappointment were not sufficient to stop the course of events; shortly after the message from Ottawa arrived, the Royal Air Force began to attack Egypt's airfields. The latest development kindled St. Laurent's anger anew.

Except for an expression of 'regret' by the Minister for External Affairs on October 30 that Britain and France had 'found it necessary to take action while the Security Council was discussing the matter', the government gave no indication of its attitude to the Canadian public until the reply to Eden was dispatched. Nevertheless, to the reporters who crowded into the corridor between the Prime Minister's Office and the Privy Council Chamber, St. Laurent's displeasure was evident. Asked by one of them if he shared Pearson's 'regret', he turned on the questioner, his eyes flashing, and snapped that he was 'having nothing further to say about that'. When a decision had been taken by the government, he would let it be known; in the meantime, he was not going to reveal what might be running through his own mind. He did announce that the permit to export the twenty-four fighter planes to Israel had been suspended.

By the time the Canadian cabinet met again on Thursday morning, November 1, the international situation had deteriorated still further. Nehru had condemned the Royal Air Force attacks on Egyptian airfields as a 'naked aggression'; a former Indian governor general recommended that India leave the Commonwealth, and urged Pakistan and Ceylon to do so as well. British and French troop landings in the area were clearly imminent, Nasser had ordered ships sunk in the Suez Canal to block the waterway and had presumably appealed to Russia for help, and the United States warships were reported to be patrolling the possible invasion route in the eastern Mediterranean. In New York, the General Assembly of the United Nations was scheduled to meet that afternoon, and Canada's two mother countries were bound to be severely condemned by a large majority of members. Pearson had telephoned to London and Washington the previous evening to see if the British and American governments could be persuaded to support a proposal for a United Nations force; just before the cabinet meeting, word was received from both capitals that the two governments welcomed the proposal as an eventual or ultimate solution, but considered it too complicated to serve their respective interests in the immediate future. . . .

In cabinet, Pearson outlined the most recent developments and submitted two guide-lines as the basis for Canada's attitude. First, he suggested, everything possible should be done to avoid Britain and France's being arraigned before the United Nations on charges of conspiring to commit an act of war against a weak and sovereign state. Second, a way must be found of imposing the authority of the United Nations in the Middle East through the creation of an international police force. If at all possible, the British and French troops, about to land in the canal zone, should be incorporated into such a force in order to get those two countries back on the side of legality. Because of the divergence of views within the cabinet, the minister was careful not to ask for detailed and specific instructions from his colleagues; it was simply agreed that he should fly to New York immediately, and see what he could do to extricate the British and French from the impossible situation into which they were plunging deeper and deeper by the hour. He was to consult the Prime Minister by telephone if a decision had to be taken, and the other ministers would be on hand if another cabinet meeting was required. Pearson left the Council Chamber early in order to fly to New York for the meeting of the General Assembly that was scheduled to begin later that same afternoon. When St. Laurent emerged, he was in a more relaxed mood, and told the tenacious newspapermen that he hoped Canada would not have to take a position on the United States resolution that was to be discussed in New York that evening.

Pearson arrived at United Nations headquarters too late to have his name placed on the list of speakers, but he began immediately to consult his many friends, and particularly the members of the British and American delegations. In an impromptu conference with Dulles during the dinner recess, he urged the United States Secretary of State to cease his insistence on an early vote, or at least to accept an amendment providing for some sort of 'negotiating machinery' rather than simply condemning America's closest allies. Engaged in a game of oneupmanship with the Soviet Union, Dulles was determined to go on record at once as condemning the aggressors. Asked in turn whether he would support the United States resolution, Pearson said that he had not yet received instructions from Ottawa, but that he had hoped personally for a more constructive proposal. 'We're interested in helping Britain and France,' he stated frankly. 'I would like to make it possible for them to withdraw with as little loss of face as possible, and bring them back into re-alignment with the United States.' 'That's not possible at this time,' Dulles replied. 'They've damaged the whole cause of freedom by placing us in an inferior position morally to the Communists. We could be having a showdown with Russia right now over this Hungary situation but for their actions.' He appeared even less interested than the British in a United Nations force, Eden having at least offered to hand over control of the area to such a unit once the military situation was stabilized.

By the time Pearson telephoned St. Laurent shortly before ten o'clock that evening, he had abandoned hope of transforming into a United Nations force the British and French units approaching Egyptian territory, and was casting about for a more acceptable alternative. In order to maintain his freedom of action to put forward a proposal for a United Nations force with maximum chance of acceptance, he recommended to the Prime Minister that Canada abstain from voting on the American resolution. If the British and French could be persuaded to accept such a Canadian plan, he explained, they can be seen to be complying with the United Nations wishes and thereby upholding the Charter. That way they're off the hook.' 'Can you persuade the Assembly to go along?' St. Laurent asked somewhat dubiously. 'We'll try,' came the reply. The Prime Minister said that he would consult some of their cabinet colleagues and call back. After a series of telephone calls to minister's residences, he advised Pearson to go ahead.

The vote on the American resolution was taken about 3 a.m. on the morning of November 2; sixty-five nations supported it, five were opposed, and six, including Canada, abstained.

L. B. Pearson, *The Crisis in the Middle East, October-December, 1956* (Ottawa: Queen's Printer, 1957), p. 8-11. Reproduced with permission. Pearson's Address to the U.N. General Assembly, 2 November, 1956.

An International Peace
and Police Force

I rise not to take part in this debate, because the debate is over. The vote has been taken. But I do wish to explain the abstention of my delegation on that vote.

It is never easy to explain an abstention, and in this case it is particularly difficult because we are in favour of some parts of this resolution, and also because this resolution deals with a complicated question.

Because we are in favour of some parts of the resolution, we could not vote against it, especially as, in our opinion, it is a moderate proposal couched in reasonable and objective terms, without unfair or unbalanced condemnation; and also, by referring to violations by both sides to the armistice agreements, it puts, I think, recent action by the United Kingdom and France—and rightly—against the background of those repeated violations and provocations.

We support the effort being made to bring the fighting to an end. We support it, among other reasons, because we regret that force was used in the circumstances that face us at this time. . . . This is the first time that action has been taken under the 'Uniting for Peace' resolution, and I confess to a feeling of sadness, indeed, even distress, at not being able to support the position taken by two countries whose ties with my country are and will remain close and intimate; two countries which have contributed so much to man's progress and freedom under law; and two countries which are Canada's mother countries.

I regret the use of military force in the circumstances which we have been discussing, but I regret also that there was not more time, before a vote had to be taken, for consideration of the best way to bring about that kind of cease-fire which would have enduring and beneficial results. I think that we were entitled to that time, for this is not only a tragic moment for the countries and peoples immediately affected, but it is an equally difficult time for the United Nations itself. I know, of course, that the situation is of special and, indeed, poignant urgency, a human urgency, and that action could not be postponed by dragging out a discussion, as has been done so often in this Assembly. I do feel, however, that had that time, which has always, to my knowledge, in the past been permitted for adequate examination of even the most critical and urgent resolution, been available on this occasion, the result might have been a better resolution. Such a short delay would not, I think, have done harm, but, in the long run, would have helped those in the area who need help most at this time.

Why do I say this? In the first place, our resolution, though it has been adopted, is only a recommendation, and its moral effect would have been greater if it could have received a more unanimous vote in this Assembly—which might have been possible if there had been somewhat more delay.

Secondly, this recommendation which we have adopted cannot be effective without the compliance of those to whom it is addressed and who have to carry it out. I had ventured to hope that, by a short delay and in informal talks, we might have made some headway, or at least have tried to make some headway, in securing a favourable response, before the vote was taken, from those governments and delegations which will be responsible for carrying it out.

I consider that there is one great omission from this resolution, which has already been pointed out by previous speakers—more particularly by the representative of New Zealand, who has preceded me. This resolution does provide for a cease-fire, and I admit that that is of first importance and urgency. But, alongside a cease-fire and a withdrawal of troops, it does not provide for any steps to be taken by the United Nations for a peace settlement, without which a cease-fire will be only of temporary value at best. Surely, we should have used this opportunity to link a cease-fire to the absolute necessity of a political settlement in Palestine and for the Suez, and perhaps we might also have been able to recommend a procedure by which this absolutely essential process might begin. . . .

I believe that there is another omission from this resolution, to which attention has also already been directed. The armed forces of Israel and Egypt are to withdraw, or, if you like, to return to the armistice lines, where presumably, if this is done, they will once again face each other in fear and hatred. What then? What then, six months from now? Are we to go through all this again? Are we to return to the *status quo*? Such a return would not

be to a position of security or even to a tolerable position, but would be a return to terror, bloodshed, strife, incidents, charges and counter-charges, and ultimately another explosion which the United Nations armistice commission would be powerless to prevent and possibly even to investigate.

I therefore would have liked to see a provision in this resolution—and this has been mentioned by previous speakers —authorizing the Secretary-General to begin to make arrangements with member governments for a United Nations force large enough to keep these borders at peace while a political settlement is being worked out. I regret exceedingly that time has not been given to follow up this idea, which was mentioned also by the representative of the United Kingdom in his first speech . . . and I hope that even now, when action on the resolution has been completed, it may not be too late to give consideration to this matter. My own Government would be glad to recommend Canadian participation in such a United Nations force, a truly international peace and police force.

We have a duty here. We also—or, should I say, we had—an opportunity. Our resolution may deal with one aspect of our duty—an urgent, a terribly urgent, aspect. But, as I see it, it does nothing to seize that opportunity which, if it had been seized, might have brought some real peace and a decent existence, or hope for such, to the people of that part of the world. There was no time on this occasion for us to seize the opportunity in this resolution. My delegation therefore felt, because of the inadequacy of the resolution in this respect, that we had no alternative in the circumstances but to abstain in the voting.

Toronto *Globe and Mail*, November 3, 1956; editorial.

Mr. Pearson Abstains

The Canadian Government added nothing to its prestige—or to Canada's— by its conduct at this week's emergency meeting of the United Nations General Assembly. External Affairs Minister Pearson did not actually cast Canada's vote against the Anglo-French effort to restore peace in the Middle East; but his abstention from voting had the same effect— assisting, in a passive way, the adoption of a United States resolution urging the British and French to withdraw.

After the vote had been called, with Canada and five other nations abstaining, Mr. Pearson got up and explained. The Canadian delegation, he said, found the U.S.-sponsored resolution "inadequate"; it called for all the nations involved in the Middle East fighting to lay down their arms—but offered nothing beyond that, no means of ensuring the arms would remain laid down. Mr. Pearson said that the ceasefire urged by the resolution should be linked "to the absolute necessity of a political settlement in Palestine". He went on:

So I would have liked to see in this resolution a provision authorizing the Security Council to make arrangements with member Governments for a UN force large enough to keep the borders at peace and prevent the shooting and forays across them while a practical settlement is worked out, as it must be.

Mr. Pearson's point is excellent. Even if the four Powers concerned instantly obeyed the General Assembly's appeal to stop fighting, how long would the fighting stay stopped? It would only be a matter of time before the Israelis once again attacked the Egyptians, or the Egyptians the Israelis. Once again, the Middle East would be in an uproar, once again the Suez Canal would be endangered, and once again Britain and France would have to intervene, as they are intervening now, to restore peace and protect the canal. And once again, we suppose, the UN General Assembly would be called into an emergency meeting to discuss the British and French "aggression".

Mr. Pearson wants no more of this nonsense; hence his proposal for a Middle East police force that would maintain order while a permanent settlement was being worked out between Israel and her neighbors. But why a UN police force? No such body exists, or has any prospect of coming into existence. It would have been more practical to suggest a force drawn from the North Atlantic Treaty Organization—which at least has men and arms.

And why did the External Affairs Minister delay his criticism of the U.S. resolution until it had gone to a vote and been adopted: until, that is, it was too late for the criticism to do any good? Had he spoken before the resolution was voted upon, it could have been amended as he suggested—would have been amended, in the light of the favorable U.S. response to his suggestion. But speaking after the vote, Mr. Pearson did nothing more than justify his abstention; if, indeed, he did that.

It is not as if the idea of a Middle East police force hit Mr. Pearson suddenly, while the votes were being taken. He proposed it himself—had he forgotten?—in a House of Commons speech away back last February; saying then, as he said at the UN this week, that Canada would be willing to contribute to such a force. And this newspaper has been pressing the need of a Middle East force for the last five years. . . .

It gives this newspaper no satisfaction to have been proved right, since the proof consists of bloody fighting and, worse, the disintegration of the whole Western Alliance. But right, we were. And the Canadian Government has been disastrously wrong in its timidity—first, turning a blind eye to the Middle East; then, when it did see the need to police that area, failing to press home its views in Washington; and all of the time giving tacit approval to United States actions and attitudes which prepared the debacle there.

But the debacle, when it came, did not confine itself to the Middle East. Canada is deeply, inextricably, involved in it. The chickens of apathy, irresponsibility and me-tooism have come home to roost at Ottawa; and it will take more than UN speeches to drive them away.

House of Commons *Debates*, November 26, 1956, pp. 19-42.

The Supermen of Europe

RIGHT HON. L. S. ST. LAURENT (PRIME MINISTER): . . . Originally there was this motion proposed which has been construed, and I think rightly so, as placing some blame on the Israelis, some blame on the French and some blame on the British for having taken the law into their own hands when what had to be dealt with was already before the security council of the United Nations. These gentlemen who utter these high-flown phrases seem to forget that the nations of the world signed the charter of the United Nations and thereby undertook to use peaceful means to settle possible disputes and not to resort to the use of force.

I have been scandalized more than once by the attitude of the larger powers, the big powers as we call them, who have all too frequently treated the charter of the United Nations as an instrument with which to regiment smaller nations and as an instrument which did not have to be considered when their own so-called vital interests were at stake. I have been told, with respect to the veto, that if the Russians had not insisted upon it the United States and the United Kingdom would have insisted upon it, because they could not allow this crowd of smaller nations to deal decisively with questions which con-

cerned their vital interests.

AN HON. MEMBER: Why should they?

MR. ST. LAURENT (QUEBEC EAST): Because the members of the smaller nations are human beings just as are their people; because the era when the supermen of Europe could govern the whole world has and is coming pretty close to an end.

MR. FERGUSON: Throwing Canada to the slaughterhouse.

MR. ST. LAURENT (QUEBEC EAST): Perhaps the hon. gentleman would do better to listen than—I will not attempt to qualify them—to make that kind of remark. I think it would be better for his own reputation if he did.

It has been said that Canada has been humiliated by the action of Colonel Nasser and has been made to submit to the requirements of Colonel Nasser. That is just one of those wild assertions for which there is absolutely no foundation in fact. The original resolution provided that the United Nations in its efforts to make peace in the world would not start their efforts to make peace by making war. It was going to introduce a police force to supervise the observance of the cessation of hostilities, but it was going to do that with the consent of the country in which those forces were going to operate. It was not going to fight its way into that country. That was the resolution which was adopted without any opposition, although with a certain number of abstentions.

At that time the secretary general of the United Nations gave us the chance to participate in this force, and gave it to those who were willing and anxious, as we have been willing and anxious since 1945, to have a United Nations force ready to deal with recalcitrants in the fulfilment of their obligations under the charter. The suggestion was made that each nation should supply something like a battalion or other self-contained unit.

We consider that every battalion in the Canadian forces would feel it an honour to be called upon to perform this duty, but there was one battalion which was next in line in the rotation of service in connection with the Canadian contingent to the NATO forces in Europe, and that was the Queen's Own. It seemed to us that all the other battalions would recognize that that battalion, having been groomed and being on the point of being called upon to replace another battalion in Europe, would naturally be the one which we would consider and which we would think of first to take on this new duty in pursuit of the objectives of the United Nations. That battalion happened to be the Queen's Own Rifles. It was suggested, I am told, although we were not present at the negotiations, that Colonel Nasser said that that would be regarded by the Egyptians as being a battalion of the Queen of England.

AN HON. MEMBER: What is wrong with that?

MR. GREEN: What about the Queen of Canada?

MR. ST. LAURENT (QUEBEC EAST): In my view nothing is wrong with it except it is the Queen of Canada's Own Rifles. No Colonel Nasser nor anything that is said here, unless it amounts to a successful vote of no confidence in this government, nor anything published in the papers which are trying to belittle the actions of Canada in this instance, is going to persuade us that we have no right to have that glorious battalion continue to be called the Queen's Own Rifles.

SOME HON. MEMBERS: Oh, oh.

MR. ST. LAURENT (QUEBEC EAST): No one is going to make me admit that it is not the Queen of Canada's Own Rifles that bear that glorious title.

SOME HON. MEMBERS: Oh, oh.

SOME HON. MEMBERS: Hear, hear.

MR. ST. LAURENT (QUEBEC EAST): Now, we felt that the sending of a battalion over into the Sinai desert was not just the right thing to do for men who had the training and who were anxious to perform the service for which we were sending them there. We did not think we should dump 900 or 1,000 men into a desert and think they were going to be looked after properly and were going to be kept in fit condition to perform the services for which they were going there. So we decided at once that in readying the Queen's Own Rifles for that expedition there would be added supplementary forces that could ensure for them the establishment that would be necessary for them to carry out their functions properly and, to make assurance doubly sure, we said we would have the *Magnificent* loaded with provisions, that we would have a hospital unit on it and that it would serve as a floating base so our men would be sure that until proper army services were organized on a land base in Egypt there would be the possibility for them to get the right kind of treatment, the treatment necessary in order to enable them to fulfil their mission. It was pretty effectively demonstrated, in spite of what has been said by hon. gentlemen in some parts of the house about a lot of money having been spent on our forces with nothing to show for it, that within a very short time we were able to move everything required to put a battalion in the field, and indeed, we could put several battalions in the field if it were necessary to do so. . . .

The original resolution provided that there had to be consent of the government of the country where the United Nations force was going to operate. But that is all that requires the consent of the government of the country where the force is to operate. It is a United Nations operation. It is the United Nations that is going to determine the composition of the force going there. It is the United Nations that will determine where in that country the force will be stationed and when and how long it will be there.

Having accepted the condition in the resolution, it is our view, and I think the view of practically everyone at the United Nations, that the other modalities of the operation of this force are things to be determined, independently of Colonel Nasser or of anyone else in Egypt, by the United Nations on its responsibility to discharge the undertaking it has assumed in the interests of peace in the world.

The amendment before us reads in part as follows:

. . . this house regrets that Your Excellency's advisers (1) have followed a course of gratuitous condemnation of the action of the United Kingdom and France which was designed to prevent a major war in the Suez area . . .

There has been no gratuitous condemnation of the action of the United Kingdom. On the first resolution that was introduced by the United States and supported by a very large number of members of the United Nations, the Canadian delegation abstained and declared it was abstaining because it was an insufficient resolution. It provided merely for a cease-fire and nothing more. That was not good enough, because just as soon as that might become spent we would be back in the same position we were in before. There was abstention by the Canadian delegation because there was applied there something which hon. gentlemen opposite have very

violently resented when it was applied here in a very modified form. The United Nations assembly applied closure and determined that there would be three speakers supporting the resolution, three speakers opposing the resolution and that the vote would then be taken. As we were neither supporting nor opposing the resolution, we could not be one of those three; and there was no move to amend the resolution. . . .

On that resolution there was no gratuitous or other condemnation by Canada but there has been an expression of regret that certain members of the United Nations had felt it necessary to take the law into their own hands when the matter was before the security council; and there was an expression of regret that what took place in the Middle East was used as a screen to obscure the horrible actions, the horrible international crimes, that were being committed in mid-Europe at the same time. Events in the Middle East made it more difficult to marshal world opinion in unanimous and vigorous condemnation of what was taking place in Hungary at that very moment.

That is what we regretted. We feel that there can come out of this situation one that will be better than that which existed previously. It is our hope and it has been our objective to get all those in the western alliance to which my hon. friend referred working together toward the common objective of a settlement of the mid-Eastern situation that will be lasting and that will involve the recognition of the existence of Israel as a state set up by the United Nations and something which the United Nations is in honour bound to defend and to see maintained. It is our hope that there will be some kind of a lasting settlement—I will not say a permanent one because permanence is rarely found in any human activities or human achievements—though it is difficult to find with whom in all those Arab nations a settlement could be made that would take into account the real interests of the population of each of those countries. It is difficult to find anyone who can form the kind of a government which would take the over-all broad view of the interests of the whole population and not the interests of a small group of the population. . . .

MR. HOWARD C. GREEN (VANCOUVER-QUADRA): . . . Feelings on these questions raised by the Suez crisis, Mr. Speaker, are running very deep in Canada, far deeper I believe than the government has the slightest conception. Listening to the Prime Minister I could not help but think he has been living in some other land altogether so far as public reaction to these issues is concerned, and particularly reaction to the attitude of the Canadian government.

This attitude has come as a great shock to millions of Canadian people. In Vancouver the story broke in the headlines on October 31, and I must admit that even I was shocked, although the stand taken was just in line with the stand this government has been taking for the last 10 years. It has been going steadily in the direction of the stand taken on this occasion. This time they happened to get caught. They spoke off the cuff before they had a nice, cover-up explanation prepared. Here we have the headlines, "Canada Turns Her Back on U.K."—it should have been the U.K. and France—"Supports U.S.". This is a dispatch by Mr. Leiterman and it begins this way:

With a wrench that will make history, Canada turned her back on Great Britain Tuesday night. . . .

Then he went on to point out the ill-concealed annoyance shown by the minister for external affairs when he was interviewed on this particular day. Mr. Leiterman had this to say:

Mr. Pearson had three possible courses. He could have supported Britain. He could have supported the U.S. or he could, like Australia in the security council, have abstained and said nothing at all.

Hesitantly, almost as if surprised at his own boldness he chose in effect to desert Britain and "associate" Canada with the United States.

That was on October 31.

MR. PEARSON: May I ask the hon. member a question? Would he tell me to what he is referring in reading that newspaper, what vote?

MR. GREEN: I am referring to a report of a press conference or an interview by the minister with the press, and the date of the report in the Vancouver *Province* is October 31. This was only the beginning. The minister went down to the United Nations, I believe it was on November 2, after the United Kingdom and France had vetoed the resolution brought into the security council, and he voted with Russia and the United States against the United Kingdom and France to put this question on the agenda of the assembly.

MR. PEARSON: Everybody else did, too.

MR. GREEN: Let the minister and the government laugh it off. This afternoon the Prime Minister was very careful not to refer to that. He had not a word to say about that particular vote. He talked about—

MR. ST. LAURENT (QUEBEC EAST): He very firmly approves of that vote.

MR. BROOKS: That does not make it right.

MR. ST. LAURENT (QUEBEC EAST): And the fact that you say it is wrong does not make it wrong.

MR. GREEN: The Prime Minister had an opportunity to make his speech this afternoon, and perhaps he will allow me to make mine.

This afternoon the Prime Minister said that when the vote came up about the cease-fire, then Canada abstained. He did not explain that while the minister for external affairs abstained, in his speech the minister showed very clearly that he was condemning the United Kingdom and France. The Prime Minister should have made that clear. This has been the course followed by this government right down through the piece since this serious situation first arose.

Again, just two days ago in the assembly of the United Nations when the second resolution about the cease-fire was under discussion the minister got up and said that this was all wrong, there had already been a resolution passed and the United Kingdom, France and Israel were complying with it. They had already taken steps to comply with the resolution and this second resolution should not be passed. Then the Canadian government did not have the courage to get up and vote against it. Only the United Kingdom, France, Israel, Australia and New Zealand voted against that foolish and provocative resolution. The Canadian government, representing the land of courageous people, did not have the backbone to get up and vote against that resolution; they were so busy currying favour with the United States.

The feature of the speech the Prime Minister delivered today, Mr. Speaker, was the anger, almost the hatred he showed in his remarks. I wish the Canadian people could have been here to watch him.

MR. ST. LAURENT (QUEBEC EAST): So do I.

MR. GREEN: He made a violent attack on the big nations.

MR. GARSON: It is too bad they cannot hear you.

MR. GREEN: He talked about the use of the veto. The veto was written into the United Nations charter because the big nations have to carry a great deal of responsibility. But the Prime Minister pushed that aside and talked about the life of a person in a small nation being as valuable as in a big nation.

MR. HOSKING: Is that not true?

MR. GREEN: It is just dragging a red herring across the trail. Then he went on to talk about the United Kingdom and France taking the law into their own hands, and in effect the Prime Minister lumped the United Kingdom and France with Russia in his condemnation.

MR. ST. LAURENT (QUEBEC EAST): How silly can you be?

MR. GREEN: Then he made this amazing statement. He said, "The era of supermen in Europe is coming to an end". I suppose he considers that all the supermen are in the Canadian government. If they are not all in the Canadian government, then I presume the opinion of this same Prime Minister is that they are in the United States government. Here you have the prime minister of France and Prime Minister Eden of the United Kingdom. They do not claim to be supermen. I am amazed at the Prime Minister of Canada making slurring remarks of that kind this afternoon. Those men in the United Kingdom and France are simply doing the best they can for their people; they are trying to give good leadership. I suppose the Prime Minister of Canada sneers at Sir Winston Churchill as a superman and includes him in his nasty, biting remarks this afternoon. His whole attitude this afternoon was one of bitterness.

MR. PICKERSGILL: We have one doing that right now.

MR. GREEN: The Uncle Louis kissing babies went out the window this afternoon; so smug, so full of self-righteousness, so hypocritical.

Part IV

Decline and Fall?

The triumph of peacekeeping at Suez boosted Canadian prestige to a new peak throughout the world. Canada had found the formula that ended a dangerous military conflict in the Middle East and had contributed troops in substantial numbers to the United Nations Emergency Force. Equally significant, perhaps, Canada had fulfilled its historic function as the bridge between Europe and the new world, and in the aftermath of the Suez invasion it often seemed as if Britain and France could communicate with the United States only by way of Ottawa.

However sweet the triumph of Pearson diplomacy, it was to be brief. In 1957 the Canadian electorate rejected the St. Laurent government and put in its place the Progressive Conservative party under John G. Diefenbaker. A second election in 1958 returned the Conservatives with an overwhelming mandate, but the new administration was to have little good fortune in its conduct of foreign policy. Part of this was unquestionably the product of government ineptitude; but part was the product of circumstances beyond the government's control.

The condition of world affairs at the end of the 1950s was radically different from what it had been in 1945. The European powers had recovered their strength, China was a genuine great power, and Japan had risen from the ashes to become a giant in the Pacific. Canada had progressed too, but its growth was not sufficient for the nation to retain the abnormal influence it had exercised earlier. Equally important was the revolution in military technology that escalated the cost of sophisticated defence equipment beyond the reach of all but the great powers. The age of overkill was upon us and it was an expensive age. Finally, to add to the increasing woes of the Diefenbaker government, the Canadian economic boom that had rocketed along for more than a decade was drawing to a close with the 1950s, and unemployment and recession became powerful factors affecting the country. The stage was set for difficulties and they were not long in coming.

One of the first decisions the new government faced on its accession to power was the question of North American air defence. Before its defeat the Liberal government had virtually completed negotiations with the United States for a North American Air Defence Command, and the Conservatives, rushed by their military advisers, had little choice other than to accept the *fait accompli*. But because of the government's curious insistence on claiming that NORAD fell under the North Atlantic Treaty, and because of the fuzzy nature of the agreement itself, there was substantial debate in the House of Commons about NORAD. In retrospect what does seem clear in all this is that the Diefenbaker government at some stage committed Canada to equipping its NORAD contingent (and its air and ground troops in NATO) with nuclear armed weaponry. To the soldiers, there was no question but that Canadian forces should have the best weapons available, and this view is clearly expressed in the extract from the pamphlet by General Charles Foulkes, the chairman of the Chiefs of Staff Committee at the time the NORAD agreement was signed.

The military issues, however, were not the only ones. The Diefenbaker government was very hesitant to accept nuclear weapons, largely because it feared a public outcry if it made Canada a "nuclear power." In addition, the New Democratic Party and the Liberals, now led by Lester Pearson, adopted a position in opposition to the acquisition of nuclear weapons. The question became an urgent one on January 3, 1963 when the retiring Supreme Commander of

NATO, General Lauris Norstad, held a press conference in Ottawa. Norstad was the first senior NATO officer to state flatly that Canada was committed to accepting nuclear weapons for its forces overseas and to imply that the commitment was not being kept. On January 12, in part at least as a result of Norstad's statement, Liberal leader Pearson reversed his position on nuclear arms, a decision that appalled some newspapers like Montreal's *Le Devoir*, and the question of acquiring the warheads now became a straight political fight. With the government in a minority position as a result of the 1962 elections, it was clear that its fate hung in the balance.

Over the course of the next few weeks the Diefenbaker government battled desperately for its life. It had been clear for some time that the Cabinet was badly split on the question, and there were increasing rumours of possible resignations. Congenitally unable to make up his mind, the Prime Minister wavered and vacillated, delivering a speech in Parliament on January 25 that was evidently inaccurate. Or so the United States Department of State indicated when on January 30, 1963, it issued a press release that flatly contradicted the Canadian leader. The fall of the government was certain now, and with the resignation of the Minister of National Defence, the inevitable occurred in February.

The ensuing election was fought in large part on the question of nuclear arms and American interference in Canadian affairs. That the Americans had intervened was certain; what was in doubt was their justification for so doing. Shortly before the election the Americans intervened again, this time unwittingly and in a fashion that probably aided Mr. Diefenbaker more than his opponents. Testimony given by Defense Secretary McNamara to a U.S. House of Representatives Subcommittee cast some doubt on the value of the Bomarc anti-aircraft missile with which the RCAF's NORAD forces were equipped. Although this testimony was used by the Conservatives to suggest that the Americans were foisting off obsolete equipment on Canada, it was to little avail. The Pearson Liberals scornfully pointed out that if the Bomarcs were worthless Diefenbaker should never have accepted them, won the election, and within months had the nuclear warheads in place.

The agonizing conflict over nuclear weapons had produced grave disquiet in the minds of many Canadians about the state of Canadian-American relations. Did public squabbles with the United States hurt Canada? Were the Americans willing and able to use economic retaliation to bring a balky Canadian government to heel? Was Canada becoming little more than a satellite? These questions and others were examined by Arnold Heeney, a distinguished Canadian civil servant who had served as Ambassador to Washington and as Chairman of the Canadian section of the International Joint Commission, and Livingston Merchant, an American diplomat who had been Ambassador in Ottawa. Their conclusions, published in 1965, emphasized "quiet diplomacy," a belief that disagreements should stay within the official family and not become public property. This approach was also largely shared by A. F. W. Plumptre, a former civil servant who had held both diplomatic posts and key positions in the Department of Finance. Pauline Jewett, however, as befits an academic political scientist and former Liberal Member of Parliament, was a bit more skeptical in her discussion of retaliation. According to

Miss Jewett, Canadian policy-makers often find themselves doing things because the Americans want them—not because they are desired by Canadians. Possible confirmation of Miss Jewett's view can be inferred from a letter sent by Prime Minister Pearson to a group of Toronto academics who had protested his government's policy on Viet Nam. Pearson implied that Canada benefits from its links with the United States and that these could not be jeopardized merely for the luxury of speaking out.

Serious attention was also being paid by scholars and officials alike to Canada's NATO commitments. The North Atlantic Treaty has to be renewed in 1969, and the debate began early. Some critics of Canadian policy, like John Warnock, a Saskatchewan political scientist, believed that the only course for the country was to withdraw from all military alliances. Others, like Saul Silverman, disagreed and maintained that Canada should press for Treaty revision. This, Silverman said, is more realistic, for NATO can become a counterweight to the United States and so fill the role that Britain once played for Canada. Above all there are the political and military realities of the 1960s and 1970s. These are discussed by Paddy Sherman, the editor of the Vancouver *Province*, in two articles that set out the problems that will require decisions from the Trudeau government.

The problems are perhaps insoluble. NATO, NORAD, the Americans, the Russians —all are genuine dilemmas, and few of the choices open to the policy-makers seem likely to be satisfactory. The tragedy is that so few of the options will be determined from Ottawa.

The Norad Agreement in *External Affairs*,
June, 1958.

The Norad Agreement

CANADIAN EMBASSY
WASHINGTON, D.C.

No. 263   May 12, 1958.

Sir,

I have the honour to refer to discussions which have taken place between the Canadian and the United States authorities concerning the necessity for integration of operational control of Canadian and United States Air Defences and, in particular, to the study and recommendations of the Canada-United States Military Study Group. These studies led to the joint announcement of August 1, 1957, by the Minister of National Defence of Canada and the Secretary of Defence of the United States, indicating that our two governments had agreed to the setting up of a system of integrated operational control for the air defences in the continental United States, Canada and Alaska under an integrated command responsible to the Chiefs of Staff of both countries. Pursuant to the announcement of August 1, 1957, an integrated headquarters known as the North American Air Defence Command (NORAD) has been established on an interim basis at Colorado Springs, Colorado.

For some years prior to the establishment of NORAD, it had been recognized that the air defence of Canada and the United States must be considered as a single problem. However, arrangements which existed between Canada and the United States provided only for the co-ordination of separate Canadian and United States air defence plans, but did not provide for the authoritative control of all air defence weapons which must be employed against an attacker.

The advent of nuclear weapons, the great improvements in the means of effecting their delivery, and the requirements of the air defence control systems demand rapid decisions to keep pace with the speed and tempo of technological developments. To counter the threat and to achieve maximum effectiveness of the air defence system, defensive operations must commence as early as possible and enemy forces must be kept constantly engaged. Arrangements for the co-ordination of national plans requiring consultation between national commanders before implementation had become inadequate in the face of a possible sudden attack, with little or no warning. It was essential, therefore, to have in existence in peacetime an organization, including the weapons, facilities and command structure, which could operate at the outset of hostilities in accordance with a single air defence plan approved in advance by national authorities.

Studies made by representatives of our two Governments led to the conclusion that the problem of the air defence of our two countries could best be met by delegating to an integrated headquarters, the task of exercising operational control over combat units of the national forces made available for the air defence of the two countries. Futhermore, the principle of an integrated headquarters exercising operational control over assigned forces has been well established in various parts of the North Atlantic Treaty area. The Canada-United States region is an integral part of the NATO area. In support of the strategic objectives established in NATO for the Canada-United States region and in accordance with the provisions of the North Atlantic Treaty, our two Governments have, by establishing the North American Air Defence Command, recognized the desirability of integrating headquarters exercising operational control over assigned air defence forces. The agreed integration is intended to assist the two Governments to develop and maintain their individual and collective capacity to resist air attack on their territories in North America in mutual self-defence.

The two Governments consider that the establishment of integrated air defence arrangements of the nature described increases the importance of the fullest possible consultation between the two Governments on all matters affecting the joint defence of North America, and that defence co-operation between them can be worked out on a mutually satisfactory basis only if such consultation is regularly and consistently undertaken.

In view of the foregoing considerations and on the basis of the experience gained in the operation on an interim basis of the North American Air Defence Command, my Government proposes that the following principles should govern the future organization and operations of the North American Air Defence Command.

1) The Commander-in-Chief NORAD (CINCNORAD) will be responsible to the Chiefs of Staff Committee of Can-

ada and the Joint Chiefs of Staff of the United States, who in turn are responsible to their respective Governments. He will operate within a concept of air defence approved by the appropriate authorities of our two Governments, who will bear in mind their objectives in the defence of the Canada-United States region of the NATO area.

2) The North American Air Defence Command will include such combat units and individuals as are specifically allocated to it by the two Governments. The jurisdiction of the Commander-in-Chief, NORAD, over those units and individuals is limited to operational control as hereinafter defined.

3) "Operational Control" is the power to direct, co-ordinate, and control the operational activities of forces assigned, attached or otherwise made available. No permanent changes of station would be made without approval of the higher national authority concerned. Temporary reinforcement from one area to another, including the crossing of the International Boundary, to meet operational requirements will be within the authority of commanders having operational control. The basic command organization for the air defence forces of the two countries, including administration, discipline, internal organization and unit training, shall be exercised by national commanders responsible to their national authorities.

4) The appointment of CINCNORAD and his Deputy must be approved by the Canadian and United States Governments. They will not be from the same country, and CINCNORAD staff shall be an integrated joint staff composed of officers of both countries. During the absence of CINCNORAD, command will pass to the Deputy Com-

mander.

5) The North Atlantic Treaty Organization will continue to be kept informed through the Canada-United States Regional Planning Group of arrangements for the air defence of North America.

6) The plans and procedures to be followed by NORAD in wartime shall be formulated and approved in peacetime by appropriate national authorities and shall be capable of rapid implementation in an emergency. Any plans or procedures recommended by NORAD which bear on the responsibilities of civilian departments or agencies of the two Governments shall be referred for decision by the appropriate military authorities to those agencies and departments and may be the subject of intergovernmental co-ordination.

7) Terms of reference for CINCNORAD and his Deputy will be consistent with the foregoing principles. Changes in these terms of reference may be made by agreement between the Canadian Chiefs of Staff Committee and the United States Joint Chiefs of Staff, with approval of higher authority as appropriate, provided that these changes are in consonance with the principles set out in this Note.

8) The question of the financing of expenditures connected with the operation of the integrated headquarters of the North American Air Defence Command will be settled by mutual agreement between appropriate agencies of the two Governments.

9) The North American Air Defence Command shall be maintained in operation for a period of ten years or such shorter period as shall be agreed by both countries in the light of their mutual defence interests, and their objectives under the terms of the North Atlantic Treaty. The terms of this Agreement may be reviewed upon request of either country at any time.

10) The Agreement between parties to the North Atlantic Treaty regarding the status of their forces signed in London on June 19, 1951, shall apply.

11) The release to the public of information by CINCNORAD on matters of interest to Canada and the United States of America will in all cases be the subject of prior consultation and agreement between appropriate agencies of the two Governments.

If the United States Government concurs in the principles set out above, I propose that this Note and your reply should constitute an Agreement between our two Governments effective from the date of your reply.

Accept, Sir, the renewed assurances of my highest consideration.

"N. A. Robertson"
Ambassador of Canada.

The Honourable John Foster Dulles,
Secretary of State of the United States,
Washington, D.C.

DEPARTMENT OF STATE
WASHINGTON, D.C.

May 12, 1958.
Excellency,

I have the honour to refer to Your Excellency's Note No. 263 of May 12, 1958 proposing on behalf of the Canadian Government certain principles to govern the future organization and operation of the North American Air Defence Command (NORAD).

I am pleased to inform you that my

Government concurs in the principles set forth in your Note. My Government further agrees with your proposal that your Note and this reply shall constitute an agreement between the two Governments, effective today.

Accept, Excellency, the renewed assurances of my highest consideration.
"Christian A. Herter"
for the Secretary of State.
His Excellency Norman Robertson,
Ambassador of Canada.

House of Commons *Debates*, June 11, 1958, pp. 1041-53.

The Norad Debate, 1958

HON. G. R. PEARKES (MINISTER OF NATIONAL DEFENCE): . . . The Leader of the Opposition asked for information as to the principles and procedures under which our air force will operate under this plan, that is the NORAD plan. He also asked various questions regarding the system of command.

The note on NORAD states quite clearly that the commander in chief, NORAD, will be responsible to the chiefs of staff committee of Canada and the joint chiefs of staff of the United States, who in turn are responsible to their respective governments. Then it goes on to say that he will operate within the concept of air defence approved by the appropriate authorities of the two governments, who will bear in mind the objectives for the defence of the Canadian-United States regions of NATO.

Then later in paragraph 6 it states:

The plans and procedures to be followed by NORAD in wartime shall be formulated and approved in peacetime by appropriate national authorities and shall be capable of rapid implementation in an emergency.

In paragraph 3 it defines "operational control". Since the Leader of the Opposition and I served during the first war this term "operational control" has been invented. It was not one we understood in those days long ago. I have therefore endeavoured, and perhaps it is wishful thinking, to put down in a very few sentences what I feel is the function of the headquarters of NORAD at Colorado Springs, both in peace and war. I hope I will not confuse the issue even further.

In peacetime the function will be to develop plans and procedures to be used in war. These plans and procedures would be agreed upon in peacetime and be ready for immediate use in an emergency. I might add that these plans are being worked out, modified and improved continuously. There is always a plan which could be put into effect, but that may only be a temporary plan awaiting further modification and ultimate approval, we hope, by the governments concerned.

These plans as submitted by the commander in chief of NORAD will be reviewed, amended and approved by the chiefs of staff of both countries. It will be a responsibility of the commander in chief of NORAD to formulate a general pattern of training and the general supervision of practice exercises in order to ensure the readiness of the forces and facilities which may be available to him in time of emergency.

In war it will be his responsibility to direct the air operations in accordance with the plans that have been agreed to in peacetime. Once the air battle is joined, NORAD will keep the subordinate commanders informed of the over-all air situation, and he will be in a position to reinforce threatened areas with any forces that might be available. He exercises that command, so far as Canada is concerned —again I have used the word "command", and I should have said operational control. He exercises that operational control through the headquarters of the air defence command of the R.C.A.F. at St. Hubert.

Perhaps a situation such as this might occur. Unidentified aircraft are located on the radar screen of the distant warning line. These aircraft are seen to be approaching Canada. It is then the responsibility of the officer commanding the air defence command of the R.C.A.F. to dispatch interceptors with the idea of identifying the planes. The radar screen, of course, could not give any definite identification. It would eventually be able to give some estimate of the number of tracks there were, or in other words the number of aircraft which were approaching Canada.

Assuming that these aircraft were a number of enemy aircraft and that they had been identified as such by the aircraft sent up by the officer commanding at St. Hubert, the officer commanding at St. Hubert would then direct interceptors to engage the enemy, once it had been established that these aircraft were of hostile intent. At the same time the information reached the officer commanding at St. Hubert the same information would have been passed to the commander in chief of NORAD. The commander in Chief of NORAD might also be getting other radar recordings from other parts of the continent of North America. He would report those to the officer commanding the R.C.A.F. air defence force. If the number of hostile planes moving through Canadian air space approaching the various targets were more numerous than could be dealt with by the squadrons of the R.C.A.F. under the command of the air defence commander at St. Hubert, the commander in chief NORAD could and would send United States air force fighter squadrons to assist the R.C.A.F. in their task of intercepting these bombers.

I see several ways in which this assistance might be given. The commander in chief NORAD might instruct the officer commanding the R.C.A.F. at St. Hubert to direct all the Canadian planes against a certain group of hostile bombers which were attacking, let us say by way of illustration those which were moving down through the Mackenzie basin. As to another group which might at the same time be attacking across Labrador, the commander in chief at Colorado Springs could say that he would look after that group with United States air force squadrons.

In such instance the R.C.A.F. commander would direct those planes which were perhaps originally going to engage the bombers over Labrador to divert and go to the Mackenzie valley. It must be remembered that from the time the interceptor takes off from its airport until it actually becomes ready for engagement, it is under constant direction from the control system of the Pinetree line which is directing that aircraft, so that it approaches and changes its route according to the changes of route taken by the hostile planes. Hence it is in constant touch with command headquarters at St. Hubert. . . .

The hon. member for Essex East [Mr. Paul Martin] asked whether it was not true that the United States will concentrate on missiles and that manned aircraft will be operated by Canadians only. Of course that is not true; the Americans are manning piloted aircraft today which, if an emergency arose, would be available to assist the Royal Canadian Air Force, and as far as I know it is the intention of the United States to continue to man piloted interceptors for a long time to come. They are, of course, carrying out work on research and actually have in operation certain missiles which would be available in a battle for the protection of the North American continent. Canada is also carrying out investigations and is training men in the use of missiles, which perhaps in the not too distant future may be required to supplement the defence of our country.

The hon. member for Essex East next asked if it were not true that the service chiefs could pull units out of NORAD when they saw fit. Again the answer is in the negative. As will be seen in the note it says that North American air defence command will include certain combat units and individuals as are specifically allocated by the two governments. No service chief can withdraw a unit which has been definitely allocated to a certain command by a government.

The next question was whether Canada will continue to contribute its air division to NATO forces in Europe. Of course we are going to continue to have those forces in Europe, and no doubt the house will recall that when the president of the West German republic was here recently the Prime Minister gave an emphatic promise that as long as Canadian forces were required in Europe they would remain there. At page 772 of *Hansard* for June 2, 1958, the Prime Minister used the following words:

I wish to make it clear that whatever threats may be made against those nations which believe in the mission of NATO and the necessity for its continuance, Canada will maintain forces in Europe as long as international disquiet and justifiable fears require Canadian participation.

I merely quote that as the most recent statement on this subject, and I am sure the hon. member did not really believe it was likely that the Canadian government would withdraw those troops just because we were making an even

greater effort to provide for the security of this continent.

MR. MARTIN (ESSEX EAST): Withdraw or reduce.

MR. PEARKES: Withdraw or reduce.

The next point with which I would like to deal is the question of timing. Suggestions have been made in this house that we should not have acted as we did last summer with respect to this headquarters, be it of a temporary or a permanent nature; and I always understood that it would be of a temporary nature until the formal notes had established it. I did not emphasize that position at the time; perhaps I should have done, but I took it for granted that it would be considered as a temporary appointment until such time as it was confirmed in the formal note.

The question was, should we have acted then or should we have waited until the formal note had been agreed to by both governments and had been discussed here in parliament? We did gain ten months because, as experience has shown, the formal note was only recently received and has been discussed in parliament yesterday and today at really the first opportunity which has been available during this session. The note was not ready during the last session of parliament. It may be said that it should have been done more quickly, but it was not done more quickly and I do not know how it could have been done more quickly.

Should we have waited? I would like to ask hon. members to consider the situation as it was last summer. Russia had refused to accept the resolution on disarmament or the limitation of arms which had been endorsed by a very large number of the western nations. Russia had walked out of the disarmament conference, and at that time had just launched its first earth satellite. There was a good deal of concern, not only on this continent but in Europe, and there was a speeding up of defensive arrangements. . . .

At that time there was great concern, and the Prime Minister of the United Kingdom came out to discuss the international situation with the President of the United States and the Prime Minister of Canada. I submit that it was only prudent for this government to press on as quickly as possible, have the two commanders concerned get together, set up their staffs and bring up to date a plan for the defence of this continent. It is my opinion that it would have been unwise to have delayed longer and to have waited, in the circumstances which existed in the world a year ago, until several months later when the formal notes might have been presented. . . .

MR. HAROLD E. WINCH (VANCOUVER EAST): . . . I was most interested to read back on May 20 in various newspapers across the country a statement by a Canadian Press staff writer to the effect that the Canada-United States agreement on the air defence of North America must rank as one of the fuzziest international documents of recent times. That certainly was my impression at the time, and I know that everyone in this chamber had a heartfelt hope that when this matter finally came up for discussion the fuzziness would be cleared away and that a plain explanation would be given with regard to this treaty and the principles of its application.

Mr. Speaker, one can only speak for oneself, but I wish to state that in my estimation the entire situation still seems to be in a welter of confusion and contradiction; even the statements made by hon. members on the government side during this debate have done nothing to clear up the discrepancies. I cannot reconcile the statements made in the past by the Prime Minister (Mr. Diefenbaker) and by the Minister of National Defence (Mr. Pearkes). They have not yet been explained. Government speakers have been endeavouring to argue—or make it clear as far as they can, I suppose—that NORAD is an emanation of NATO and that political approval of NORAD therefore flows directly from approval of NATO. The Prime Minister had this to say on December 21, as reported page 2721 of *Hansard:*

I want to re-emphasize what I pointed out there, and it was accepted as a fact, that these integrated forces are an integral part of the NATO military structure in the Canada-United States region.

It was not so many days after the Prime Minister made that statement that the Leader of the Opposition (Mr. Pearson), on January 4, asked a question of the Minister of National Defence which is to be found on page 2865 of *Hansard* of that date. He asked a question as follows:

Is it the intention of the government, when agreement has been reached with the United States on the political arrangements covering the defence organization, to submit that political agreement to the NATO council for discussion with the NATO partners in the hope, perhaps, that an agreement of this kind can be made an integral part of the NATO organization?

To that question the Minister of National Defence made the reply to be found on page 2866 of *Hansard,* and he said:

That matter would, of course, have to be discussed with the United States. I cannot make any firm commitment. I can only express a personal opinion which it would not be wise for me to express here. It would have to be discussed, as the hon. gentleman knows, with the United States.

So, Mr. Speaker, here we have the Prime Minister stating that NORAD was an integral part of NATO, and then we have the Minister of National Defence saying he could not say whether it was or not without discussing it with the United States. That contradiction has not yet been cleared up, either yesterday or today. As a matter of fact, the only definite statement we have on the subject whatsoever —and I say this though it may hurt the feelings of the Secretary of State for External Affairs—is the clear-cut statement made by Mr. Spaak as quoted verbatim by the Leader of the Opposition last evening.

Now, let us turn directly to the formal notes with which we are actually dealing. What does this document say?

It says this:

In view of the foregoing considerations and on the basis of the experience gained in the operation on an interim basis of the North American air defence command, my government proposes that the following principles should govern the future organization and operation of the North American air defence command.

(1) The commander-in-chief NORAD will be responsible to the chiefs of staff committee of Canada and the joint chiefs of staff of the United States, who in turn are responsible to their respective governments.

Where is NATO there? NATO is just not there at all. The formal note continues and says, in paragraph 2:

The North American air defence command will include such combat units and individuals as are specifically allocated to it by the two governments.

Let us review that very briefly: "In view of the foregoing considerations and on the basis of the experience gained in

the operation of the North American air defence command" I would have thought that the Minister of National Defence or, at least, the Prime Minister, would have told us just what experience was gained in the operation on an interim basis of the North American air defence command, because we were told last night at about a quarter to ten by the Minister of National Defence that no Canadian squadrons have yet been allocated to NORAD, and I have yet to read anywhere that the United States has allocated any to NORAD either. It would be interesting to know that too. But on the basis of what we do know with regard to our own country, namely that no squadrons have been allocated to NORAD, just what is the experience that has been gained in the operation which has convinced the government that there should now be this Canada-United States agreement as has been outlined and as is now before us for consideration?

I say, "for consideration" and not for ratification because there is already a signed treaty in existence between the two governments. This brings to mind another point which I think is worthy of the utmost consideration, and that is that a treaty between Canada and the United States of this nature is most certainly a matter of external relations and is, surely, just the type of subject which we have established a standing committee on external affairs to consider. I am amazed that on a foreign relations question of this importance and nature action of this sort should not have been taken. As I have said, on the basis of the exchange as outlined in the formal notes I can find nothing which would constitute NORAD as an integral part of NATO....

As I said, we in this group have always supported to the fullest extent the concept of collective security and collective defence but we are still in the dark as to the direct relationship in conformity with NATO that exists as a result of the introduction of the NORAD treaty agreement with the United States. We strongly feel we have not been given the information which as members of the House of Commons we are entitled to receive which would give us a satisfactory understanding of the situation. There is still too much confusion and contradiction. I have already mentioned one example of the squadron control.

I suppose we cannot challenge the statement of the Minister of National Defence to the effect that the strategic air command planes of the United States air force do not fly over or from Canada and yet on the same day that statement was made the Prime Minister announced that permission had now been granted for the establishment of tanker refuelling stations in Canada. There may be a logical explanation but we have not heard it yet as to why the United States should want to establish tanker refuelling stations in Canada if United States planes are not flying over or from Canada.

There are many questions which have not been satisfactorily answered. Several contradictions have not been reconciled. The confusion has not been cleared away. I do not think hon. members of this house should be expected to reach a decision on this matter until such time as the confusion has been eliminated and the conflicting statements of ministers of the present government have been reconciled and until we have been taken into the confidence of the government as completely as possible within security provisions to enable us to appreciate the necessity for this action and be convinced that this is a direct part of the NATO command.

General Charles Foulkes, "Canadian Defence Policy in a Nuclear Age," *Behind the Headlines*, XXI (May, 1961). Reprinted by permission of The Canadian Institute of International Affairs and the Author.

A Soldier's View of Defence, 1961

CANADIAN DEFENCE POLICY: THE ALTERNATIVES

There appear from time to time criticisms of defence policy and suggested solutions to the defence problem in Canada. These proposals range from the suggestion that Canada should become a nuclear power with its own deterrent to various forms of neutrality. In the light of this background of the development of defence policy it might be helpful to discuss some of these proposals in search of a better answer to the present defence dilemma.

The question of neutrality

When in search of a national solution to avoid nuclear destruction it is only natural to turn to the age-old fallacy of neutrality, even though it is obvious to all that neutrality did not save Belgium in the First World War nor Holland in the second conflict. Would neutrality really save Canada from destruction in an all out nuclear war involving the United States and the Soviet Union? While Canada can revoke its solemn treaties with its friends, it cannot negate geography. Canada is physically joined to the United States just like the Siamese twins. If one of the twins gets hurt the other one suffers. It is just as impossible to separate the defence of Canada from that of the United States as it would be to separate the Siamese twins and expect them to survive. In a nuclear war Canada could not hope to escape grave damage and loss of life. Radiation, blast and fallout have no respect for national boundaries. What would Canada achieve from neutrality? Certainly not immunity from destruction. On the contrary, it would lose its influence with the United States and with its NATO partners, and it is doubtful if it would enhance its prestige in the United Nations.

A further suggestion has been put forward that Canada should withdraw its forces from the NATO command in Europe, cancel the air defence arrangements with the United States and place all the Canadian armed forces under the United Nations. In order to examine carefully this proposal it might be advisable to deal with the withdrawal of Canadian forces from the NATO commands and later examine the feasibility and desirability of placing the forces under the United Nations.

Should Canada withdraw from NATO?

It has been mentioned earlier that our contribution to the shield forces in Europe consists of a Brigade Group of three battalions and supporting troops, and an Air Division of 12 squadrons. As far as the Brigade Group is concerned, from a purely military standpoint, its withdrawal would not be significant. With the build-up of the German forces the Brigade should be taken out of its present forward role, and the Germans should take over the defending of their own border.

Whether the Brigade should be given another role or brought home is a political decision. However, this is the only operational role the Army has, and it is doubtful if you can maintain a fighting force just by practising survival.

The Air Division is being re-equipped. Eight of the present day-fighter squadrons are to be converted to a reconnaissance strike role and are to be equipped with the F-104 strike aircraft. This new role requires the use of a small atomic bomb, and although the aircraft is useless in this role without it, so far arrangements for obtaining these weapons have not been completed. There is no role for this formation in Canada and, therefore, if it is brought home, it would probably be disbanded.

While, from a purely military standpoint, the European partners should now be able to look after their own territorial defence, there are serious political and psychological considerations. A decision to bring the Canadian troops home might be misinterpreted by Mr. Khrushchev as the beginning of the breakup of NATO (which is of course one of the Soviet Union's announced aims) and by our partners in NATO as the start of Canadian neutrality or withdrawal to *Fortress America*.

Should Canada withdraw from NORAD?

This is a question that is generally misunderstood. As mentioned earlier, the decision to undertake joint air defence was made in 1946 not in 1958. The setting up of the integrated headquarters in Colorado Springs which became known as NORAD was the last step in co-ordinating the whole of the air defence of the continent which had been developed over the past fifteen years. Some of the argument for the abandonment of the air defence

organization may be based on the assumption that bomber attacks are now outmoded and therefore there is no need for such defences. Bombers are still the most accurate and flexible delivery system for mass destruction weapons. Rockets are now being developed which can be launched from bomber aircraft at long ranges, something like 1000 miles, and these rockets carry a megaton warhead. This provides a new form of mobility to the retaliatory weapon and decreases the risk of destruction of the deterrent by a first strike. The U.K. have abandoned their extensive *Blue Strike* missile programme because of its vulnerability and are planning to adopt the U.S. Skybolt airborne missile in their Vulcan bombers. It is my opinion that it is premature to abandon an efficient working system until we are sure that the Russians have scrapped all their bombers and it has been established that the NORAD organization is of no use against the airborne type of missile. It should be remembered also that NORAD is responsible for the operation of the ballistic missile early warning system which is now in operation. A satellite early warning system known as MIDAS will come into operation in about 1965. If and when a missile defence system is developed, NORAD will operate the system.

There is also another important advantage to Canada in fully co-operating with the U.S. in the defence of this continent. This action puts Canada in a preferential position because, as we are full partners in the defence of North America, we have to be consulted every time the U.S. contemplates using force anywhere in the world. This consultation is necessary as this use of force may bring about retaliation and our joint air defences must be in a high state of readiness.

Therefore, we are in a very favourable position to influence U.S. policy. This is worth keeping, and I see little to be gained and much to be lost in severing our close defence relations with the United States. Right enough, we should not spend much more on bomber defence, but it is important to keep this close and intimate defence relationship.

Should Canada commit all its forces to the U.N.?

As mentioned earlier, we have been aware of possible U.N. commitments since 1946. Since that time Canada has played a part second to no other country in providing military personnel for United Nations mediatory forces and for the international truce commissions in Indochina. This has been a very important contribution by Canada to the maintenance of stability in the Middle East, Southeast Asia and Africa, and the provision of such forces is given a high priority in Canadian defence planning. It would be helpful, of course, if a United Nations Emergency Force could be set up on a permanent stand-by basis to avoid improvisation in emergencies. If this could be done, Canada should certainly make its appropriate contribution. There has, however, been too much opposition to this proposal on the part of the Soviet bloc and the uncommitted countries to allow it to be accomplished. In addition, it has had to be recognized that there are different requirements for each emergency. In Indochina the need was largely for officers. For the United Nations Emergency Force in the Middle East we were asked to supply officers and men in customary military formations. In the Congo, there were political reasons for preferring African and Asian troops, and Canada was asked for specialists such as signallers and air

force transport personnel.

While the policy of our services should be flexible enough to cope with these important requests for international service, it is quite another matter to suggest that the provision of such forces should be the sole aim of our military preparations. We cannot have a healthy army, navy, or air force without a rounded programme.

It should be borne in mind, futhermore, that these international mediatory functions are quite different in kind from broader ideas of a United Nations army or police force with which they are often confused. They are quite different from the United Nations Command which fought in Korea. This latter was composed of components from armed forces of various countries supplementing the army of the United States, which also directed the military strategy. The job of the United Nations forces in the Middle East and the Congo is to supervise not to fight against aggression. It may be that eventually this concept of an international force will grow into the reality of a United Nations armed force able to enforce the will of the United Nations. It is very hard to see, however, how such a force to combat aggression can have any meaning until the great powers have drastically disarmed. Until that time, what kind of international army could resist the armies of the Soviet Union or China—or even of Israel or Cuba? We can all hope that the day of disarmament and an international police force will come, but it would be a grave mistake to base our defence policy on the illusion that that day had come.

To say, therefore, that Canada should put all its forces at the disposal of the United Nations is to talk nonsense. The United Nations, as now constituted, cannot dispose of forces in this way. The

Security Council can ask member governments to contribute their forces in certain ways to help keep the peace. When called upon to do so, the best contribution a country can make is to produce troops from effective and well-trained national forces. It should be constant Canadian policy to make our armed forces available for United Nations service and even to declare that they will be used only for purposes consistent with the U.N. Charter. This does not mean, however, that Canada or any other country is expected to turn over its forces to the direction of a non-existent United Nations command to be used in accordance with the will of any fleeting majority in the Security Council or the General Assembly. . . .

There is left the problem of providing tactical nuclear weapons for the Canadian forces. This issue still seems to be in question and deserves close examination.

Should Canada possess tactical nuclear weapons?

There is a tendency for some critics to lump together tactical nuclear weapons, *e.g.* warheads for the *Honest John* support weapon, and mass destruction weapons such as the multi-megaton cobalt bomb, and condemn the acquisition of all types of nuclear weapons. This type of approach condemns the weapon because of the nature of the explosive content and not because of its destructive power. These critics ignore the problem of Canadian troops facing an adversary armed with superior nuclear weapons. Therefore, it may be helpful in understanding this complicated issue first, to discuss the types of weapons required by the Canadian forces and the proposals for storage, control and custody of the nuclear components before giving consideration to the desirability of acquiring these weapons.

Canada has accepted a forward task for the Brigade Group in the Shield forces in Europe which requires heavy support for its infantry. The Government has agreed to provide for this support the *Honest John* 762 mm. close-support rocket which requires an atomic warhead. This is the same equipment which is being used by the other NATO partners in the Shield force.

As I mentioned earlier, the air division is being re-equipped. Eight of the day-fighter squadrons are being converted to reconnaissance strike squadrons, and the Government has decided to equip these squadrons with the F-104 strike aircraft which is to be armed with a small atomic bomb. To carry out these roles which the Government has accepted, these atomic weapons are necessary. Canadian maritime forces of ships and aircraft have been allotted an anti-submarine role in the North Atlantic. The most effective method of carrying out their tasks is by using atomic depth charges and atomic torpedoes. These weapons are essential to deal with the missile-carrying atomic submarine which has the capability of attacking Canadian ports and shipping.

The *Bomarc* missile requires an atomic warhead and two of these air defence missiles will be located in Canada. If any new fighters are procured to replace the CF-100, these fighters will require an air-to-air atomic missile. These warheads will be supplied and maintained by the United States. They will be stockpiled under NATO or national arrangements, guarded by NATO or national forces as applicable but will be maintained by and remain in the custody of the U.S. until released by the President to the Supreme Allied Commander (SACEUR) or the country concerned. The reason for this veto on their use is to ensure that the weapons are used only for the purpose intended; that is, for the defence of the NATO area. This appears to be a very prudent safeguard.

This issue is sometimes clouded by the objection to the U.S. maintaining custody of the nuclear components. The statement is frequently made that Canada should not have anything to do with weapons that are not completely under Canadian control. This fear does not stand up to close examination. These weapons are manufactured and paid for by the U.S. and are not *bought* by Canada; they remain the property of the United States. They are provided solely for joint use or for multilateral defence of the NATO area which includes Canada. The U.S. law restricts the release of nuclear components to the President. This is a safeguard to ensure that they are not used for any other purpose. This release is not an order to use them; it is only a release to the country concerned. The decision to use the weapons, like the decision to go to war, is a national government decision. . . .

The only remaining issue is whether these nuclear components for tactical nuclear weapons should be acquired from the United States for use by the Canadian armed forces in Europe, in the North Atlantic and in Canada.

From a purely military standpoint there is no doubt that in order to carry out the tasks that the Government has accepted in Europe, in the Atlantic and in North America, these nuclear weapons and warheads are required. To ask the Canadian serviceman to fight with weapons inferior to those of the enemy has never been Canadian policy and I hope it never will be. The Prime Minister has said on several occasions that the Canadian forces will be well-equipped and trained for the Canadian share in balanced, collective defence. If for any reason the most modern and efficient weapons are not to be obtained, then the roles and tasks that Canada has accepted should be revoked or modified. Under no circumstances, however, should the Canadian serviceman be expected to carry out military tasks with equipment inferior to that of the enemy.

Peyton Lyon, *Canada in World Affairs,* Vol. XII: *1961-63* (Toronto: Oxford University Press, 1968).

The Norstad Press Conference, 1963

. . . On January 3 General Lauris Norstad came to Canada in the course of taking his leave of the fifteen governments that he had served as supreme commander on NATO's most important front. He had gained a reputation for championing the interests of the alliance at the expense of his relations with his own government in Washington, and in the capitals of the European members he was received warmly by the top national leaders. President de Gaulle was exceptionally cordial. However, Mr. Diefenbaker, although back from Nassau, elected not to see the distinguished visitor. General Norstad called on the Governor-General, and since Mr. Harkness was out of town, his host during the day was the Associate Minister of Defence, M. Pierre Sévigny. The highlight of the visit was a thirty-five minute press conference which transformed the nuclear arms debate in Canada. About half of it dealt with Canada's commitments in NATO; because of the various motives later attributed to General Norstad, it seems advisable to cite in full the relevant portions of the transcript. In his opening

statement, the General stressed the accomplishments of NATO and concluded: "Your Government, by its contribution, by the presence of its forces, has made an outstanding contribution." The third question raised the main issue:

Q. Well, Sir, have you always been satisfied with Canada's contribution to NATO even though it was non-nuclear all along?

A. It's a mistake for anyone ever to say he is satisfied with anything. . . . Canada has made certain commitments . . . which bear a very reasonable relationship . . . to Canada's ability to commit forces. . . . Canada has met those commitments in numbers and, in general, in quality during the entire life of the alliance. So Canada has been really quite outstanding in meeting its NATO commitments.

Q. General, do you consider that Canada has committed itself to provide its Starfighter squadrons in Europe with tactical nuclear weapons?

A. That is perhaps a question you should direct to the Minister rather than to me, but my answer to that is "Yes". This has been a commitment that was made, the continuation of the commitment that existed before, and as the air division is re-equipped that air division will continue to be committed to NATO and will continue to play an extremely, an increasingly important role.

Q. In the field of tactical nuclear . . .?

A. That's right.

Q. I'm sorry, Sir,—will play an extremely important role with or without tactical nuclear weapons?

A. I would hope with both. Is Air Marshal Miller here? I don't want to release anything you people haven't released here on this.

[Air Marshall Miller, Chairman, Chiefs of Staff: I think you're right on that; quite right on that . . . (then inaudible).]

NORSTAD: We established a NATO requirement for a certain number of strike squadrons. This includes tactical atomic strike squadrons and Canada committed some of its force to meet this NATO established requirement. And this we depend upon. Again, we depend upon it particularly because of the quality of that air division.

Q. Does it mean, Sir, that if Canada does not accept nuclear weapons for these aeroplanes that she is not actually fulfilling her NATO commitments?

A. I believe that's right. She would be meeting it in force but not under the terms of the requirements that have been established by NATO. I'd like to say that with all forces (there's always a tendency to get too black and white on this question of atomic weapons). Now, let me emphasize again the importance of conventional forces. We have established that requirement back as I say to '55, '56, and '57. It's absolutely essential that that should be met. That requirement cannot be met by atomic weapons. Nor can conventional weapons meet all the requirements of atomic weapons. I would hope that at least a substantial part of our forces could perhaps have a dual capacity; but there is a snare and a delusion involved in this, because you can't say we'll go conventional or we'll go atomic. You've got to commit something for a period of time because it takes hours, and in some cases days, and sometimes longer, to make the change; but there will be a balance throughout the whole alliance with conventional and atomic forces, and we are depending upon Canada to produce some of the tactical atomic strike forces.

Q. General, did you say that you believe that Canada has committed this Starfighter group to tactical weapons?

A. No doubt—I know that they have committed the Starfighters, yes.

Q. Could you say that this commitment is given in writing anywhere?

A. I don't know the answer to that one. The commitment, certainly, to provide the units is in writing as has been repeated on several occasions and I cannot specifically recall where it states whether they are going to be atomic or not.

Q. Sir, do the Starfighters have any capability, in your view, with conventional weapons?

A. They could have. But I think that the minimum number that is required for the atomic—for the deterrent—to make the deterrent effective, that is for these atomic strike forces, we should not, in my judgment, degrade their deterrent value by making them conventional. We should have other conventional forces. We should not degrade their deterrent value by making them conventional.

Q. General, would the nuclear weapons be available to the division in case of emergency?

A. Yes.

Q. How long would it take to make the nuclear weapons available?

A. This is all done on the basis of Allied arrangements, Allied policies, Allied plans and principles. There is a NATO atomic stockpile. This is a supply system. Let's deglamourize this—we are talking too much about nuclear weapons for my taste, as a matter of fact, because this is not the only thing in this business, by any means. We have a stockpile, a supply system in NATO.

This was established by the heads of Governments in 1957. Look at it as a supply system. It is developed to meet the requirements of the NATO forces under the NATO plans, regardless of nationality or command affiliation or geographical location. So they would be able to service the Canadian squadrons on the same basis that, for instance, they can service the American squadrons. There is no difference whatsoever —although there is no proliferation as far as control is concerned, because these weapons are held in the hands of the country of their source until they are actually used. But they can be made available just as fast to a French squadron, to a Belgian squadron, to a Dutch squadron, to a German squadron, to a British squadron or to a Canadian squadron, as they could to an American squadron.

Q. Yes, but subject to bilateral agreement . . .

A. Yes, this is subject to bilateral agreement.

Q. Would the crews be trained to use the atomic weapons?

A. Under the bilateral agreement, yes. It does take a bilateral agreement because under the American atomic energy law, para. 144 (b), if there is a bilateral agreement between two countries concerned then the information can be made available which will permit the training with these weapons. And this is being done with almost all the countries of the alliance at the present time.

Q. Sir, does this mean that before Canada's NATO forces could be equipped with nuclear weapons that we would have to have a bilateral agreement with the United States?

A. That's quite correct. There would have to be a bilateral agreement. This is a technical agreement. This is not a policy agreement.

Q. Lacking a bilateral agreement, how long does it take to train crews?

A. You can't train them without a bilateral agreement.

Q. What I mean is after you get such an agreement, how long would it take?

A. Well, I should know the answer to that question. Too long! It's a matter of —I think Air Marshal Miller started this off in the first place—Frank, I think it's about six months, isn't it three to six months minimum?

MILLER: Yes, but it could be done under six months.

NORSTAD: It takes some time; it takes a considerable period of time.

Q. Does this mean that there is an existing bilateral agreement between Canada and the United States?

A. No, No, I don't think this exists. This has been subject to discussion but does not exist.

Q. This also means, then, that our crews have not had this training?

A. That's correct. But then, of course, they don't have the equipment at the present time to use this. This will come up when the Starfighters come up. . . .

Q. It is then fair to say that Canada has not met her 1957 NATO. . . .

A. No, I think that would be unfair to say that. This is all relative but, as I said before, Canada is one of the two, perhaps three, countries who have done their best in meeting their commitments in every sense. I don't want to pick out any specific point.

Q. Do we understand, Sir, that the whole of the Air Division has been committed to go atomic and that no part of it can be used . . .

A. Gentlemen, I think that's a question

you ought to direct to your own government. Can we drop this subject for the moment. I think we are spending too much time on it. Certainly there must be something else interesting to Canadians*

*From a transcript of the Department of National Defence.

Toronto *Globe and Mail,* January 14, 1963. Report of Address by Pearson.

The Pearson Flipflop

In dealing with our friends, we must assume that a change of government would not normally mean a sudden and unilateral renunciation of the treaty obligations they have undertaken. Our friends have the same right to assume that the commitments of Canada are the commitments of the nation; that they will not automatically disappear with a change of government. . . .

The Canadian government in 1959 agreed that the role of our overseas air division in NATO should be changed to the very important one of strike-reconnaissance. The Liberal Opposition in Parliament opposed this new and changed commitment. Nevertheless it was undertaken for Canada.

The aircraft for this role, American "Starfighters", CF-104's, in the RCAF, are now being delivered to discharge this commitment.

For this purpose, they are designed to be armed with nuclear warheads. We know that they cannot effectively do the job in question without such warheads. That's the commitment.

The government, however, after committing us to expenditures of hundreds of millions of dollars on these planes, has not made up its mind . . . whether to accept the warheads or not. . . .

At home, our Bomarc missiles—ground to air—are in the same state of impotence. The government must have decided, back in 1959, that the two Bomarc bases are important links in the continental defence chain. We Liberals at the time thought they were wrong in this . . . but the decision was made for Canada. Yet it is perfectly clear that these missiles are useless without nuclear warheads and that these cannot be secured and used at once in an emergency. Plans have to be made in advance; agreements reached with the United States for that purpose.

Our Bomarc missiles, for instance, stood useless in the alert during the Cuban crisis. That crisis also showed how absurd it is to think that a decision could be made and that quick, effective action could be taken after the emergency developed.

. . . the Canadian government . . . should end at once its evasion of responsibility, by discharging the commitments it has already accepted for Canada. It can only do this by accepting nuclear warheads for those defensive tactical weapons which cannot effectively be used without them, but which we have agreed to use. . . .

The Canadian government should support the strengthening of NATO conventional forces so that undue reliance would not have to be placed on nuclear tactical weapons for defence against every attack; even a limited and conventional one.

Canada should not . . . contribute to the strategic, nuclear deterrent . . . We should oppose any additional independent and national nuclear force. . . .

The government should re-examine at once the whole basis of Canadian defence policy. In particular, it should discuss with the United States and with NATO a role for Canada in continental and collective defence which would be more realistic and effective for Canada than the present one . . . However, until the present role is changed, a new Liberal government would put Canada's armed services in the position to discharge fully commitments undertaken for Canada by its predecessor.

Le Devoir, January 15, 1963; editorial.

Mr. Pearson's Acrobatics

The declaration Mr. Pearson has just made on the subject of nuclear arms is all the more astonishing because it flagrantly contradicts the previous attitudes of the Liberal leader as well as the resolution adopted by the Liberal Party Convention two years ago.

In January 1961, when the problem of nuclear warheads for the Bomarcs and for the Canadian troops in Europe had already become acute and was under discussion, Mr. Pearson gave a vigorous address to the Liberal Party Convention, which was the complete opposite of Saturday's declaration. At that time he extolled closer cooperation with NATO and rejected any military integration limited to the North American continent. He added that Canada must not become a minor partner in U.S. defence and that we must not acquire or use nuclear arms under any form of either national or joint control.

This speech was reported in the newspapers and Mr. Pearson did not dispute their accounts. Further, the Liberal Party Convention had correctly interpreted the speech of its leader and had turned it into a resolution stipulating that no Liberal government should acquire, manufacture or use nuclear arms, whether they were under the sole control of Canada or under the joint control of the U.S. and Canada; the resolution went further in saying that Canada's role in NORAD should be limited to that of detection, identification and alert, and that Canada should relinquish its participation in interceptors for NORAD.

A few days later, in a speech in Toronto, Mr. Pearson said that if the acquisition of nuclear arms became a necessity for the defence of Canada, it would be necessary for them to be under the control of NATO; he added that this necessity had not arisen at the present time.

After yet another few weeks, the Liberal leader suddenly discovered that he had been misunderstood at the party convention, and that he had merely declared that if Canada were to become a non-nuclear power she would not need NORAD. In addition, he rejected the party resolution on the interceptors and said that our obsolete CF-100s should be replaced by more modern interceptors, but armed only with conventional warheads.

At the end of February 1961, Mr. Diefenbaker paid a visit to Mr. Kennedy in Washington to discuss relations between the two countries concerning NORAD, and on this occasion Mr. Pearson arrived at another conclusion: that if the Canadian government decided to accept nuclear arms, this would have some bearing on the policy of the Liberal Party, particularly if the Liberals came to power after the arms were accepted.

This not only contradicted the party resolution, but in effect Mr. Pearson said to Mr. Diefenbaker: hurry up and accept nuclear warheads, and then I shall merely have to accept the *fait accompli*. In this way the Liberals would have the best of it, for they would be able to denounce the Conservative government but would not have to take a difficult decision themselves.

Now Mr. Diefenbaker has not moved, the elections are over and more elections are upon us. Mr. Pearson now finds another way of escape. He recommends that nuclear arms be accepted in order to fulfill obligations already undertaken by Ottawa. The Liberal leader can foresee that the government will do nothing before the elections, so he keeps ahead of the game. If he obtains the victory he counts on or hopes for, he will accept nuclear warheads whilst blaming the Conservative government which undertook to accept them. His manoeuvrings can be read between the lines.

Two years ago Mr. Pearson reckoned that a bilateral agreement with the U.S. for the use of nuclear arms was inacceptable and dangerous because Canada would become a minor partner in the defences of a great power; in other words, a nuclear satellite of the Pentagon.

Today he views the problem through the other end of the telescope: in order to accept its responsibilities and fulfill its undertakings, Canada must "agree to arm with nuclear warheads its strategic arms for defensive purposes which cannot be used effectively without such warheads."

This fine piece of reasoning applies to the Bomarc missiles, which were already only of marginal value in 1961, and whose uselessness had become steadily more evident in the last two years as a result of the Soviet bombers armed with missiles similar to the "Skybolt," and of the Soviet submarines carrying missiles similar to the "Polaris" missiles.

This is only the military side of the problem, which in the circumstances seems less grave than the political aspect. In January 1961 Mr. Pearson objected to nuclear warheads under bilateral control, and said that if one day Canada had to accept nuclear arms it would have to be under the multilateral control of NATO.

Now, today, when the Liberal leader speaks of our undertakings towards NATO with respect to nuclear arms, he causes confusion and plays on words in a way which deceives no one. Our armed forces in Europe are part of the NATO forces, it is true. But there is no multilateral control in NATO, as such, over nuclear arms. The European troops which have nuclear arms receive them from the U.S., as a result not of the Atlantic Pact but of a series of bilateral agreements which each of these countries has with Washington. In each case, it is the American military commander who controls the use of these arms.

There exists in principle a joint control, but it is obvious that the major role is played by the Pentagon. Otherwise the President could not provide these arms because a congressional law forbids complete surrender of nuclear warheads. It is an agreement of this kind, a bilateral agreement with the U.S., which we would have to conclude in order to give our troops the warheads for the Honest John missiles which they already have in Europe.

Mr. Pearson uses a clever metaphor to justify what he condemned two years ago. The Americans will have their finger on the trigger, but Canada will have its finger on the safety catch. If control is divided on a physical or military basis, it will still be partly bad, since the disproportion between the partners destroys any chance of equality or equilibrium: but the gravest problem is that the safety catch is a political matter. It is well known, particularly since the Cuban crisis, that the safety catch doesn't prevent the trigger from acting unilaterally and independently.

A senior officer of the Canadian

army, Major-general Macklin, insists that the military value of these arms has never been proved and that we should not accept them. He adds that the U.S. has a striking force five times that of the Russians, and we cannot contribute anything to it. If Mr. Pearson is to convince us, he will have to find other arguments than those he used on Saturday. The main result of his latest speech is to have turned a great many of the electors against his party.

PAUL SAURIOL

House of Commons *Debates*, January 25, 1963, pp. 3128-3137.

Diefenbaker on Nuclear

Weapons for Canada

[MR. DIEFENBAKER]: . . . During 1958 the Canadian government studied intensively the arms required by Canadian forces in modern circumstances, and we reached the decision we would provide aircraft for the purposes of NATO. At that time I made it perfectly clear, as I shall point out in a moment, that those forces would have to be equipped, in order to be fully effective, with defensive nuclear weapons if and when the need arose. That was recognized in taking the decision that was announced in September, 1958, to install Bomarc anti-aircraft missiles in Canada.

The Leader of the Opposition would have you understand that there has been no change; once you do a thing you should stay. In 1958, when the Bomarc was first laid down as a plan, the great challenge to North America was believed to be bombers carrying bombs. That is what we thought. Today that is changed. More and more there is a phasing out in connection with the bomber threat as more and more intercontinental ballistic missiles are increasing in number. Those are some of the stands we have taken and I set forth the views of the government on February

20, 1959, as quoted by the Leader of the Opposition. In accordance with that statement we proceeded to acquire equipment, aircraft, launchers and other items necessary to enable the Canadian forces to be ready to use defensive nuclear weapons if and when that became necessary.

In May, 1959, the supreme commander of NATO forces visited Ottawa and proposed to the government that the first Canadian air division in Europe should undertake a strike reconnaissance role to protect the NATO forces aircraft from the first attack on them. That we placed before the House of Commons. The government considered the proposal, and early in July announced its decision in the house to accept this role and to equip eight squadrons of the division to discharge it. Our ambassador informed the NATO council of this decision.

While nothing was specified about arming the aircraft with nuclear weapons it was realized by all that this would be desirable and that nuclear weapons should be available as and when required, under joint control, in NATO stockpiles in accordance with the general NATO decision of December, 1957, to which I have referred. Similarly, but less important, plans were made in connection with short-range defensive missiles.

Now, sir, that is all in the past. Those are the stands which we took. Those are the views that we placed before parliament in detail; and that is what surprises me, that the Leader of the Opposition, after his return from the United States a few weeks ago and after the interview with General Norstad, suddenly realized what was actually the fact. He suddenly realized that there should be some action taken, and I am going to deal with that because when I follow him in his equivocating stand throughout the past five years—if I can do it—I shall place before the house something of what I spoke so frequently . . . of a bold and imaginative policy, straightforward and courageous. . . .

We have spent billions of dollars on defence since world war II. Much of what has been spent might be considered by some to have been wasted, but if it had not been for the defences we built up, and those associated with us, our freedom might long since have disappeared. Since the time we entered into these commitments I have referred to things which have changed greatly. It was not a mistake to take measures to ensure the necessary security, on the basis of the information we had then, even though in the light of subsequent events some of the things that were done had been proven, as with every country, to be unnecessary. . . .

Every now and then some new white hope of rocketry goes into the scrap pile. We established the Bomarc, the two units. They are effective over an area of only a few hundred miles. They are effective only against aircraft. People talk about change. Who would have thought three years ago that today the fear would be an attack with intercontinental ballistic missiles? This program cost Canada some $14 million. The United States put up the major portion of the total cost. I do not want to repeat, but it is necessary to do so, that with the advent more and more into intercontinental ballistic missiles the bomber carrier is less and less the threat that it was.

So what should we do? Should we carry on with what we have done in the past, merely for the purpose of saying, "Well, we started, and having started and having proceeded, we will continue"? Should we do this in an area where mistakes are made? I am not dealing with those mistakes at the moment; but should we continue with such programs, in the light of changing circumstances? These were not mistakes in judgment at the time, but the failure to be able to look ahead and read the mind of Khrushchev and those associated with him in the presidium. More and more the nuclear deterrent is becoming of such a nature that more nuclear arms will add nothing materially to our defences. Greater and greater emphasis must be placed on conventional arms and conventional forces. We in Canada took a lead in that connection. In the month of September, 1961 we increased the numbers of our conventional forces. There was criticism at the time.

I was in Nassau. I formed certain ideas. I read the communique that was issued there and I come to certain conclusions based on that communique. Those conclusions are as follows, and these are the views expressed also by the United States under secretary of state, George W. Ball: that nuclear war is indivisible; that there should be no further development of new nuclear power anywhere in the world; that nuclear weapons as a universal deterrent is a dangerous solution. Today an attempt is being made by the United States to have the NATO nations increase their conventional arms. The Nassau agreement seemed to accept these three principles as basic, and to carry them out both countries agreed to assign to NATO part of their existing nuclear force as the nucleus of a multilateral force. . . .

I propose to review some of the views expressed by this government on the question of defence and to go back over some of the various statements which have been made. I do this because it seems passing strange to me that the Leader of the Opposition only found them out after his trip to the United States—or only revealed that he had found them out then.

I say this because I dealt with the situation in detail here in the House of Commons on February 20, 1959. I ask hon. members to read *Hansard*. They will find I said this—

MR. MARTIN (ESSEX EAST): What page, please?

MR. DIEFENBAKER: Page 1223. I said that in keeping with the determination that Canada should carry out its task in a balanced, collective defence—

In keeping with that determination, careful thought is being given to the principles which in our opinion are applicable to the acquisition and control of nuclear weapons. The government's decisions of last autumn to acquire Bomarc missiles for air defence and Lacrosse missiles for the Canadian army—

One doesn't hear anything more about Lacrosse missiles—

—were based on the best expert advice available on the need to strengthen Canada's air defence against the threat to this continent and on its determination to continue an effective contribution to the NATO shield.

The full potential of these defensive weapons is achieved only when they are armed with nuclear warheads. The government is, therefore, examining with the United States government questions connected with the acquisition of nuclear warheads for Bomarc and other defensive weapons for use by the Canadian forces in Canada, and the storage of warheads in Canada. Problems connected with the arming of the Canadian brigade in Europe with short range nuclear weapons for NATO's defence tasks are also being studied.

It set this out in great detail. There is no concealment. There is complete revelation of what we are doing. I could read from *Hansard* year by year. As found at page 1223 of *Hansard* for 1959, I said this:

It is our intention to provide Canadian forces with modern and efficient weapons to enable them to fulfill their respective roles . . . it is the policy of the Canadian government not to undertake the production of nuclear weapons in Canada . . . We must reluctantly admit the need in present circumstances for nuclear weapons of a defensive character.

Then again as the Leader of the Opposition said, on a number of occasions I stated that there was no expectation of an early conclusion of a formal agreement. On January 18, 1960, as found at page 73 of *Hansard,* I said this:

Eventually Canadian forces may require certain nuclear weapons if Canadian forces are to be kept effective.

Then again:

Negotiations are proceeding with the United States in order that the necessary weapons can be made available for Canadian defence units if and when they are required.

That was always of the essence throughout in the stand that we took. I cannot comment in detail on these negotiations but I wish to state that arrangements for the safeguarding and security of all such weapons in Canada will be subject to Canadian approval and consent. Then again on February 9, 1960:

If and when Canada does acquire nuclear weapons it will be in accordance with our own national policies and with our obligations under the north Atlantic treaty. . . .

There has been no suggestion at any time of any watering down of that stand. Then again on September 20, 1961:

However, and I emphasize this, in each of the instruments that we have, the Bomarc and the Voodoos, nuclear weapons could be used. The defensive weapons requirements of Canada and the need for the preservation of security will be the overriding consideration in the mind of this government.

And so on throughout the entire piece. Then, as well in various speeches made outside of the House of Commons I underlined this fact, namely that we were in a position where nuclear weapons could be secured and would be secured in the event that the circumstances at the time made such a course reasonable and necessary. I went further in that connection when I said this:

Would you in 1961, faced by the overwhelming power of Soviet might in East Germany close to West Berlin with large divisions fully armed, would you place in the hands of those who guard the portals of freedom nothing but bows and arrows? They would stand against overwhelming power— it is as simple as that.

Throughout the election campaign I followed the same course. In the two speeches I made before the United Nations I asked, as had the Secretary of State for External Affairs, and as did the Leader of the Opposition today, for the abolition of nuclear weapons, the end of nuclear weapons, the systematic control of missiles designed to deliver nuclear weapons of mass destruction, the designation and inspection of launching sites for missiles, the abolition of biological and chemical weapons and the outline of outer space for military purposes. That has been our course throughout.

During the election campaign, however, with the change in circumstances that had been taking place from the point of view of defence, I outlined the position of this party in a speech which I made in Brockville. It was not too successful, judging by the results, but I spoke there during the campaign and I said this:

We shall not, so long as we are pursuing the ways of disarmament, allow the extension of the nuclear family into Canada . . . We do not intend to allow the spread of

nuclear arms beyond the nations which now have them.

Those in short are the views expressed, with one exception. Today the Leader of the Opposition said that when we brought into Canada the 60 F-101B interceptors, it was clearly understood that they would be armed with nuclear weapons. On June 12, 1961, I set out in detail the arrangements that had been arrived at between Canada and the United States. I think I had better read from it:

—for some time representatives of the Canadian and United States governments have been working on an agreement relating to the defence of Canada, more particularly to air defence and to the Canada-United States production sharing program. The objective of such an agreement was to reflect the desire of both governments to ensure more effective use of the productive capacities, skills and resources of each country and at the same time to demonstrate our mutual determination to improve the defensive strength of NATO and particularly of NORAD under it . . .

In consideration of the financial and other benefits which will accrue to the United States as a result of Canada's assumption of additional responsibilities under the Pine Tree agreements, Canada will be furnished with 66 F-101B interceptor aircraft and appropriate support equipment. These aircraft, title to which will be vested in Canada, will be armed with conventional weapons.

Today the Leader of the Opposition said otherwise. That is the background. That is the recital of some of the stands we have taken and which are consistent throughout and which, when read in conjunction one with the other reveal the situation as we saw it. The Leader of the Opposition said, "Let us be bold; we have a policy. The government has not a policy but we have a policy". Well, I am not going to follow the Leader of the Opposition throughout the entire course of his migrations through change in connection with this problem, but I am going to refer to some of the oscillations and vacillations. I am going to try to carry hon. members through the jungle of uncertainty that he built up on behalf of the opposition during a period of several years.

In 1958 he proposed that nations manufacturing atomic weapons should agree not to do so in the future. But that did not prevent him from approving the continuing increasing sale of Canadian uranium to the United States, the chief buyer and the chief maker of atomic weapons. Furthermore, regarding the use of nuclear weapons by Canadian forces he said on the 17th of March, 1960: "There is every doubt and confusion".

What was the stand of the Liberal party? On January 18, 1960, he said: "We should not accept baby nuclear bombs or missiles." On July 15, 1960 he said: "The middle powers should have a self-denying ordinance in nuclear weapons." On August 5, 1960 he said: "Canada should get out of Bomarc operation." Hon. members will have difficulty following me though I am reading from the same gentleman. . . .

To summarize our viewpoint, there is a will to peace, as the Secretary of State for External Affairs said yesterday. There is progress being made. We must maintain our defence. We shall not allow Canada to be placed in a subservient or unsovereign position. We shall follow the course that we have been following—one that has been consistent. It has been one of calm consideration of the matters as they arise.

We know, as the Leader of the Opposition said, that the way to prevent nuclear war is to prevent it. What course should we take at this time? I emphasize what I have already stated, that we shall at all times carry out whatever our responsibilities are. I have said that strategic changes are taking place in the thinking of the western world, and there is general recognition that the nuclear deterrent will not be strengthened by the expansion of the nuclear family. With these improvements in the international situation, this is no time for hardened decisions that cannot be altered. We must be flexible and fluid, for no one can anticipate what Khrushchev will do.

A meeting is about to take place in Ottawa of the NATO nations. They will meet here on May 21 to 23 and the very fact that they are meeting here indicates the attitude towards Canada and the feeling of the NATO nations towards her. As was said by the Leader of the Opposition when they met here previously, it represented a recognition that Canada had a very important part to play.

What shall our attitude be? It will not be one of recklessness, not one of making final decisions in the face of a changing world. I mentioned Nassau a moment ago and, as one examines what took place there, he realizes that we are living in a new and changing world of defence realism.

The Leader of the Opposition says all the F-104G aircraft have been delivered.

MR. PEARSON: I never said that.

MR. DIEFENBAKER: You did not say that? I am sorry. My interpretation was that he repeated over and over again that that was so. The total number that has been delivered is one squadron. Following SACEUR's recommendation, as we saw the situation in 1959 and as I said earlier in my remarks, we undertook to equip our squadrons assigned to NATO for a strike reconnaissance role, which role would include the mission of delivering nuclear weapons. No one was under any misunderstanding in that connection. Parliament approved this program and appropriated the funds.

I have said earlier that all the nations made mistakes, $3 billions worth of mistakes and more, up to 1960 but the fact that a mistake may have been made, or may not have been made, should not be a basis for the continuation of a policy just because to admit it would be wrong. Delivery of the F-104G has commenced, but the strike reconnaissance role has been placed under doubt by the recent Nassau declaration concerning nuclear arms, as well as other developments both technical and political in the defence field. It will be necessary, therefore, at this meeting in May, for Canada to give consideration to this matter and we will, in co-operation with the nations of NATO, undertake a clarification of our role in NATO defence plans and disposition.

We are united in NATO. We have never and will never consent to Canada breaking any of her pledged words or undertakings. It is at that meeting, where there will be reviewed the entire collective defence policy, that we shall secure from the other member nations their views, and on the basis of that we will be in a position to make a decision, a consistent decision, first to maintain our undertakings and second, to execute, if that be the view, the maintenance of our collective defence. In the meantime the training of Canadian forces in the use of these weapon systems can continue.

So far as NORAD is concerned I have said at the beginning of my remarks that Canada's sovereignty must be maintained. We shall continue our negotiations. They have been going on quite forcibly for two months or more.

MR. HARKNESS: For two or three months.

MR. DIEFENBAKER: Yes, they have been going on for two or three months. Sometimes I wonder whether that is the reason the Leader of the Opposition rushed in with his statement the other day, because he found that out and knew about it. But there was never any concealment of the fact. We will negotiate with the United States so that, as I said earlier, in case of need nuclear war heads will be made readily available. In other words, we will be in a position to determine finally, in the interests of Canada and our allies, the course to be followed in the light of changing circumstances in the disarmament field, which have become encouraging recently through Khrushchev's acceptance of even a minimum observation of nuclear testing. We will discuss with the nations of NATO the new concept of a nuclear force for NATO. If that concept at Nassau is carried into effect, much of our planning in the past will pass out of existence.

Mr. Chairman, it so easy to say what should be done. Conscientiously and honestly we have tried, in the face of changing conditions, to bring about peace. We do not want to do anything at this time to rock the boat. If in the progress of disarmament it is found that we are beginning to approach that new era that all of us look forward to, the NATO nations meeting together can make that determination in agreement that is best for each and all. If, on the other hand, there is going to be set up a multilateral nuclear force, then all our planning to date, or most of it, will be of little or no consequence. I know they say, "Make decisions. Be concrete; be direct". Mr. Chairman, recklessness was never evidence of decisiveness. We will, as a result of the fullest discussion and consideration, determine a course which I believe now means a vast alteration in all the defensive techniques that we have accepted in the last few years, and we will come back to parliament and place before it the considered view of this government.

MR. HELLYER: You will come back when?

MR. DIEFENBAKER: I throw this back to the opposition. We never sold Canada. We have never in any way made undertakings that we have not carried out. Canada has a proud record. The opposition should not try, for political purposes, to besmirch that record. All of us should be true Canadians when facing a problem that touches the heartstrings of each and every one of us. My prayer is that we will be directed in this matter. Some may ridicule that belief on my part. I believe that the western world has been directed by God in the last few years, or there would have been no survival. I believe that will continue. My prayer is that we shall so live as to maintain not only the integrity of Canada and its high reputation by carrying out our responsibilities, but at the same time that we will be right, that the Canadian people will be able to say that, whatever decision is made, it was made with every consideration being given to all those moral and psychological things that form one's make-up.

I would rather be right, Mr. Chairman, so that those who come after may say, "He refused to be stampeded. He refused to act on the impulse of the moment. He and his colleagues together, with the support of the Canadian parliament, brought about a policy, in co-operation with their allies and by influence over their allies, that led to the achievement of peace".

United States, Department of State, Press Release, January 30, 1963.

American Intervention: the State Department Press Release

UNITED STATES AND CANADIAN NEGOTIATIONS REGARDING NUCLEAR WEAPONS

The Department has received a number of inquiries concerning the disclosure during a recent debate in the Canadian House of Commons regarding negotiations over the past two or three months between the United States and Canadian Governments relating to nuclear weapons for Canadian armed forces.

In 1958 the Canadian Government decided to adopt the Bomarc-B weapons systems. Accordingly two Bomarc-B squadrons were deployed to Canada where they would serve the double purpose of protecting Montreal and Toronto as well as the U.S. deterrent force. The Bomarc-B was not designed to carry any conventional warhead. The matter of making available a nuclear warhead for it and for other nuclear-capable weapons systems acquired by Canada has been the subject of inconclusive discussions between the two Governments. The installation of the two Bomarc-B batteries in Canada without

nuclear warheads was completed in 1962.

In addition to the Bomarc-B, a similar problem exists with respect to the modern supersonic jet interceptor with which the RCAF has been provided. Without nuclear air defence warheads, they operate at far less than their full potential effectiveness.

Shortly after the Cuban crisis in October 1962, the Canadian Government proposed confidential discussions concerning circumstances under which there might be provision of nuclear weapons for Canadian armed forces in Canada and Europe. These discussions have been exploratory in nature; the Canadian Government has not as yet proposed any arrangement sufficiently practical to contribute effectively to North American defense.

The discussions between the two Governments have also involved possible arrangements for the provision of nuclear weapons for Canadian NATO forces in Europe, similar to the arrangements which the United States has made with many of our other NATO allies.

During the debate in the House of Commons various references were made to recent discussions at Nassau. The agreements made at Nassau have been fully published. They raise no question of the appropriateness of nuclear weapons for Canadian forces in fulfilling their NATO or NORAD obligations.

Reference was also made in the debate to the need of NATO for increased conventional forces. A flexible and balanced defense requires increased conventional forces, but conventional forces are not an alternative to effective NATO or NORAD defense arrangements using nuclear-capable weapons systems. NORAD is designed to defend the North American continent against air attack. The Soviet bomber fleet will remain at least throughout this decade a significant element in the Soviet strike force. An effective continental defense against this common threat is necessary.

The provision of nuclear weapons to Canadian forces would not involve an expansion of independent nuclear capability, or an increase in the "nuclear club". As in the case of other allies, custody of U.S. nuclear weapons would remain with the United States. Joint control fully consistent with national sovereignty can be worked out to cover the use of such weapons by Canadian forces.

Cited in Jon B. McLin, *Canada's Changing Defence Policy, 1957-63* (Baltimore: Johns Hopkins Press, 1967), pp. 164-165. Reprinted by permission of the Johns Hopkins Press.

The Worth of the Bomarcs

. . . On March 29, a transcript of the testimony was released which Secretary of Defense McNamara had given to the House Military Appropriations Subcommittee the previous February 6. It included the following passage:

Mr. Minshall—No hearings of this subcommittee would be complete unless I at least mentioned in passing the word "Bomarc."

Mr. Flood—You are speaking of the woman I love.

Mr. Minshall—I notice on page 55 of your statement you pointed out: 'As I pointed out last year, the Air Force's Bomarc missile suffered from essentially the same defects as manned interceptors (deleted). Nevertheless, we plan to continue the Bomarc force (deleted), since the large initial investment costs are already behind us.' If I remember correctly, including the cost of SAGE and the Bomarc missile itself, all the research and development, we put somewhere between $3 billions and $4 billions into this program. I just wonder if it is as ineffective as you now agree it is, why we even put any money into the operational cost of this weapon when it is so useless.

Secretary McNamara—The operational costs are really not extensive. Since we have put such a heavy investment in the weapons system itself and in the controls for it, the SAGE controls, it seemed wise to us to continue to deploy it at least as far ahead as we can see.

Mr. Minshall—We are trying to cut down at every corner of the budget. These sites take men to man. I am sure it will run into millions of dollars just for operations and maintenance.

Secretary McNamara—Yes, the Bomarc looks to us to cost on the order of $20 mil-

lions a year to operate.

Mr. Minshall—That to me is an awful lot of money.

Secretary McNamara—For the protection we get I do not believe it is an unreasonable amount.

Mr. Minshall—The protection is practically nil, Mr. Secretary, as you said here in your statement. The sites are soft, SAGE is soft.

Secretary McNamara—We can correct for some of these deficiencies. We are considering further dispersal of those Bomarcs. The problem with the dispersal alternatives is it costs money to disperse. We have a series of alternatives underway that we hope will allow us to increase their effectiveness. In any case, I would hesitate to cancel their deployment if we saved no more than $20 millions a year. . . .

. . . At the very least, they would cause the Soviets to target missiles against them and thereby increase their missile requirements or draw missiles onto these Bomarc targets that would otherwise be available for other targets.

Mr. Flood—Here is another chance for another McNamara hard decision.

Secretary McNamara—If there were any real amount of money to be saved, I would propose taking them out, but for $20 millions a year I think we are getting our money's worth.

Mr. Minshall—In view of the statement you just made, Mr. Secretary, why do we not leave the Jupiter missiles in Italy and Turkey? If we have to draw enemy fire, that is a good place to draw it.

Mr. Flood—If we scratch Bomarc, we have stuck the Canadians for a whole mess of them and we have another problem on our border.

Secretary McNamara—As they are deployed, they draw more fire than those Jupiter missiles will.

Mr. Minshall—All I can say is, these turned out to be very expensive targets.

Secretary McNamara—They did, I agree with you fully.*

*U.S., Congress, House, Committee on Appropriations, *Hearings before the Subcommittee on Department of Defense Appropriations*, 88th Cong., 1st Sess., 1963, Part 1, pp. 512, 13.

A.D.P. Heeney and Livingston Merchant, *Canada and the United States Principles for Partnership* (Ottawa: Queen's Printer, 1965). Reproduced with permission.

Getting Along with the Americans: A Diplomatic View

29. The mutual involvement of the two countries and peoples has also complicated, on both sides, the problems arising from the disparity in power. In most—though not all—of their bilateral affairs the capacity of the United States to benefit or harm Canadian interests is greater than that of Canada to affect the prosperity and security of the United States. Canadians are more conscious than Americans of this element in their dealings with the United States. On the other hand, the United States, pre-occupied with the responsibilities of world power, may sometimes be inhibited in its bilateral dealings by considerations which do not operate directly on Canadian attitudes. Here restraint is required of both sides.

30. Canadians sometimes feel that, because they are so close, so "American", there is a disposition on the part of the United States to expect more of Canada than of other allies—as in setting other countries a good example—reflecting a tendency to apply to Canada a kind of "double standard" of international conduct. The result is sometimes to tempt Canadians into demonstrating their independence by adopting positions divergent from those of the United States. In a quite different sense, Americans are inclined sometimes to suspect the application of a "double standard" on the part of Canada when, for example, in an international negotiation, the United States is urged to be "reasonable", to make unilateral concessions to break a logjam which has been created by the intransigence of others. For Canadians cannot but be disturbingly aware that, despite their underlying confidence in the basic motives of the United States, Canada could be involved inevitably in the consequences of United States' decisions in circumstances over which Canadians had little influence or control. Such tendencies, on each side, arising from mutual involvement, inequality and the facts of international life, should be recognized but not exaggerated. . . .

39. We are convinced that the cornerstone of a healthy relationship between our two countries is timely and sufficient consultation in candour and good faith at whatever level or levels of government is appropriate to the nature and importance of the subject. To consult in this fashion, however, cannot be taken to imply that agreement must always result. The purpose rather is that each be enabled to hear and weigh the other's views. The outcome will depend upon the circumstances of the case and, ultimately, upon the judgment by each of its national interest. . . .

54. We now turn to the essence of consultation and to certain guidelines which, in our judgment, should be observed by our two governments in their dealings with each other:

(a) In the first place, every effort should be made to begin the consultative process sufficiently early to provide reasonable time for each party to consider and give full weight to the views and interests of the other. This will help to satisfy each side that its position on any issue is being seriously examined. It will also improve the chances of resolving difficulties and, where no detours around roadblocks are to be found, it can ease the shock of impending collision.

(b) In certain fields where combined efforts are called for, such as continental air defence arrangements and joint development of resources, there is obvious advantage in having the consultative process begin at the planning stage so as to facilitate concurrent formulation of policy.

(c) There will be in the future—as in the past—cases where, by reason of what is deemed an overriding need for speed or secrecy, the process of consultation must be telescoped. This is a fact of life which must be recognized, but the judgment in such circumstances should be that of the highest authority.

(d) While all crises are not predictable, many—probably most—can be foreseen as possible. For this reason the process of consultation should provide for continuous exchanges of views between the appropriate authorities of the two governments over the whole range of looming problems, including mutual exposure to any relevant contingency planning.

(e) Consultation should be initiated whenever one of the two governments is in the process of formulating important policies or planning actions which would have an appreciable impact on the other. The responsibility for initiating consultation in such cases rests on the party approaching decision or con-

templating action.

(f) Existing mechanisms for consultation should be utilized in order to ensure prompt and continuous access by one government to the other.

(g) Many problems between our two governments are susceptible of solution only through the quiet, private and patient examination of facts in the search for accommodation. It should be regarded as incumbent on both parties during this time-consuming process to avoid, so far as possible, the adoption of public positions which can contribute unnecessarily to public division and difference.

(h) Each government has a responsibility to ensure that its own procedure for intragovernmental consideration of subjects which affect the other country operates promptly, effectively and consistently so as to facilitate the consultative process.

55.   We recognize that the kind of consultation which we have described has different implications for our respective governments. These derive primarily from the wide disparity in power and international responsibility which we have already underlined. In consultations with the United States, Canadian authorities must have confidence that the practice of quiet diplomacy is not only neighbourly and convenient to the United States but that it is in fact more effective than the alternative of raising a row and being unpleasant in public. By the same token, the United States authorities must be satisfied that, in such consultations, Canada will have sympathetic regard for the world-wide preoccupations and responsibilities of the United States. . . .

78.   The need is clear for our two governments to confirm the practice of intimate, timely and continuing consul-

tation on all matters of common concern, at the appropriate level, employing such machinery and procedures as are most effective for this purpose.

79.   As partners in NATO, and sharing responsibility for the air defence of this continent, Canada and the United States have similar policies and share important common obligations. In the conduct and development of their unique bilateral relationship, however, the two countries must have regard for the wider responsibilities and interests of each in the world and their obligations under various treaties and other arrangements to which each is party.

80.   This principle has a particular bearing upon our affairs in relation to the heavy responsibilities borne by the United States, generally as the leader of the free world and specifically under its network of mutual defence treaties around the globe. It is important and reasonable that Canadian authorities should have careful regard for the United States Government's position in this world context and, in the absence of special Canadian interests or obligations, avoid so far as possible, public disagreement especially upon critical issues. This is not to say that the Canadian Government should automatically and uniformly concur in foreign policy decisions taken by the United States Government. Different estimates of efficacy and appropriateness or degree of risk generate honest differences of opinion among the closest allies. The Canadian Government cannot renounce its right to independent judgment and decision in the "vast external realm". On its part, Canada has special relations and obligations, some of which the United States does not share but of which it should take account, in particular with Great Britain and the other states of the Commonwealth, with France, and with certain other nations.

81.   It is in the abiding interest of both countries that, wherever possible, divergent views between the two governments should be expressed and if possible resolved in private, through diplomatic channels. Only a firm mutual resolve and the necessary practical arrangements to keep the totality of the relationship in good and friendly working order can enable our countries to avoid needless frictions and minimize the consequences of disagreement.

A. F. W. Plumptre, *et. al,* "Retaliation: The Price of Independence," in Stephen Clarkson, ed., *An Independent Foreign Policy for Canada?* (Toronto: McClelland and Stewart, 1968). Reprinted by permission of The Canadian Publishers, McClelland and Stewart Limited, Toronto.

Getting Along with the Americans: Retaliation?

A. F. W. Plumptre: *Tit for Tat*

The basic difficulty in dealing with the question of retaliation may well lie only partly in the concept itself but equally in the closely related notion of "an independent foreign policy." The more "independent" (in some sense) our policy becomes, the more likely it is to provoke "retaliation."

I have spent much of the past twenty-five years in various official positions in Ottawa, Washington and Paris. Throughout that period I was trying to help formulate and execute something that could with justice be called an independent Canadian foreign policy. And yet I can only remember two or three occasions, in regard to rather specific issues, on which either the word or the concept of "retaliation" against Canada entered into consideration. . . .

. . . most governments, and certainly a government as well-served as the Canadian, will always formulate its foreign policy in pretty full knowledge of what the effects of its policy, what the repercussions of its policy, will be abroad. It will indeed weigh the pros and cons of each action, and weigh them carefully. The repercussions of its actions abroad may be in Government circles; in business or financial circles. But I do not think we should generally use the word "retaliation" to describe such repercussions. They are simply part of the day to day assessments involved in judgment-forming and policy-making. In some ways the conduct of external affairs resembles a game of chess. Each move takes into account all previous moves by *both* players, and their possible future moves; but it is a mistake to describe any particular move as retaliation for the last one.

I suggest that the word retaliation is properly reserved for something different, a tit for tat that must be unpleasant for the recipients.

Put in this crude way, the danger of anything deserving the name retaliation is minimal. "Pressure," yes, "retaliation," no. If Canada adopts a measure like the magazine tax that is clearly unwelcome in various quarters in the United States, we may be reasonably sure that certain identifiable forces will be set in motion against us. This possibility may well affect the outcome of a disagreement between ourselves and the Americans in GATT or in some other international arena; but the process is not well described as "retaliation." A country moves purposefully, yet somewhat cumbersomely, towards its objectives. It is neither within its power nor its purpose, in most cases, to "punish" or to "slap back at" other countries that get in its way. Retaliation is a game that Latin American dictatorships might play with each other; but it is not really a game for grown-up countries. . . .

Canadians, particularly Canadians of the post-war generation, may need to be reminded how extremely careful the Canadian Government was throughout World War II to keep off the list of countries that received U.S. aid—a list that in the end included all or virtually all of the other allies of the United States.

However, our independence of the American aid programme does not render us impervious to the results of other American actions; far from it. And in this regard we must remember that the US government can hurt Canada unintentionally as well as intentionally—like the big pig that just rolls over onto the little piglets. For the piglet, life, liberty and the pursuit of happiness can only be bought at the price of eternal vigilance. . . .

I do not remember whether, at the particular moment when we announced our magazine tax, there were on their way through Congress any bills that were designed to give new support to US interests at the expense of Canadian—for example whether our lead and zinc exports, or our exports of motor-car parts, or any other of the Canadian exports that are under perennial attack in Congress were under attack then. If so, one can guess that the bill, whatever it was, got a little farther along the Congressional path before it was killed than it otherwise would have done. Perhaps it even got as far as President Eisenhower's desk for his signature or his veto. One can see him reaching for the red pen to record a veto. At that very moment Henry Luce of *Time* calls to alert him to the new infamy that is abroad in Canada. So he puts back the pen, telling his aide that this one will have to have some more thought. Then he ruminates on the state of his political situation wondering whether he can afford to continue to protect Canadian interests if Louis St. Laurent is going to stab him in the most sensitive section of the press.

Very human. But is he pondering "retaliation"? Again, the word does not fit either the facts or the feeling of the situation.

If we did decide to call it "retaliation," we would have to recall that we are really in as good a position to retaliate against the United States as they are against us. Not only do their exports to us far exceed our exports to them, but we have all those lovely investments of theirs to stick pins into—publishing houses, oil companies and many, many others. Just as in Washington there is a long queue of people lined up to get something for themselves at the expense of Canadians, so there is a similar line-up in Ottawa of Canadians who would like to get something at the expense of Americans.

And yet, even this is the wrong way to look at the matter. It is true that there are erosive rats at work all the time in each capital to undermine our international agreements. But these are entered into because, on balance, each agreement in each country helps more than it hurts. In the long run, the successful erosion of treaties by the rats in Ottawa would hurt Canadians as much as Americans. Similarly, erosion in Washington would hurt Americans as much as Canadians. This is why each country supports each agreement.

So, after all, when he picks up his red pen again and vetoes the anti-Canadian bill before him, President Eisenhower is acting for the US interests involved and not for the Canadian interests. And if that is so, what has become of the last vestiges of the concept of "retaliation"? . . .

Pauline Jewett: *The Menace is the Message*
. . . I think the term "retaliation" should and does apply to lawful situations, to acts that are well within the law. Cer-

tainly this is how it is understood in political circles. I cannot, of course, speak for all political circles, but I do recall very well the use of the word "retaliation" on many occasions, within my own party and in Parliament, while I was a Liberal MP. It was used chiefly in the context of Canadian-American relations when the fear was expressed that the US would "retaliate" against Canada, through some specific act or policy (quite legal), should Canada pursue a certain course of action.

I could give several concrete examples of this but the most vivid in my memory concerns the magazine legislation of 1964 which excluded Canadian advertisements in American journals from tax exemption and so gave Canadian journals protection. The Liberal caucus was generally in favour of this legislation and also in favour of having it include *Time* and *Reader's Digest*. There was only one individual strongly opposed to the latter and he had *Reader's Digest*— a large employer—in his riding! The cabinet, I gather, was a bit more split, being closer no doubt to political reality. The "political reality" in this instance was, quite simply, fear of American retaliation. Members of caucus had it explained to them by members of cabinet that, should the government go ahead and include *Time* and *Reader's Digest,* Washington (in response, no doubt, to domestic pressures) would "retaliate" against us. A tentative agreement on some particular matter (automobiles perhaps?) would not go through. Or the President would cease supporting us vis-à-vis Congress with respect to some proposed Congressional act.

Maybe we politicians are just naïve. After all, we are not in the State Department or External where people "know" that these things are not going to happen. But I can only say that the fear was there and that past experience had shown that it was justified. Professor Safarian notes that there have been few occasions when we suffered the act of retaliation. But there have been a sufficient number of times when we feared its possibility that the threat of retaliation has conditioned governmental attitudes into general timidity.

What concerns one most about all this is the mesmerizing effect it has on Canadian policy-makers. Instead of doing things that they think are desirable or that the Canadian public may want done, our policy-makers do things that the American public or the American government or powerful American pressure-groups want. Not always, of course. Not on bread-and-butter issues like selling wheat to China. But on broader matters of foreign policy like *recognizing* China or the war in Vietnam, our governments waffle. They do not take the positions that either their own judgment or, in many instances, Canadian public opinion demands.

Lester Pearson, "Canada the United States and Vietnam," Statements and Speeches No. 67/8.

Getting Along with the Americans: Economic Reality?

CANADA, THE UNITED STATES AND VIETNAM

Text of the Reply by the Prime Minister, the Right Honourable L. B. Pearson, to Representations from a Group of University Professors, including the Faculty Committee on Vietnam at Victoria College, University of Toronto, March 10, 1967.

I need hardly tell you that the situation in Vietnam is one to which the Government attaches great importance in the formulation of Canadian foreign policy. That importance reflects not only the implications of the problem for world peace and the international processes of change by peaceful means but also the concern which the Government shares with responsible citizens at the toll the hostilities are taking in terms of human suffering as well as of wasted resources and lost opportunities for human betterment. On these points, I think there can be few differences of opinion. . . .

. . . I realize, as the public debate over Vietnam here and elsewhere over the past few years has shown, that it is possible to arrive at different assessments of the rights and wrongs of the various positions represented in the conflict. This in inevitable, and, in the long run, useful, in a free society, always provided, of course, that the differences of opinion are genuine and based on the fullest possible range of facts. But, whatever the view one might hold about the origins and development of a situation such as we face in Vietnam today, I believe that the right and proper course for the Canadian policy-maker is to seek to establish that element of common ground on which any approach to a solution must ultimately rest.

This is precisely the direction in which we have attempted to bring Canadian influence to bear—the search for common ground as a base for a solution to the Vietnam crisis by means other than the use of force. We have spoken publicly about our belief that a military solution is neither practicable nor desirable and we have encouraged the two sides to enter into direct contact to prepare the ground for formal negotiations at the earliest practicable time. . . .

As I have said, I am convinced that the Vietnam conflict will ultimately have to be resolved by way of negotiation. But I do not think that a Geneva-type conference (or, indeed, any other conference) will come about simply because the Canadian Government declares publicly that this would be a good idea. It will come about only when those who are at this time opposed to such a conference can be convinced that it would be in their best interests to attend and negotiate in a genuine desire to achieve results. And, in the process, confidential and quiet arguments by a responsible government are usually more effective than public ones. . . .

In short, the more complex and dangerous the problem, the greater is the need for calm and deliberate diplomacy. That may sound like an expression of timidity to some of the proponents of political activism at Canadian universities and elsewhere today. I can only assure them, with all the personal conviction I can command, that in my view it is the only way in which results can be achieved. . . .

As far as the bombing of North Vietnam is concerned, there is not the slightest doubt in my mind that this is one of the key elements, if not the key element, in the situation at the present time. You may recall that I was one of the first to suggest publicly that a pause in these activities might provide openings for negotiations. Subsequently, I have repeatedly stressed that I would be glad to see the bombing stopped, Northern infiltration into the South stopped, and unconditional peace talks begin. This has been and will remain, in broad outline, the Canadian Government's position—a position which we have adopted not in a spirit of timidity but in a sense of reality, because we believe it corresponds to the facts and because we believe that a negotiation involves reciprocal commitments. Any other position taken by the Government, I am convinced, would be unhelpful.

In your letter you also called upon the Government to reveal all military production contracts related in any way to the Vietnam war, and to consider refusing to sell arms to the U.S.A. until the intervention in Vietnam ceases. While I can appreciate the sense of concern reflected in your suggestions, I think it might be helpful if I were to try to put this question in a somewhat broader perspective than the problem of the Vietnam war alone.

Relations between Canada and the U.S.A. in this field are currently covered by the Defence Production Sharing Agreements of 1959 and 1963, but in fact they go back much farther and find their origins in the Hyde Park Declaration of 1941. During this extended period of co-operation between the two countries, a very close relationship has grown up not only between the Canadian defence industrial base and its U.S. counterpart but also between the Canadian and U.S. defence equipment procurement agencies. This relationship is both necessary and logical not only as part of collective defence but also in order to meet our own national defence commitments effectively and economically. Equipments required by modern defence forces to meet even limited roles such as peace keeping are both technically sophisticated and very costly to develop and, because Canada's quantitative needs are generally very small, it is not economical for us to meet our total requirements solely from our own resources. Thus we must take advantage of large-scale production in allied countries. As the U.S.A. is the world leader in the advanced technologies involved, and because real advantages can be gained by following common North American design and production standards, the U.S.A. becomes a natural source for much of our defence equipment. The U.S.-Canadian production-sharing arrangements enable the Canadian Government to acquire from the U.S.A. a great deal of the nation's essential defence equipment at the lowest possible cost, while at the same time permitting us to offset the resulting drain on the economy by reciprocal sales to the U.S.A. Under these agreements, by reason of longer production runs, Canadian industry is able to participate competitively in U.S. research, development, and production programmes, and is exempted from the "Buy American" Act for these purposes. From a long-term point of view, another major benefit to Canada is the large contribution which these agreements have made and are continuing to make to Canadian industrial research and development capabilities, which, in turn, are fundamental to the maintenance of an advanced technology in Canada.

In this connection, I should perhaps point out that the greater part of U.S. military procurement in Canada consists not of weapons in the conventional sense but rather of electronic equipment, transport aircraft, and various kinds of components and sub-systems. In many cases, the Canadian industries which have developed such products to meet U.S. and continental defence requirements have, at the same time, been able to develop related products with a civil application or have been able to use the technology so acquired to advance their general capabilities. For a broad range of reasons, therefore, it is clear that the imposition of an embargo on the export of military equipment to the U.S.A., and concomitant termination of the Production Sharing Agreements, would have far-reaching consequences which no Canadian Government could contemplate with equanimity. It would be interpreted as a notice of withdrawal on our part from continental defence and even from the collective defence arrangements of the Atlantic alliance.

Saul N. Silverman, "Canada and NATO Revision," *Canadian Dimension*, Vol. 3, 1966, pp. 34-36. Reprinted by permission of *Canadian Dimension*, a magazine of the left, published in Winnipeg, Manitoba.

Revise NATO

After August 1969, NATO members will be free to leave the alliance. No doubt, many Canadians will urge that Canada give the required one-year's notice (Art. 13) and exercise this option. I suggest that Canada can better serve her interest in world stability by opting for NATO revision rather than for NATO's demise.

Even if there had not been serious debate within the alliance during the last few years, NATO revision would be overdue by the end of the decade. The world within which NATO operates differs significantly from that of 1949, when the alliance was negotiated and the treaty signed. The Soviet posture toward the West is neither as militant nor as exclusively military as it was in the last years of the Stalin era. Europe has recovered economically and has gone on to an unprecedented boom; the European states no longer cower behind the American nuclear shield, and De Gaulle's political initiatives evoke some sympathy in other quarters. Nuclear proliferation is now a reality, and most important, Europe is no longer the main area of global political confrontation. A new world politics in which the older East-West conflict is cut across by a multiple revolution center-ing in the developing countries, dwarfs the Cold War of the late 1940's and the 1950's. Given these changes, and its inability to develop to meet new challenges and new conditions, NATO has become moribund the last few years, an arena for debate over the distribution of power within the coalition rather than a useful instrument either for defence or for collective diplomacy aimed at détente.

Yet, a revival and reshaping of NATO can be a more palatable alternative than those which might develop given NATO's demise. The earlier priority of collective defence would, in such a revised NATO, be absorbed into a broader goal of shaping and focussing relations among the alliance partners, creating conditions of interdependence that could counterbalance destabilizing initiatives by any single member of the alliance. For Canada, a general interest in enhancing stability in the Atlantic area could be supplemented by a particular interest in finding a diplomatic balance, to take the place of the one we lost with the decline of British power, to the power of our immediate neighbour, the United States.

NATO Revision or Non-alignment?

Canadian foreign policy has traditionally sought an arena in which our ability to manoeuvre among powerful and competing forces would be harnessed to the achievement of marginal advantage to ourselves. One set of forces has been played against another to gain room within which national unity and socio-economic development—the internal values which "independence" has served—could be furthered. The traditional simple balance between British and American influence is obviously no longer possible. Canada must therefore seek a wider balance, a broader constellation of nations within which to operate.

Which of the available diplomatic constellations offers the most potential advantage to Canada? One suggested constellation is the United Nations. No one can seriously propose that Canada not do all in its power to further the UN cause. But this body encompasses such large and diffuse congeries of nations that any diplomacy of manoeuvre ultimately means choosing among coalitions within the U.N. Another constellation, often suggested as a counter to excessive reliance upon the United States, is the Commonwealth. But the Commonwealth, as the Rhodesian and other crises have amply demonstrated, has not developed into a framework for collective diplomacy. Rather, it tends to present a ceremonial facade to the outside world; behind the facade, more and more discontent is being expressed at the practical inadequacies of the Commonwealth. If Canada wishes to exert influence in world politics, it must look to diplomatic constellations characterized by some real focus of interests, even if identity of interests continues to be elusive. For all its faults, NATO offers the greatest potential for a diplomatic coalition within which a Canadian diplomacy of manoeuver be possible.

The only other possibility frequently mentioned is a policy of Canadian non-alignment. In the main, the advocates of non-alignment seem to be concerned less with advancing the merits of their suggested policy than with presenting arguments against Canada's present defence and foreign policy orientation; however, their serious arguments against NATO and Canada's role in the alliance deserve to be considered.

The nonaligners object to NATO as a destabilizing influence in world politics and argue that Canadian withdrawal would be a noble blow for greater international stability; they contend that NATO intrinsically limits Canada's independent initiatives on the diplomatic scene.

What would happen if NATO were to vanish from the scene? It seems likely that NATO might give way to even more unstable alternatives. Let us consider two such possibilities. . . .

CANADA'S INTEREST IN NATO REVISION

If NATO as a whole should dissolve, there is no doubt that one of two developments would follow—either of which would lead to greater instability than presently prevails. One possibility is that the present U.S.-German relationship, now partially mediated by the presence of other actors within the coalition, would become an open bilateral alliance. The U.S. would become more committed to a pro-Bonn solution to the division of Germany, and West Germany would be emboldened by the possession of advanced weapons which she would claim as the price of such an alliance. A second possibility, particularly if the demise of NATO were to coincide with a catastrophic American defeat in Southeast Asia, would be retreat into a "Fortress America" variant of isolationism, with the United States armed to the teeth and "loaded for bear" and, moreover, freed from the need to give any consideration to the interests and opinions of non-existent allies. Either of these possibilities is dangerous. The United States would be pushed into much more belligerent positions than it presently occupies vis-a-vis the Soviet Union and would be cut off from the moderating opinions of its present European allies. The dangers which we see today arising out of the Viet Nam crisis would, under these circumstances, be compounded ten-fold. . . .

If we look at these alternatives, a multilateral western alliance, hopefully a reshaped NATO with considerable room for in-coalition manoeuver aimed at re-straining and focussing the policies of its more powerful member, appears infinitely less dangerous than the kind of alignments that might replace NATO.

The argument that Canada's commit-ment to NATO seriously acts to inhibit her taking initiatives in world politics is two-fold. Major stress is placed on the allegation that Canada has forfeited her leading role among non-aligned countries by adhering to NATO. That Canada ever had such a role among the non-aligned or could gain significant leadership or influ-ence in their councils remains to be demonstrated. While many nations view Canada rather kindly, when they notice her at all, nowhere in the "third world" is there evident any yearning for Cana-dian leadership or influence. If Canadian delusions of grandeur were to become widely known outside her own borders, they would provoke ridicule or contempt —ridicule at the spectacle of a political entity that cannot reconcile its own nation-al divisions aspiring to bridge the diversity among the congeries of nations—contempt at the arrogance behind this posture of penny-ante "neo-colonialism," the "Ca-uck's burden," articulated not by the powers of high finance but by university and newspaper intellectuals. It is time that Canada stopped deceiving herself in this fashion. Canada should help the under-developed nations in practical fashion whenever possible, but Canadians should not aspire to a position of "leadership" which is neither deserved nor expected.

The second, more empirical aspect of the argument that NATO inhibits Cana-dian diplomatic initiatives can be dealt with by even the most cursory glance at the record. While Canada has not been noted for the sort of major breakthroughs that only the super-powers, if they were willing, could undertake, she has to her credit a fine record as a diplomatic tech-nician—a responsible "middle power" tinkering with the devices of diplomacy to enhance the degree of flexibility pos-sible in world politics. A few examples come readily to mind: in 1955, in the United Nations, Canada (Mr. Martin then headed our UN delegation) negotiated the compromise that led to breaking the long-standing logjam over admission of new members and paved the way (for better or worse) to the present greatly-expanded UN in which the developing countries play so significant a role; in 1956, Mr. Pearson negotiated the formula whereby the UN entered into the settlement of the Suez crisis and, in so doing, established the precedent for the present plethora of UN peace forces; . . .

We are all aware that Canada's at-tempt to use the alliance to her own ad-vantage backfired. Canada did not de-velop, economically, as quickly as wartime prophets thought would be the case; at the same time, European recovery and the re-assertion of the influence of some of the apparently prostrate members of the alli-ance proceeded more rapidly than had been anticipated. Instead of becoming the third power in the alliance, Canada was relegated to a role in the Greek chorus. Two institutional developments enhanced this regression of Canada's position. NATO paid only lip-service to the kind of joint planning agencies that had func-tioned during the war, in which Canada had been able to maximize her influence. Further, the Korean War led the United States to take a much more active role in NATO and to attempt to convert it from a military coalition to an appendage of its own armed forces. In the end, the Ameri-can goal was partially frustrated—NATO never developed either the strength, in terms of combat-ready divisions, or the degree of unified military command that the Pentagon desired. But in the process of NATO evolution, Canada's purpose was frustrated also.

Now the question of shaping the coalition is once more on the agenda. This time, the dominant theme, I would suggest, is less that of collective defence (though this still remains important) than the co-ordination of power relations in the Atlantic area. Canada's positive purpose remains the same: to seek to enhance its own in-coalition bargaining position. Her negative interest is to forestall the development of alternatives to NATO that would lead to greater instability and that would have the effect of shutting the door on a Canadian role in coalition decision-making. Is there hope that Canada's interests can be realized in the course of rebuilding Atlantic institutions?

Some aspects of the changed international situation (compared to 1948-1949) favour a Canadian advantage from NATO revision. Since the Soviet threat is less overt, the European nations involved in NATO renegotiation, while still interested in establishing a credible minimum deterrent posture vis-a-vis the East, are more likely than they were in the late 1940's and early 1950's to view favourably attempts to create a balance of power and influence within the Atlantic superstructure. Canada's interests are, then, likely to be complemented by those of some of the European partners. Secondly, France represents a powerful agency for in-coalition diplomatic balance, and Canada has less reason than does the U.S. to fear the effects of De Gaulle's manoeuvres. De Gaulle, too, realizes the risks involved in driving the United States into the arms of West Germany; despite officially-inspired propaganda on this side of the Atlantic, it appears likely (especially if one has regard to the French diplomatic tradition) that the General aims less at the disruption of the alliance than at enhancing his bargaining position for the coming round of negotiations on the shape of the post-NATO coalition. . . .

Canada's tasks in preparing for the coming NATO revision is three-fold. A positive foreign policy depends on the existence of a viable domestic polity; if Canadians wish to enhance their influence abroad, they must, in the next few years, arrive at at least a provisional resolution of their own domestic discontents. Secondly, Canada must become highly innovative in her tactical diplomatic alignments in the preparatory stage of negotiations and during the negotiations themselves. If Canada seeks the transformation of NATO into a more politically and economically oriented coalition, it must align itself with the more positive aspects of the Gaullist position—not only in Europe but to a considerable extent in Asia as well. Ethnically Canada possesses the passport for the transition from a British or American-oriented policy to one which, while retaining some aspects of our older ties, boldly moves toward a closer relationship with the New Europe. Finally, and perhaps most important, Canadians must free themselves of the miasma of self-congratulatory or over-belligerent delusions about foreign affairs and start a real debate, focussing on those options which are realistically attainable in the next decade or so. One thing is clear: Canada cannot, with either profit or honour, retreat into a spirit-world of narcissistic self-contemplation. Our future lies in wider associations of interdependence; the task, in the coming years, is to begin to forge the bonds through which interdependence can be achieved.

John N. Warnock, "Canada and the Alliance System," *Canadian Dimension*, Vol. 3, 1966, pp. 36-39. Reprinted by permission of *Canadian Dimension*, a magazine of the left, published in Winnipeg, Manitoba.

Scrap NATO

The press conference of President de Gaulle on February 22, 1966, finally seems to have brought to the attention of the American public the fact that the North Atlantic Treaty Organization, as it now exists, will cease to operate after April 4, 1969, the date provided in the Treaty for "opting out." But the full impact of the French position apparently has not been noticed by Canadians. While we are accustomed to little public participation in foreign policy, in this case there seems to be no official or informed comment. Paul Martin has indicated that Canadian policy should be to "not rock the boat," the traditional Calvin Coolidge-Mackenzie King approach to serious problems.

The French have announced that after April 4, 1966, all forces, French as well as other foreign troops stationed in France, will be under French command. At a minimum this seems to indicate that the 26,000 American troops must be moved to other NATO countries and that the NATO "infrastructure" must also be shifted. This latest move is a natural continuation of French protests against Anglo-American domination and a "second-class" French role in the Alliance. In the past France has refused to "integrate" her navy and air force under NATO command, noting that the British and American forces had remained outside. When the United States refused to include France along with Britain under the special arrangements for exchange of nuclear information in 1958, President de Gaulle announced that France would build her own nuclear force and would insist on control over all nuclear weapons stationed on her territory.

There is no question but that the formal structure of NATO has always been dominated by Britain and the United States. The two important military commands, the European Command and the Atlantic Command, have always been headed by Americans. Of the five subordinate commands in Europe, only one, the Central Europe Command, has ever been headed by a French officer. Of the seventeen top command positions, seven are held by Americans, eight by British, with one French and one Belgian officer. In theory, the commands are subordinate to the Standing Group, the representatives of the Chiefs-of-Staff of France, Britain and the United States. However, the Standing Group is located in Washington and has lost any real military influence. The Supreme Allied Commander Europe, always an American General, is the Central authority in the Alliance, and he answers directly to the President of the United States.

With the creation of the unified command structure in the early 1950's, NATO was transformed from a military alliance into an organization which the United States clearly dominated and in which she made the decisions. With the time limits of technological warfare what they are to-day, if war did start in Europe there would be no time to consult 15 member nations for approval of action. The Supreme Allied Commander would either act automatically, under contingency plans, or if time permitted, consult with the President. Thus, the Treaty today is far from the original one which proclaimed that in case of attack the parties, individually or collectively, would take "such action as it deems necessary, including the use of armed force, to restore and maintain the security of the North Atlantic area." Lester B. Pearson, then Foreign Minister, assured Canada that in case of aggression the government would consult Parliament first. In the United States, the Truman Administration made it clear that action would not be taken without Congressional approval. This is out of the question to-day.

U.S. domination is evident, however, in other more important matters. The nuclear "sword" of NATO, the Strategic Air Command's fleet of bombers and ICBMs, remains solely under the control of the United States. Furthermore, the United States has retained a degree of control over the use of tactical nuclear weapons by the members of NATO, including Canada, who have acquired their use. In theory, they cannot be activated without the approval of the United States. . . .

CANADA'S ROLE IN NATO

What, then, is the future role for Canada in NATO? Certainly her military contribution is negligible. The Army Brigade stationed in Germany consists of about 6,200 men, about three-tenths of 1 per cent (.3%) of the NATO land forces. Since the advent of the Pearson Government, in 1963, it has included four batteries of nuclear-armed Honest John

missiles. Even then the missile was cumbersome, immobile and generally obsolete, and in any case it was widely agreed that NATO could not fight a tactical nuclear war and survive.

The RCAF maintains one Air Division in Europe, eight squadrons of CF-104 Starfighters. This constitutes only 200 of NATO's 5,500 tactical aircraft. In 1959, the Diefenbaker Government agreed to convert the Air Division from a defensive to an offensive role. In case of war, the Canadian Air Division is scheduled to drop nuclear bombs, up to the megaton range, on predetermined cities and other targets in Eastern Europe. Even in 1959 there was no need for this additional nuclear power, which merely added to what is termed the West's "overkill capacity."

Quite obviously, NATO could get along without the Canadian military contribution; this has even been admitted by Liberals. But Canadian participation has always been defended on the ground that we must shoulder our share of the responsibility in order to set a good example and to provide moral support for the alliance. It is also argued that Canada would lose its influence in NATO decision-making if it reneged on its military contribution. This is a specious argument, for it assumes that Canada now has influence, which it quite obviously does not. As well, it is argued that the United States, with her own deterrent, is protecting us all from invasion by the Soviet Union. Subordination is often the price we must pay for security. Somehow, it is difficult to picture the Soviet Union poised on the border of the Canadian Arctic, restrained only by American nuclear power.

Participation in this military alliance has been a source of continued embarrassment to Canada and has provoked a bad conscience in many political leaders. Some have rationalized Canadian participation in NATO on the grounds that a transatlantic alliance broadens the base of Canadian defence. They state it operates to help keep Canada from falling completely into a bi-lateral defence system, which could only mean total subordination to the United States. Since Canadian governments have not made any real effort to bring the NORAD system under NATO, and have, almost enthusiastically, entered into various military agreements with the United States since 1940, this argument seems rather weak.

From the beginning, Canada has insisted that the alliance should be more than just a military system. In order to move toward an "Atlantic Community," it should also have as a goal further co-operation in the economic and cultural field. The first result of this was the well-known Article II in the Treaty, called the "Canadian article." Such a role has been consistently opposed by the United States and Britain and is probably the most ignored part of the treaty. The limited NATO membership does not offer a sensible system for further Atlantic economic co-operation. The creation of the OECD, in 1961, should have ended this argument once and for all. Yet, this dead article still serves both the Liberals and the New Democrats as a rationalization for involvement in the alliance. . . .

EXIT FOR CANADA

What is Canada going to do? Undoubtedly she will muddle along, trying to sweep the problem under the rug, following her traditional policy of "partnership" with the United States. Using our past as a guide, we cannot expect more. If, in the short run, NATO breaks down or is transformed into a series of bilateral alliances, Canada will become even more obviously a satellite of the United States. When will continental integration stop? Will we end up a Yugoslavia? . . . a Poland? . . . or a Latvia?

We are already in a sort of commonwealth relationship similar to that of Puerto Rico. Sooner or later, we have to face this problem. Perhaps we already have. If NATO breaks up, I would not be happy living in a country which decides to remain closely aligned with the United States. On the other hand, I would not want to live in a country which gives its support to an "Atlantic Community" based on white supremacy and coupled with a desire to preserve an increasingly affluent society at the expense of keeping the undeveloped world in a state of quasi-slavery.

The only alternative is to withdraw from the military alliances. While it may be very doubtful that this will ever happen, it is a possibility and must be considered. I have not discussed the North American defense system yet because nobody can really take Canadian participation seriously. The system never provided a defence for the United States, either against missiles or bombers. In the past the three-tier system of radar detection served a purpose, but this was replaced in 1961 by the Ballistic Missiles Early Warning System stationed in Alaska, Greenland and Britain. No Canadian contribution or participation is needed. In the U.S. Defence budget presented in 1965 Secretary McNamara declared that NORAD was obsolete and was being phased out. Right now it only serves a political purpose—keeping Canada tied with the United States. An attractive alternative role was proposed in 1959 by Harry Pope, joint Canadian-Russian operation of the radar system both ways as a step toward peace, but this was ignored then and appears to be dead today in spite of the detente.

But withdrawal from the system of military alliances does not mean that all of a sudden Canada is going to emerge as a leader of the non-aligned world, or even as an influential member. As a rich, white country, with a long past of close association with colonial powers, there will always be suspicion. But today Canada has no influence in international politics and is generally viewed as a meek spokesman for the United States. Prior to the admission of the new states, Canada did play a role as a mediator at the United Nations; since 1960 this role has been usurped by the non-aligned powers. While every politician lauds Canada's role in UN peace-keeping operations, they refuse to admit that this is rapidly changing. Even during the 1956 Suez crisis, the Queen's Own Rifles were refused because of their colonial identification. Canadian troops were not accepted for the UN Congo operation whereas those from Sweden, Austria and Ireland were accepted. The UN refused the Canadian offer of troops for the operation in West New Guinea. Canadian troops could be used in Cyprus only because all parties concerned were associated with NATO.

Basically the choice for Canada is whether to play a passive or active role in international politics. The easy answer is the present passive role as a dependency of the United States. This itself involves a moral choice, that we believe American policy is right and therefore choose to follow. But if Canada is to play an active part in international politics today it can only be as a non-aligned power. This would be a difficult policy to undertake, for it would require a break with the past. But it could also have some beneficial domestic results. I agree with Professor Paul Painchaud of College Jean de Brebeuf that this is the only issue that can unite French and English Canada.

But there is a positive aspect of this policy choice in the international arena. Canada could begin a movement to build and maintain co-operation between the white and the non-white world. She could become the first developed country to make a serious effort to close the widening gap between the international North and South. However, any effective policy in this direction would require significant changes and disruptions of normal international intercourse. As a minimum it would call for the elimination of the ridiculous Canadian defense expenditure. Such a change would make participation in military alliances even more irrelevant than today; indeed, they would be a general handicap. But some Western country must undertake this task, even if it is too little and too late.

Paddy Sherman, "Politics will keep Canada in NATO," *Vancouver Province*, September 14, 16, 1968.

NATO Military Realities

When (or should it be if?) Prime Minister Trudeau explains his upcoming decision on whether Canada should stay in or pull out of NATO, most Canadians will be in for a considerable shock.

They will find that the reasons they have assumed over the years for Canada's participation are no longer the real reasons.

And they are likely to learn that although Canada's military contribution is costly and marked by expensive errors, Canada will continue in NATO—at a greater cost than before.

The main reason for all this is that Canada's involvement, which began as a military matter, is now regarded as a primarily political affair.

A common public reaction until recently was that Canada was in NATO because of an agreement made 20 years ago that would prevent the Russians from invading Europe. That agreement was outdated, the argument went, and therefore Canada should do as France did, and pull out her forces.

This reaction changed somewhat with the invasion of Czechoslovakia, but not much; people who felt that way insisted that NATO's lack of action showed it

was powerless anyway against Russia.

However, to top-level people in both the Defence Department and the External Affairs Department in Ottawa, that lack of action was a highly intelligent and deliberate response completely in keeping with NATO's basic political role.

Nobody seriously suggests, particularly after the speed and precision of the Russian advance into Czechoslovakia, that NATO's military forces could hold the Russians from an aggressive sweep across Europe. At best they could slow them down a day or two, long enough to give the U.S. Congress time to decide if it would use nuclear weapons against Russia.

The real worry, Trudeau is being told by his experts, is that any significant change in the present lineup of either NATO or the Warsaw Pact nations will make Russia nervous and jittery, thus greatly increasing the risk of war. Czechoslovakia emphasized their warning.

What would happen if Canada decided to quit? Other countries are under pressure to get out for economy reasons. If they followed, the real new role of NATO would fall apart—there would no longer be an international alliance keeping Germany in check.

Germany is the strongest European nation apart from Russia. If she were suddenly alone, who would stop her from acquiring her own nuclear weapons—a prospect that already ignites a bitter fear in Russia?

Would she then drive hard for unification with East Germany, which Russia would resist violently—and which the other NATO countries have quietly refused to push for, although they pay lip-service?

If Britain and the U.S., who vanquished Germany, remained the only allies on her soil, Germany would be furious and dissatisfied. And if everybody went, would Germany be content to have no nuclear weapons of her own, relying only on an American promise to consider using missiles if the Russians invaded in a battle over re-unification?

These are the basic political arguments being placed before the prime minister as he tries to make up his mind.

In short, they suggest that as long as NATO is present, even a NATO that Russia could lick, the Russians will be content, for NATO will be containing their most-feared rival in Europe. If Canada goes in the present climate the elaborate bloc structure that holds back Russian worries will disintegrate. Does Canada intend to be the bloc-buster?

In addition to the major reasoning, Canada has other, more selfish, political interests. Despite claims that Canada would enhance its prestige by moving out and taking a lofty stance, the reverse is true, Mr. Trudeau is being told.

Many doors now open because of her NATO commitment would close. Nobody would tell us of major plans or developments as freely as before. We would have no major political forum in Europe in which to further our national interests, particularly involving trade.

Consequently when the NATO ministers begin their important talks in Brussels in December, Canada is likely to continue to deal herself in, and try to breathe new life into Article Two of the Treaty. This provides for economic co-operation among the NATO countries.

But the cost of continuing membership in NATO is likely to be high. . . .

In terms of the integrated, efficiency-conscious armed forces dreamed of by Canada's new military planners, Canada's long-standing NATO contingent of 10,000 men in Europe is costly and far from ideal.

The annual bill for it is around $150 million, and it is likely to go considerably higher. In fact, any significant change in its role is likely to increase the present fixed defence budget of $1.7 billion.

The present set-up is open to considerable criticism. Under the cabinet's NATO re-appraisal, it is getting that criticism.

For example, Canada's soldiers and airmen in Europe use widely separated bases, with different supply lines, adding to servicing costs. The roles of both our air and army contingents there are different from the roles for which the bulk of our forces are trained at home.

The airmen fly the CF-104, a nuclear attack bomber for which there is no role in Canada. Special training facilities are needed. The same applies to the armored brigade. Both the planes and the tanks are due to be replaced with new models before many years. Canada has already been asked to take part in joint development of a new NATO aircraft, a costly step she is reluctant to take.

It must be remembered, in all this, that Canada's biggest commitment to NATO is in naval strength, primarily intended to detect submarines. That role, too, is under study, but withdrawal of the naval forces from NATO could virtually end the life of the navy.

The most delicate question at the moment, however, is the future of the forces in Europe. The government has three options open to it: It can get out now; it can stay in a little longer and stall; or it can plunge at once into a new role costing hundreds of millions of dollars.

In the light of the political reasoning, a quick get-out is now virtually out of the question. Even if it were not, removing our troops from Europe is of itself no answer to demands to cut costs. The basic cost of the forces is about $14,000 per man in general personnel charges. It takes as much money to keep a man sitting in Canada as in Europe. The extra European costs are relatively minor. If we pulled out our 10,000 men only to save money, we'd have to fire them all back into civilian life.

If we stay in and stall, the life of our present equipment is less than seven years. That means two years or so from now we would still have to decide whether to go into new models or pull out and disband.

The third option is the most attractive politically—and the most expensive. It is to drop our nuclear bomber and tank role, and replace it with a highly mobile airborne cavalry function that would specialize not in massive resistance but in crisis management.

That means a whole range of new vehicles, principally helicopters, which are among the most expensive of all to operate. The defence planners found this out to their chagrin when they investigated it as a potentially cheaper way to retain our European presence. Estimates for the conversion now run as high as three-quarters of a billion dollars. And it would cost twice as much as that to keep the troops in Canada with enough fast jets to get them into Europe rapidly, a concept that would also fit them into a United Nations police-type role.

Therefore either of these possibilities is likely to send the budget close to the $2 billion mark.

How acceptable is all this politically? Internationally it would be welcomed. There is a certain status-symbol rating conferred among members of defence alliances according to the amount of money they will spend to support their principles. Such spending is measured in relation to the gross national product.

In this field, Canada is close to the bottom of the NATO alliance. Her defence spending runs around 2.8 per cent of GNP, compared with a NATO range of three to five per cent and a 10 per cent rate for the U.S. and Russia.

But the political reaction at home is likely to be quite different.

It is hardly likely that Mr. Trudeau could provoke a happy public reaction to the thought of an increased defence budget if he persisted in the old reasoning for NATO. Even after Czechoslovakia there is too much public feeling that Russia fears only the prospect of nuclear missiles, not NATO tanks.

If he is to get public acceptance of the new attitude to NATO, in fact, he must embark on the sort of full and frank educational campaign among the voters that he often mentions. It will need to be a major and most sophisticated campaign. In fact, it and the policy he intends to sell may well prove one of the biggest undertakings of his term in office.

Part V

New Possibilities,
New Problems

The choices posed by alliance politics are hard indeed. Fortunately there still remain other areas in which Canada can exercise some influence, and according to some observers these are precisely the areas that should be developed to the fullest. But if some new opportunities offer themselves there are new problems, too, noticeably in the growing unrest in Quebec and in the increasing influence of France in the affairs of the province.

Of the opportunities, perhaps the most attractive and idealistic is peacekeeping. It was in this area that Lester Pearson achieved world prominence for Canada in 1956. And Canada, unique among the nations of the world, was represented on each and every peacekeeping body established by the United Nations. After he became Prime Minister, Pearson continued his interest in the problems of peacekeeping, and in an article published in *Maclean's* in 1964, he advanced some specific proposals and suggestions on ways to increase the effectiveness of this device. Already, however, the academics were beginning to train their guns on peacekeeping, and sometimes their fire was deadly accurate. The article by Donald Gordon, a University of Alberta professor, raised some fundamental questions about the value of peacekeeping in general and about Canada's interest in it. Professor J. L. Granatstein of York University, however, still sees real value in international peacekeeping, both for its calming effects in troubled areas and for the role it potentially offers Canadians in an area more or less removed from alliance pressures.

And what of the Commonwealth? The Empire was in decay throughout the 1950s and 1960s. The "gentlemen's club" of white Dominions was dead and gone, and after Suez in 1956 not even an essential community of interest could be said to remain. Equally important in the decline of Empire was the drastic diminution of British strength in the age of the superpowers. Still, something remained, often intangible, often limited only to the fact that the members spoke English and were trained in roughly similar educational and political traditions. For Canada, the benefits offered by the Commonwealth tie were perhaps limited, but some benefits did exist. The pamphlet by Professor K. A. MacKirdy, the University of Waterloo historian who died in 1968, underlines these advantages.

Potentially of greater significance to Canada's world role—and possibly of enormous significance in terms of purely Canadian needs—was the emergence of the French Commonwealth—*la Francophonie*. Still not formalized, still little more than a loose association of French-speaking nations, Francophonie seemed to offer a way for French Canadians to find a role abroad. More, it seemed to offer the opportunity for Canada to develop a genuinely bicultural foreign policy. Clearly as Jean Morrison pointed out in her article on Francophonie, if Canada did not seize the initiative Quebec would. By 1968, there was every indication that Ottawa was moving forcefully to solidify Canadian links with the French-speaking world.

This was significant, for the entire question of Quebec's role in the world had become a matter of public comment after President De Gaulle's visit to Quebec in 1967. In a now famous address at the Hotel de Ville in Montreal, the French President seemed to provide encouragement for the separatist minority in Quebec with his call for a *"Québec libre."* This address roused English Canadian fears, as did the participation of Quebec's education minister, M. Car-

dinal, in an international educational conference in the African state of Gabon. There Cardinal was treated as the representative of a sovereign state, a condition of affairs that Ottawa was not disposed to disregard. The result was the publication of a White Paper by the Secretary of State for External Affairs, Mitchell Sharp, that spelled out Ottawa's position in explicit terms.

Already reaching near-paranoid proportions, Ottawa's suspicion of France reached a new peak after the "Rossillon affair" in the fall of 1968. Rossillon, an official of the French premier's office, had paid a visit to a French-speaking community in Manitoba, a visit that provoked an extraordinarily harsh reaction from the prime minister, Pierre Trudeau. Rossillon was an agitator, seemed to be the reaction, out to produce disaffection among the Franco-Manitobans. A press excerpt by Claude Ryan, the editor of the Montreal morning newspaper *Le Devoir*, gives some idea of the range of feeling in Canada after this visit.

For all the difficulty between Quebec, Ottawa, and France, there was much that was healthy in English Canada's new awareness of Quebec's international aspirations. For too long Canadian policy had been English in its orientation, formation, and implementation. Now this could never be possible. Quebec had forced Canada to become aware of the one-third of its population that spoke French—and also of the nations in Asia, Africa, and Europe that belonged to Francophonie. There were grounds for hope that out of this new understanding would yet come a more effective foreign policy and a stronger nation.

Lester Pearson, "A New Kind of Peace Force," *Maclean's,* May 2, 1964.

The Need for United Nations Peacekeeping

There have been six major efforts during the last thirty years to restore or to keep the peace by organizing international force behind international decisions.

The latest of these, in Cyprus, an effort which is just beginning, shows once again the importance of the UN for peacekeeping, but it also shows us the folly of not organizing in advance so that the UN can operate effectively in this field.

How long must the United Nations go on improvising in times of crisis? How long is the burden to be carried by a few member states, while too many others merely stand by, or obstruct?

The Canadian government was urged to volunteer a force for Cyprus, swiftly, and get it there at once. But there were no arrangements for such a UN force and no terms of reference to ensure it could do the job; no operating orders, no provision for collective financing of a UN operation.

How long must we wait before the UN makes provision in advance to deal with these local crises before they become general wars? I believe that arrangements to prevent the spread of "brushfire wars"

can be and must be made; we must have a force that can do this brushfire job, and do it well.

I believe, however, that the initiative for advance planning should come—as it has come in the past—from a country like Canada, not from a great power. It seems to me that there is a way open to us by which we can mobilize the peacekeeping resources of countries like our own. . . .

How can we, within the UN, use the experience we have gained in these actions to improve our future efforts to keep the peace? . . .

There should be advance planning and organization so that the United Nations will not have to scramble and improvise, but will be in a position to know that certain members, invited and willing to participate, will have contingents organized, equipped and ready to go.

A United Nations force sent into a danger area to keep the peace should know in advance what its responsibilities are; what it can and cannot do, and how it should operate.

It should be informed and advised by a small, permanent, military-planning-and-staff group in the secretary-general's office, which would have responsibility for the organization and operation of a UN force, once established.

The United Nations should decide that, in future, UN peacekeeping operations will be financed by the United Nations as a whole, not only by the participating members or by voluntary contributions from others. This is essential. Otherwise countries like Canada, which are asked to participate in almost all these international interventions at their own expense, will have a justifiable grievance which will eventually express itself in reluctance to continue to carry a disproportionate share of the burden.

These are Canada's views, but other UN members share them. The Nordic countries and the Netherlands have firm, largely parallel policies, and more and more governments seem to be thinking along the same lines. This prompted me last autumn at the general assembly to suggest that it might be useful to pool experience and ideas for improving United Nations peace-keeping methods. But the recent history of UN peace-keeping shows how difficult it is to bring about these conditions and get agreement on the necessary plans.

In 1958, Dag Hammarskjöld, who was then secretary-general of the UN, submitted a report to the general assembly on the experience derived from the establishment and operation of UNEF in Palestine. In this report he made suggestions for certain permanent international arrangements to meet emergencies in the future. The assembly, however, refused even to discuss this report, let alone act on it.

Why? The USSR and the communist members were adamantly opposed to the whole idea of organizing the enforcement and peace-strengthening functions of the United Nations. Certain other countries, especially some Asian ones that had only recently secured national independence, were almost equally suspicious. They appeared to dislike anything that would authorize the United Nations to put force behind international decisions in a way which might interfere with their own national policies. Lingering fears of imperialist intervention under international guise aroused their suspicions, even though the concept of UNEF—and of the secretary-general's conclusions in his report on UNEF—should have served to remove, rather than to create, such suspicions.

There were, however, other members of the United Nations—including Canada —who were strongly in favor of using the experience of UNEF to help build a permanent organization for international peace-and-police action.

Canada knew that a genuine and powerful international force under the security council was impossible because of the division among the permanent members of the council. We knew that even stand-by arrangements for limited purposes would be opposed inside the United Nations and would, in any event, have to be voluntary in character and flexible in organization. We knew that Mr. Hammarskjöld was right when he said in his report:

In view of the impossibility of determining beforehand the specific form of a United Nations presence of the type considered in this report, which would be necessary to meet adequately the requirements of a given situation, a broad decision by the general assembly should attempt to do no more than endorse certain basic principles and rules which would provide an adaptable framework for later operations that might be found necessary. In a practical sense, it is not feasible in advance of a known situation to do more than to provide for some helpful stand-by arrangements for a force or similar forms of a United Nations presence.

We also knew Mr. Hammarskjöld was right when he emphasized that the United Nations must have full authority over the constitution and control of any UN force or presence. As he put it:

A United Nations operation should always be under a leadership established by the general assembly or the security council, or on the basis of delegated authority by the secretary-general, so as to make it directly responsible to one of the main organs of the United Nations, while integrated with the secretariat in an appropriate form.

Yet, as I have pointed out, Mr. Hammarskjöld's modest proposals for organizing the peace-keeping role of the United Nations could not even be discussed, let alone adopted by the UN assembly to which they were addressed.

Can nothing be done?

Yes, something can be done: When it became clear, more than ten years ago, that the security council—because of the cold war—could not organize collective security under Article 43 of the UN charter, certain members who believe in such security as the best defense of peace did not sit back and do nothing. Balked in the United Nations itself, they organized, as a second best, collective security on a limited basis under Article 51 of the charter.

The result was NATO.

There is similar need for a new initiative today, but one to be taken inside the United Nations itself. If the UN assembly, as such, refuses to take that initiative —if it is unable to agree on permanent arrangements for a "stand-by" peace force —then why should a group of members who feel that this should be done not do something about it themselves? Why should they not discharge their own responsibilities individually and collectively by organizing a force for this purpose, one formally outside the United Nations but ready to be used on its request?

To do so would require a number of middle powers, whose credentials and whose motives are above reproach, to work out a stand-by arrangement among themselves consistent with the United Nations charter. What is needed, in fact, is an entirely new arrangement by which these nations would establish an international peace force, its contingents trained and equipped for the purpose, and operating under principles agreed on in advance.

Any such arrangement would not conflict with responsibilities arising out of existing agreements for collective action. It would be separate from and additional to them, but it would be specifically tied to carrying out United Nations decisions.

This new arrangement, at least at the beginning, could be confined to half a dozen or so middle powers. The forces provided could only be called into action on the request of the United Nations through a resolution passed for that purpose. But the forces would be ready for such a call.

The parties to the new arrangement might, indeed, set up their own consultative machinery to watch over developments, as well as a small military staff to co-ordinate the roles of separate contingents of the peace-keeping force. This kind of political and military machinery would, of course, only be necessary if it had not already been set up in the office of the UN secretary-general.

With a group of middle powers working together this way, a respectable and effective stand-by peace force could soon be brought into being ready for instant use. The arrangement governing its activities and organization would bind, of course, only those members who subscribed to it. It would, therefore, not be a United Nations agreement as such. But its machinery would come into action only on recommendation of the United Nations, and the arrangement could be formalized by the United Nations any time the assembly so decided.

In this way, if a crisis arose and there were no UN force to deal with it, the world organization would know that some members had available their own international force for preserving the peace; for carrying out and supervising UN recommendations when called on; for pacifying disturbed areas; and for putting international police force behind international decisions.

This would be an important and constructive initiative for international peace and security. If it is to have any hope of success, it must be taken by middle powers with a sense of international responsibility, who by their records are known to have no selfish or aggressive purposes in what they are trying to do.

There must be leadership to bring this about. Interested governments must be prepared to give it. As a leading middle power, with a well-known record of support for United Nations peace-keeping operations in widely spread theatres, Canada is in a unique position to take the initiative. It is prepared to do so. It is anxious to develop its close co-operation with other UN members in these vital endeavors; to explore with them means for strengthening the United Nations' capacity to act in this field and the ability of member states to participate.

Cyprus has once again demonstrated the need for a high degree of preparedness. The recurring risks and challenges of our rapidly changing world demand no less than a United Nations equipped for effective response.

Donald Gordon, "Canada as Peacekeeper," *in* King Gordon, ed., *Canada's Role as a Middle Power* (Toronto: CIIA, 1966), 51-65. Reprinted by permission of The Canadian Institute of International Affairs and the Author.

Peacekeeping:

A Muted Voice

Now, on the face of it, peace-keeping is enormously attractive. Usually there are four main reasons cited for this. None of the four is actually that valid, but these reasons have been and probably will continue for some time to be very convincing. It is very important to note the difference between "validity" and "convincingness". The fact that we feel peace-keeping is a good thing, and persuade ourselves to support it, creates just as much of a reality as an objective, sober, highly-qualified assessment of the substance of peace-keeping. In this sense we are up against a situation in which two realities can come into conflict.

The first reason for Canadian involvement in U.N. peace-keeping was suggested by Andrew Boyd of *The Economist*, in his book on the United Nations in which he paid great tribute to the "fire brigade" of the U.N. Mr. Boyd made a great fuss about the importance of Canada, the Scandanavian countries, and Ireland, as the firemen who charge from the firehouse whenever an action is deemed to be tolerable to all the major powers and is actually supported by a sufficiently strong coalition of major powers. He argued that middle powers possessed the specialized men and

equipment and the political sophistication that are necessary. They are felt to be qualified to deal with a brush fire threat which, if unchecked, will either spread into the preserves of the major powers or assume proportions that will involve major powers, whether they like it or not.

Both aspects of this kind of fire brigade efforts are thought to be quite important. The specialized skills, of course, make for a relatively cheap and relatively efficient operation (if we send in people with bows and arrows we probably will achieve the same result, but we will need more of them and this will probably cost more money). Equally, the political skills serve to reduce errors of ignorance, inexperience and, most of all, excessive idealism.

I always think of the example of the Disarmament Conference in Geneva in this regard. So far as the substance of disarmament is concerned, it is clearly up to the major powers to decide the basic issue of whether we are going to agree in principle on disarmament or not. But when it gets down to the specific drafting—working out what an agreement will mean in exact detail—(is a jeep a nuclear weapons carrier, for example)—then you need delegates from associated smaller powers who have experience and skill. You have got to know what special consequences will emerge. You have got to know the kinds of formulas and phrases and definitions that apply. In this sense, then, it is argued that as a middle power in the fire brigade our political sophistication is just as important as our specialized physical and equipment skills.

Secondly, there is the suggestion that by taking part in peace-keeping Canada enhances her influence and prestige. From a Canadian viewpoint there is the attraction of being able, in an assortment and succession of ad hoc coalitions of middle and minor powers, to gain the attention of the major powers. A single state power like Canada has one voice of comparable weight to that of, say, Texas. But in coalitions there are that many more Texases involved. And so we can command attention in a way that we might have trouble doing otherwise.

Also, to a degree, we can influence policies and their implementation. If we say we are going to take our peace-keeping baseball and go home, sometimes it matters. When it does matter—as a threat or a negotiating instrument—then we can influence a policy.

And, perhaps as the most important aspect of our enhancing of influence and prestige, we can introduce fresh dynamics into static situations. A coalition of middle and minor power can gain attention and can suggest the slightly different points of view that can help often to resolve a conflict or issue.

Now, in addition to this, it is often believed that continual activity in such successions of coalition—rubbing shoulders with the Swedes regularly, the Irish occasionally, and so on—serves to enhance the confidence, the cooperation, and the information available to us. Thus it becomes possible, in theory, for us to begin to provide a much-needed bridge between major and minor powers into the non-white areas, and so on. However, this actually may be nonsense, partly because we are a good deal smaller than our pretensions suggest, and partly because there isn't as much obsessive attention paid to Canada as we would like to believe. Other people don't inflame their navels about us as much as we do.

I was particularly reminded of this in the Congo, as a matter of fact, where I flew in one time to Stanleyville and announced triumphantly to a Congolese soldier, "I'm from Canada." His reply was "Who is he?"

The third of the four arguments for this peace-keeping idea is the argument that peace-keeping really serves domestic Canadian purposes. This probably is the most defensible point. Apart from the people actually involved in peace-keeping, who are usually either monumentally disenchanted or dangerously over-euphoric, it seems to me that peace-keeping does feed our fires of nationalism. It provides a certain element contributing to domestic unity and it suits practical partisan political needs.

Peace-keeping has overtones of romance, adventure, and intrigue. It is relatively cheap and simple of operation. Thus, inasmuch as it serves domestic purposes, peace-keeping does have much to be said for it—perhaps even more than the ill-fated vision of The North that had such a great effect on us a few years ago.

And fourthly, it is argued that peace-keeping is an inescapable task, because there are no other practical alternatives available. Thus you get buffer forces providing a physical interposition of man and equipment between potentially warring factions, with the idea that only a neutral U.N. is acceptable for the job and only a middle power is talented enough among the neutrals to be able to do the job. Also, you get various observer groups who act as recorders or sometimes even referees. And finally there are the U.N. police forces where the factor is often a question of applying a technique in terms of organization, training, numbers, and methods. In each case the middle power seems to have an advantage, mainly because the major power is disqualified, except in its own area where there are special circumstances, such as in Cyprus. . . .

Now we come to the Canadian circumstances, and it seems to me that further qualifications are needed if we are to see this as an effective arm of Canadian foreign policy. The circumstances are a reflection of problems. Some of the problems are just coming home to roost now. Some of them are a consequence of what you might call an enlightened refusal to admit the presence of problems in the past, and some are believed to outweigh the positive gains I have mentioned. And they fall into the categories of political and military concern. First of all, there are the political concerns. Five aspects are involved here.

To begin with, there is what you might call the alliance factor. The fact is that, in terms of fundamental Canadian interests, we are members of a white, "have", North American complex. We cannot end this by cutting loose the anchor chain and drifting off into the North Atlantic to become another Iceland. This is a fact of our existence. This means that, to a certain extent, we are at least likely to be and, to a certain extent in the past, have been at odds as white "have", North Americans with some of the objectives that peace-keeping has been aimed at achieving. This is especially so as the Afro-Asian states have come to change the balance of United Nations' membership. We are now reaching a stage where we should be very concerned because much of the remaining harmony in political terms between Western aims and U.N. aims is breaking down. The fact of the present U.N. crisis is adequate testimony of this, and it seems quite likely that in the future there will be peace-keeping operations presented that will involve the reverse side of the coin. We may very well be faced with the prospect—if we continue to serve a peace-keeping god

blindly—of having to serve interests that are actually opposed to our own self-interests.

Secondly, it seems to me that peace-keeping as we have known it has involved the formal application from time to time of policies which have tended to divide our own natural alliances. In this sense, it is the formal institutionalization of divisions that we should worry about. There will always be disagreements, of course. But if they can be kept in a sort of fluid pragmatic context, the process of knitting together the alliances—the process of reconciling disagreements—is much easier. If disagreements are made public and overt, as to a degree peace-keeping tends to do, then it becomes much harder to bring the allies back together for a common cause afterwards.

Such overt expressions then, as the Congo operation, tend to further the stresses and strains in an already shaky series of relationships. We may not be terribly excited about it, but it is a fact that Belgium does exist as one of our allies. Our participation in the Congo operation, our comments on the position of Belgium, and so on, have raised the principal kind of dichotomy that is involved. We were criticizing a colonial power which is part of our policy. We were also dividing ourselves against an ally and thus faced the threat of, in this case, a reduction of NATO participation. There is always a price to this kind of activity and in hard times—colonialism or not—we finally have to settle for the conclusion that our own self-interest, in terms of survival at least, has to be considered in the equation.

Thirdly, there is a muting factor. Canadian leeway is inevitably circumscribed by the tendency of many of the peace-keeping assignments we have known to force Canada to mute her voice, at least in public, on all but broad questions of policy and practice. Now sometimes this is very useful—the fact of the UNEF force in the Middle East means that we can turn to both the Arabs and the Israelis and say, "I am sorry we cannot publicly support you because we are in this U.N. operation." We secure a kind of neutral cloak which gives us the benefits of both worlds with a clear and evident excuse. But in other circumstances, where there is a specific unilateral Canadian interest, this kind of neutral cloak can be a disadvantage. For instance, the silence that we maintained on the application of Congo policies—silence on all but general assertions of our position and apologies for the U.N. Secretariat—contributed to what I would regard as unnecessary delay in securing a settlement there—a delay which added as much as three years to the operation as a whole. Now I would emphasize that this is political silence: The use of the U.N. by politicians who say, "Well this is a U.N. thing now, we don't have to comment on it, thank goodness—we won't push a Canadian position despite what the professionals may advise."

Fourthly, there is the factor of ambiguity. Inevitably, subscription to or support of any U.N. operation is going to involve compromises, because it is going to involve a wide assembly of powers with different aims and ambitions. Now, to a large degree then, as the U.N. moves from weakness to weakness, we are repeatedly being placed in the same kind of posture of weakness by association. In many ways, for instance, we had to pay a significant price by subscribing to limited U.N. terms during the first year in the Congo, when our men were not allowed to fire in defence of their own weapons. We became less impressive, less laudable,

because of this. We became somewhat the same kind of laughingstock that a good many of the U.N. troops became in the Congo in the eyes of outside observers at the time.

Fifthly, we come to the question of the domestic problem, and again I think it is the domestic aspect that we really have to bear in mind, if we are going to be at all realistic in looking at Canada right now. To a large degree, the mandarins of Ottawa keep forgetting in their statements of precise analysis, and so on, that Canada herself is basically an underdeveloped nation. We don't have the people, we don't have the time, and we don't have the money that we need to make our tentative break-through to modern technology stick with any certainty—and it's very tentative. We mislead ourselves by looking at American pictures and thinking it's Canada we are seeing. In fact, it wouldn't take much to push us back towards depression days.

Now each decision we make to venture abroad, laudable as it may be, and worthy as the motives may be, means that we are diverting men, money, and resources that we can use at home. In this sense, particularly right now in view of the biculturalism issue which is almost one of survival in Canada as we know it, we should pause and think very carefully. If we are going to send off our best diplomats and our best soldiers and our best equipment on various peace-keeping ventures, we have got to bear in mind the kind of price that we are going to have to pay domestically. I am not saying that we should turn off the tap, but I think perhaps we need to be more aware of this, at least at the political level, than we have been so far. For political reasons alone we should reassess our easy propositions about peace-keeping and ask ourselves four questions: First, are we doing that important job in fact? Secondly, are the international hostilities and frictions arising from peace-keeping worth the results we have been getting? Thirdly, are there alternative vehicles available to do the job? And finally, are we wise to increase the possibility of domestic dislocation by accepting commitments to peace-keeping?

Now, I would propose to turn to some of the military considerations of peace-keeping as they have applied to date. The hard fact is that, regardless of diplomatic triumphs, and whatever degree of prestige that has been involved, the actual provision of peace-keeping forces, the job of providing the specific men and equipment, has created a certain basic conflict in Canadian defence policy. This affects both the alliances in which we are involved—NATO, NORAD, and so forth —and the not inconsiderable job of defending Canada itself. The problem is relatively simple and relatively straightforward. Canadian and international commitments are based on forces that are small (because we are wedded for political reasons to volunteers), possessed of relatively modest budgets and, most important of all, highly specialized because we need to make up in fire power what we lack in manpower. Now, since we recognize that Canadian defence is really part and parcel of continental defence, and more realistically I would suggest Western defence, then it has to be assumed that such forces are going to be of a type that can and will be readily integrated into a similarly small and specialized group of components in the Western or North American alliance as a whole.

On the other hand, peace-keeping as we have known it so far, and presumably as it is likely to be in future, has radically different requirements. It is true that small contingents are usually required,

with the exception of the Korean and Cyprus forces but, so far as Canada is concerned, there has developed the companion assumption that such troops will be in the support area rather than the combat category.

This in some ways is a rather sensible recognition of what could be called racial sensitivity. If you send white troops, call them Canadian, British, Belgian, French, or whatever, into non-white areas and put guns in their hands that they are going to fire at non-whites, you fling them immediately into the emotional and inflamed trap of racialism. The U.N. and to a degree, I think, the Canadian government, have both recognized the possibilities of such accidental confrontations. We now are put into the support category—signals, reconnaisance squadrons, and so on. In addition, by nature of the hurried and ad hoc character of U.N. operations and the frank factor that associated U.N. units, almost necessarily, have tended to come from relatively unsophisticated nations, there is the fact that U.N. operations have needed to be relatively simple, even primitive, compared with the complex and technical devices of the Western alliance. In other words, you don't have missile systems when you go on peace-keeping, you have hand weapons. You might have an occasional Canberra bomber if you can persuade the British to close their eyes or at least behave more naturally, but that's about as far as you can go. You don't run a modern, complex, technological force.

Now the consequences of this in military terms are fairly serious. First of all, so far as the men in Canadian armed forces are concerned, U.N. operations are what could be called rusty operations— men possessed of skills are seconded to jobs where their skills are not wholly used. Men assigned to support duties work with combat units of lower caliber and efficiency. As a result, the efficiency and proficiency of Canadian and allied defence forces tends to suffer. They aren't doing the job that they are trained to do in the national, continental, and Western alliance defence context. And they are absent from the defence force, so that the capacity of our force is reduced accordingly.

Secondly, a time factor intrudes. On average, the pipe line to and from a U.N. operation ties up men and materials from two weeks to a month at each end of the usual six month tour of duty. As a consequence, the regular forces we have—the non-peace-keeping components that are in no way relieved of their still-existing responsibilities—are arbitrarily and relatively artificially shrunk as far as manpower is concerned. And, because Canada's budget experts are perhaps the most efficient of our public servants, little allowance is made for such extra manpower demands. Therefore our force capacity tends to suffer.

Finally, there are recruiting problems. Because we have tended to be the specialist people in peace-keeping—such as signals—we are up against the fact that it is not easy to recruit and, more important, retain specialists for a force which is likely, fairly frequently, to go to a primitive and, in a sense unsuitable, theatre of operations. This is partly because of the nature of the operation. It is more the fact that there is hard competition. The Canadian army nowadays is forced into the situation of having to compete with the giants of electronics and defence production. A man who has learned how to run and maintain a wireless set is a very valuable man in the domestic economy.

J. L. Granatstein, "Canada: Peacekeeper," *in* Alastair Taylor *et. al., Peacekeeping: International Challenge and Canadian Response* (Toronto: CIIA, 1968), pp. 177-187. Reprinted by permission of The Canadian Institute of International Affairs.

Peacekeeping:

To Freeze a Crisis

That Canada has played a leading role in UN peacekeeping operations is evident. What is not so evident is why. Paul Martin discussed this point in an address in 1964 when he referred to the number of operations in which Canada had participated. "It is a long and expensive list", he said, and "it is politically difficult at home because of the risks; and we get small thanks abroad for our work. We do it not for the glory but as our duty, since there are not many of us willing and able to move in quickly with an effective force." In these words the Minister was probably franker than is his custom. Canada generally has been willing to contribute to United Nations forces, and this is almost certainly the most important factor in our continuing involvement. Peacekeeping operations are troublesome, they can involve casualties, financial outlays, diplomatic difficulties, and domestic embarrassment. Very few countries are willing to expose themselves to these troubles. Canada has been, and this willingness is largely responsible for the con-

tinuing requests. All too often, however, there has been a tendency for Canadians —and this includes members of the government—to look on their peacekeeping role as qualifying them for international sainthood. In fact, however, it can be argued that Canada's efforts are eminently practical. Situated in the line of flight of Soviet and American ICBM's, Canada's only defence is peace. Anything that may lead to the attainment of this goal is in the best interests of the nation, and it is difficult to fault the argument that peacekeeping is Canada's most effective military contribution to peace. Certainly it is a more useful contribution than adding a penny's worth of powder to our American ally's overkill capacity.

Another factor of importance is that Canada is able to contribute effective forces to the UN. Our armed forces are among the most sophisticated outside those of the great powers. The RCAF now has an impressive air transport organization, capable of moving even the heaviest loads over long distances. This capacity is being increased. The Army is relatively well equipped, mobile, and well trained. Only the Navy is not geared for peacekeeping. Nonetheless the RCN has transported personnel and equipment on two occasions, and naval officers have been employed as observers. *The White Paper on Defence* of 1964 has promised an increase in Navy sea-lift capacity, and should make the RCN better able to participate in peacekeeping.

The unification of the armed forces should increase still further Canada's readiness to meet UN demands. A larger pool of technicians and specialists will be available. The ground forces, drawn from Mobile Command, will be able to operate in extreme conditions "from arctic to jungle, and to undertake tasks of varied complexity from fire-fighting to communications. The key to organization", the former Defence Minister, Paul Hellyer, has said, "will be flexibility and mobility."

Such a force seems ideally designed for peacekeeping and this has worried critics of the unification plan. Retired generals and air marshals charged that with a unified force Canada would be unable to meet its commitments to NATO and NORAD; politicians jeered after the collapse of UNEF that Hellyer's "jolly green giants" would be all dressed up with no place to go. In fact to this observer the creation of the unified force does not imply that Canada is going to abandon its membership in NATO and NORAD and concentrate on UN peacekeeping exclusively. Unification, rather, is predicated on the assumption that Canada will stay in NATO, perhaps changing the form of its commitment. Unification is predicated on the assumption that Canada will remain in NORAD, certainly until the Bomarcs rust away. And unification is also—and more hopefully—predicated on the assumption that Canada will continue to play a role in peacekeeping. What unification has done is to rationalize these roles and to make the effective completion of them possible within our limited defence budgets.

There is one other factor that has made Canada's participation the *sine qua non* of peacekeeping: the Canadian reputation for disinterested impartiality. The nation belongs to NATO and is closely tied to the United States. Despite these international drawbacks, Canada has somehow managed to preserve its image as a reasonable member of the international community. We contribute to foreign aid, and we have acquired a genuine reputation in the Commonwealth as an intermediary between the old white members and the Afro-Asian states. During the crisis of May and June 1967 this reputation for objectivity wore thin with the Arab states, and it is possible—even probable—that Canada will be unable to participate on any future peacekeeping operations in the Middle East. But the reputation still holds in other parts of the world. When combined with the willingness to participate and with the capabilities of the armed forces, this international standing marks Canada out as a likely source for troops.

The mystique of peacekeeping has been accepted without question in Canada until very recently. Until the parliamentary debates on unification of the forces, scarcely a politician disagreed with the concept. The sure-footed diplomatic skills of Mr. Pearson, his Nobel Prize, and Canada's unmatched record of UN service virtually precluded criticism. The collapse of UNEF and the precipitate withdrawal of the Canadian contingent, however, increased the doubts, and a mounting volume of criticism has been heard.

Even before the apparent change in fortune, academic doubts had started. One critic, Professor Donald Gordon, has seen both political and military drawbacks to peacekeeping. Peacekeeping, he says, has tended to separate us from our natural allies (e.g., Belgium in the Congo) and has forced Canada to mute her voice in international affairs (Professor Gordon cites the Congo and the Middle East situations as examples). Furthermore, he believes, the employment of Canadian forces on UN duties rusts valuable technical skills, hurts recruiting, and thus is damaging to Canadian, continental, and Western defence. Professor James Eayrs has also pointed out that the Canadian government tends to be too fastidious about the locales into which it commits Canadian servicemen. "Experience has shown that our government will not readily respond with offers in areas considered by one or other of the great powers as lying within its special sphere of influence. We have never intervened in Latin America", Dr. Eayrs notes. "We have been extremely anxious to avoid interposition in so-called wars of liberation . . . as in Vietnam. Finally, we have tended to attach as a condition of our interposition that the operation must be carried out under the auspices of the United Nations." When all those criteria are applied, "you should not be surprised to find very little left for us to do."

These criticisms have much force behind them. Whether or not they are fair is another thing. Certainly the argument that peacekeeping rusts skills and weakens our defence is not. Nothing is worse for an army than years of inactivity, garrison duty, and continuous repetition of training. Service in Cyprus, Egypt, and the Congo is operational service—a chance to put training into practice in field conditions. If anything, such United Nations duties should increase the skills of the serviceman. It is also extremely short-sighted to look on Canada's contributions to peacekeeping as weakening the Western defence posture. Had the Cyprus force not been formed, to cite one example, war could have resulted between two NATO allies. Could anything have been more damaging to Western defence than this? The question of Canada's proper role might also be raised. Is it to be a part of Western alliances? Or is it to press for an increase in United Nations capabilities? Without arguing the merits of either case, it should be sufficient to say that by no stretch of the imagination is there a unanimous body of opinion in Canada calling for all our defence efforts to be directed to NATO and NORAD.

The complaints about the areas to which the government has committed Canadian forces are no less unjustified. The only forces that have intervened in Latin America in recent years have come from the United States or the Organization of American States. Fortunately, Canadians were not asked to participate in these episodes, and it is doubtful if there would have been much popular support for acceptance of a request in any case. It is probably true that Canada has been anxious to avoid interposition in wars of liberation. Except for the International Control Commissions in Indochina, however, no peacekeeping bodies created by any organization have intervened in such situations. Professor Eayrs' final comment, that UN auspices seem to be a requisite for Canadian participation, also seems to be incorrect. Undoubtedly, the government would have preferred to see UN involvement in Indochina in 1954. When this proved unattainable, however, the forces were nonetheless committed. In Cyprus, on the other hand, the government's choice probably would have been a NATO or Commonwealth force.

There is one point that was not raised by Professors Eayrs and Gordon. Peacekeeping evidently remains an article of faith to the Canadian government—or at least to the Pearson government. The armed forces can do the job, and despite the recent criticisms the public is still taken with the concept. In such circumstances, would it be possible for the government to refuse to participate in a peacekeeping force even if its goals clashed with Canadian interests? The Diefenbaker government, for example, apparently had little desire to participate in ONUC in 1960, but public pressure and UN appeals forced a commitment. However, after the collapse of UNEF and after the continuing stalemate in Cyprus, the government would be remiss if it did not impose conditions before Canada joins any future UN forces. Peacekeeping is no longer enough. There is some virtue in maintaining the *status quo,* to be sure, but there is more virtue in finding a solution. *Peace-making* capability must be part of any new UN operations. Clearly, regulations are also necessary to define who can terminate an operation. And equally important, planning and organization at UN headquarters must be improved. . . .

The peacekeeping forces thus far created are difficult to classify in any meaningful fashion. There seem to have been three major types of operations: supervisory commissions; surveillance forces; and internal security forces. The supervisory commissions generally have consisted of a relatively small number of military observers capable of inspecting and reporting in a particular area. Examples of this type of force include those in Indochina, Kashmir, Palestine, and Lebanon. Surveillance forces, such as UNEF or UNYOM, on the other hand, have consisted of troops equipped with light weapons. These forces, however, had limited capabilities and could do little more than maintain a border watch. Internal security forces such as ONUC or UNFICYP, finally, seem to require large numbers of men, a high degree of mobility, and a moderate amount of fire-power. This latter type of peacekeeping operation is likely to be formed with increasing regularity in the future.

Each of these three types of forces has certain characteristics in common. In the first place, every peacekeeping operation has been improvised in haste after the failure of political means of settlement. An inevitable result of this urgency

has been inadequate planning, a factor that is complicated by the admixtures of different languages, customs, and military staff systems. All of the forces, too, have been designed with the intention of restoring or maintaining peace and not for fighting. Indeed, the right to use force in every case has been severely limited. This has caused embarrassment, especially in the Congo and in Cyprus, but as the forces operate with the consent of the host power, there is very little that can be done to get around this potential source of difficulty. The host country's rights have also extended in some cases to the right of veto over the participants in a peacekeeping force. This has caused problems for Canada in the past, and may well do so again. But there can be no doubt that the contributors should be selected with reference to their acceptability in the area in which they are to operate.

The peacekeeping operations, then, have been conceived in chaos, restricted in their powers, and hampered by clashes of language, custom, and race. Have they achieved anything despite these drawbacks? By any standard, the achievements have been substantial. Peacekeeping forces have made it relatively easy to secure and maintain a cease-fire in brush-fire war situations. They offer some assurances against gross violations of armistice agreements, and they can bring the pressure of the United Nations to bear on disputants. Unfortunately, they have been largely unsuccessful in bringing about settlements of disputes, but it is no mean accomplishment to freeze a crisis. Most important, however, peacekeeping operations have demonstrated that the smaller powers do have a role to play in a world dominated by the fear of nuclear extinction. A Canadian officer serving with UNEF in 1962 summed it all up:

Whatever else this force may be, it does foster the belief that the UN is a working reality and that editorialists are both wrong and foolish to forecast its demise. Gaza headquarters is a hodgepodge of more than two dozen representative countries. . . . It's quite a sight on Sunday nights to see Saris, turbans, business suits, fezzes, etc. A very good feeling. The brotherhood of man is still a possibility. . . .

K. A. MacKirdy, "The Commonwealth Idea," *Behind the Headlines,* XXV, October, 1965, pp. 14-18. Reprinted by permission of The Canadian Institute of International Affairs and the Estate of K. A. MacKirdy.

The Commonwealth:

Does it Exist?

Canadians, in their continuing search for the symbols and substance of distinctive national identity, have tended to overlook the potential of the Commonwealth association. This situation is partly the result of their failure to appreciate the true nature of the Commonwealth, viewing it either as a harmless alumni association of the British Empire, or seeing in it something more sinister, an external focus of loyalty for some colonially-minded, unassimilated Britons in our midst. Today's Commonwealth might be regarded as an accidental development—no political theorist could have conceived of such an unlikely association. Unlike the Hapsburg Empire of the nineteenth century, which served such a politically useful purpose, but whose full value was not realized until it was allowed to disintegrate, the Commonwealth would not have to be invented if it did not exist. It does exist, however, and offers unique opportunities for a country such as Canada.

Some of the opportunities are primarily of a domestic Canadian nature. The circumstances whereby the historical Commonwealth association permits the association of a monarchical form of government with an egalitarian, democratic society, deserve more attention than they are being given. Professor W. L. Morton pointed out in a lecture originally delivered to an American audience, later published in *The Canadian Identity* (Madison, 1961), that the nature of monarchical allegiance, even in the formality of a nationalization oath, permits a greater divergence of tolerable political and social custom than does allegiance to a Constitution. A republican constitution intensifies pressures toward uniformity, as some French Canadians have noted. The value of an appreciation of historical continuity in the functioning of the parliamentary system is another reason for preserving an association with the country which was the birthplace of the High Court of Parliament and of the system of law related to it, and with those other states in which these institutions were successfully transplanted. The problems of political integration experienced by many of the new Commonwealth members, attempting to reconcile far more numerous and diverse linguistic and cultural strains into a national entity, can help us place our problems into juster perspective. The efforts being made by a number of the Commonwealth nations in Africa, notably Ghana, to encourage the learning and use of French should arouse a sympathetic response from *les Canadiens.* Our experience also might be of value to them. It is to be hoped, however, that the sending of both French- and English-speaking troops to Cyprus, where two other founding races are having greater difficulty in evolving a *modus vivendi,* will be an exception to the form of aid Canada will be called on in the future to offer a fellow member of the Commonwealth.

The value of the multi-racial Commonwealth association in fostering Canadian national interest becomes more apparent when viewed in the context of our foreign policy. It is generally accepted that the British connection has in the past helped to preserve the separate existence of a Canada in North America. However, with the shifting power balances of the past quarter century, the present loose Commonwealth is not as effective a counterpoise to a more powerful United States. A Canada that requires external contacts and an interdependent world if it is to enjoy any room for diplomatic manoeuvering needs the Commonwealth's potential advantages to complement those of the United Nations. A relatively wealthy, technically advanced nation, with an economy highly vulnerable to shifting international trading patterns but with a population numbering less than twenty million, cannot go it alone in today's world. It can make an effective contribution on the international scene only if lines of communication are maintained throughout the world, if most problems are solved by negotiation, and if the fighting that does break out is contained at the brushfire level. The Commonwealth association is rich with potentialities for furthering these ends, but these advantages must be sought out and extracted—they are not always readily apparent. The great danger to the continued existence of the Commonwealth is that its full potentiality will not be appreciated, and that, consequently, the association will be neglected because of public apathy.

One example of the value of the association is the regular meeting of members of the Commonwealth missions to the U.N. Ever since the chairmanship of these meetings has been rotated among the members (earlier the British delegate presided), discussions have been more lively. The meetings, like most working Commonwealth sessions, are held *in camera*. The delegates are thus forced to address themselves to their peers around the table, and not to their constituents at home. Few delegates (who, it must be remembered, are acting on instruction from their governments) are converted, but a fuller appreciation of each other's position can be gained in these sessions than in the open forum of a United Nations General Assembly or Security Council debate. The upsurge of racialist sentiment apparent in the Security Council and General Assembly debates following the Belgian-American intervention at Stanleyville in late November, 1964, accentuates the importance of maintaining and enlarging a tested and established channel of communication among the various regional groupings. The lower key of Commonwealth discussions, the confidential setting of working sessions, the candour with which positions can be stated, and the fact that bonds of common interest as well as potentially divisive factors are discussed, combine to give the association a special value in the contemporary world.

FOSTERING THE SENSE OF COMMUNITY

A dividend of the Commonwealth association which deserves fuller investigation is the functioning of an informal but effective Ottawa-New Delhi axis during certain periods of international tension. On the higher diplomatic levels its operation was facilitated by the presence on both sides of persons who, through Commonwealth conferences, had frequent opportunities to meet and learn to appreciate one another's qualities. On lower levels, the co-operation of Canadians and Indians in the Indo-China observation teams, and of Canadian and Indian soldiers on the Gaza strip and on other U.N. assignments was not the result of prior friendship and mutual respect of the participating personnel, but of a common tradition of professional training. The common possession of this heritage is often discovered with surprise by those who earlier had been unaware of the extent of their indoctrination. The testimony of a young *Canadien* provides a striking example. On his return from an assignment in French-speaking West Africa he remarked, privately, that until this experience he had no idea how fundamentally British were his assumptions on political matters. . . .

In the fall of 1964 the Canadian government through the Office of External Aid arranged that the aircraft used to fly Canadian University Service Overseas personnel to their assignments in Africa and Southeast Asia would on their return flights carry the recipients of African Students' Foundation awards as well as Colombo Plan trainees. Through this relatively small expenditure of government funds two privately organized groups, one for recruiting and placing young Canadians overseas, and the other bringing African students to Canada, have had their opportunities for service greatly increased.

If the Commonwealth is to develop a clear and favourable public image of something more than a concert of convenience, a promising approach might be to provide a focus for the idealism of youth. A healthy political organism requires the conviction of a significant portion of its citizens that it represents a cause worthy of service, for some altruistic, for others, with more apparent

rewards. Much of this service can be focused within the national boundaries, but youth, and those who have retained the spirit of youth, seek adventure, and distant horizons are still inviting. Commonwealth-sponsored facilities for seeking service abroad for short or extended terms will provide another bonus to the status of sovereign independence offered by Commonwealth membership.

The opportunities for service can be found through such organizations as the recently announced Company of Young Canadians, the Canadian University Service Overseas, various exchange schemes at different levels of the educational system, exchanges in other professions and businesses, and development schemes. Most of the projects will be for a comparatively brief period of time, two to five years, although Harold Wilson, when still in opposition, suggested the organization of a career service for experts in developing countries. Viewed in historical perspective, the era of overseas aid to developing nations is likely to be a passing phase, and thus it is unlikely that the Commonwealth will become that vast system of outdoor relief for the educated classes which nineteenth century critics charged the British Empire with being. The concept of service within the nineteenth century British Empire was racially exclusive. The doctrine of trusteeship assumed the wardship of all who were not of the imperial race. In a multiracial Commonwealth the opportunities for service should be open to all who can render service. A prime task of an exchange teacher or a technician in a developing country is to work himself out of a job. By training his local replacement, that person is involved in a more difficult task than he who (in good faith) took up the white man's burden two generations ago.

He must work with people rather than for people.

Commonwealth exchanges would serve two complementary functions. Those between the developed and developing nations would exploit most fully the idealism associated with the concept of service. They would enhance the national pride of those countries, such as India, Pakistan, Ghana, and Nigeria, which, though receiving aid, could also provide experienced technical staff for projects elsewhere; i.e., there is no reason why some could not be employed in Canada. Exchanges among the nations of the "old Commonwealth" would preserve the appreciation of the additional common ties among these nations.

Jean Morrison, "Canada's Role in a French Commonwealth," *Behind the Headlines,* XXVII, October, 1967, pp. 16-26. Reprinted by permission of The Canadian Institute of International Affairs and the Author.

Canada and *Francophonie*

The recent expression of sympathetic interest in a French Commonwealth, at the federal level, is not surprising. During the last three years Canada's cultural dualism has quietly come to be accepted more and more widely in influential circles in English Canada.

The idea that Canada is made up of two major peoples and that the federal government should serve both and represent both has, of course, certain implications in the field of foreign policy. The Secretary of State for External Affairs, Mr. Paul Martin, has made this point a number of times, as he did not long ago in a speech delivered at the University of Montreal:

I have always held strongly to the belief that Canada's foreign relations, like all other basic aspects of our national policies, should express the bilingual and bicultural character of our country. The steady development of our bilateral relations with France and the French-speaking world is helping to develop that new dimension in our policy.

When the occasion permits, Mr. Martin cites the evidence of this "new dimension" in some detail: cultural agreements with France, new diplomatic missions in Francophone Africa, increased aid to French-speaking countries, growing numbers of French-speaking Canadians serving abroad under Canada's External Aid Bureau.

This policy was initiated when the Liberals returned to office after the Diefenbaker years. In 1961-62 aid earmarked for French-speaking countries was minuscule: $300,000. In 1966-67 the fund for Francophone Africa is $8.1 million, and another $2.5 million is going to Southeast Asia. In 1967-68 $12 million will be earmarked for Francophone Africa. This year 211 teachers and 65 experts are working in French Africa and another 50 or so in Laos and Cambodia. The number is expected to increase. One-third of all Canadian External Aid personnel abroad this year have been assigned to the Francophone world and 400 students from this same area are at present studying in Canada.

In his speech to the Montreal Chamber of Commerce in March 1967 Mr. Martin stated that Canada had not waited for the recent discussion about *la francophonie* before enlarging its bilateral relations with the French-speaking world. The Federal Government is spending a million dollars a year on cultural exchanges with France: at least 100 scholarships are available in Canadian universities for French students and a number are provided for Belgians and Swiss. Exchanges are developing in the field of science. Increased economic cooperation between France and Canada is under study as well as cooperative arrangements regarding defence production; officers are moving between the respective armed forces; Canadian civil servants are being trained in the French National School of Administration.

Mr. Martin accepted President Senghor's definition of *la francophonie* as

an intellectual or spiritual community of all the countries which have French as a national or official language, or where it is currently spoken.

He continued:

The aim is to bring closer together those countries which, through the French language, share a cultural heritage and have certain ways of thought and action, of looking at problems and of solving them, in common. . . . As a French-speaking country, thanks to one of its two great cultures and one of its two official languages, Canada ought to welcome this idea warmly.

La francophonie, said Mr. Martin, is already in existence, already developing through such voluntary international organizations as the associations of Francophone jurists, journalists, doctors, broadcasters and parliamentarians. He announced that the Canadian government had decided to give AUPELF an annual grant of $50,000 a year and to make an annual contribution of twice this amount, during the next five years, to the International Fund for University Cooperation.

Mr. Martin suggested, in addition, that these "spontaneous initiatives" should be strengthened and coordinated through

. . . an international organization of an essentially private nature, based on national associations of the same character, which would be independent from one another and from their governments, but would work closely with the latter and would enjoy their support. . . . The Canadian government is convinced of the value of this idea, and has undertaken to submit it to French-speaking governments. If their opinion is favourable, we shall be ready to call a meeting of their representatives to discuss the question.

This is useful ammunition to meet charges from French Canada, made from time to time, that the federal government is dominated by English Canada. Taking part in a French Commonwealth seems to be regarded in Ottawa as another proof that the present Federal government has made great strides in realizing a truly bicultural foreign policy. It can be interpreted as further response to the pressure created by the awakening of French Canada.

THE VIEW FROM QUEBEC

As far as Quebec is concerned, such commitments on the part of the Federal government by no means settle the matter. Mr. Martin made his speech on March 11. Two weeks later Cultural Affairs Minister Tremblay was in Paris for private discussions with French Cabinet ministers. In an interview with Agence France Presse, M. Tremblay stated:

Quebec intends to get an ever-increasing freedom of action in international matters, because it represents the existence of a French-speaking culture in North America. . . . It does not intend to allow Ottawa to take over the job of representing Quebec in France or on a more general plane within international bodies. . . . It wants to be heard in some other way than through the Federal government. We will not content ourselves with indirect representation diluted by the presence of the central government.

This aspect of the quiet revolution has been seriously misunderstood, or at least underestimated, in other parts of Canada. French-Canada has moved with determination and speed away from its old isolation. Dynamism at home has produced a thrust toward new relations with the Francophone community abroad. Quebec may appear to be turning its back on Ottawa, but it has been facing outward.

The drive for independence and for social and economic development in Africa has influenced French Canada in not in-considerable ways. The Algerian struggle has had a message for young separatists. If Togo, a tiny country with a population of a million and a half, can be independent and have a seat at the United Nations, why can't Quebec, with 5.5 million people, much greater resources, a much more advanced economy, exist as a separate entity? It is not only the extremists who ask this question.

The Lesage government took the first major steps to intensify Quebec's relations with the outside world.

1. In 1961 Quebec set up its own representation in Paris. France created a non-diplomatic category for the "délégation-générale" and gave it diplomatic privileges and immunity. Now a staff of twenty-five administers scholarships offered to French and Belgian students in Quebec, arranges artistic and scientific exchanges, and tries to attract French industry to the home province.

2. In February 1965 Quebec concluded a cultural agreement with France. Vigorous discussion about the constitutionality of Quebec's action ensued, inside and outside Parliament. M. Gérin-Lajoie, who as Quebec Minister of Education had signed the accord, maintained that Quebec had the right to negotiate and sign agreements in its own fields of jurisdiction. On the other hand, he declared, treaties had to be the subject of negotiations between sovereign states. Later the new Premier of Quebec, Daniel Johnson, adopted the same position.

In the House of Commons in April 1965, Opposition members charged that Quebec had started the negotiations without informing the Federal Department of External Affairs and that Cana-dian assent had been given only after the agreement had already been signed.

Mr. Pearson, however, stated that the negotiations had been conducted with the knowledge, approval and co-operation of the Federal Government, and Mr. Martin declared that France and Canada had exchanged notes on the very day of the signing. Canada, he said, had participated in three-way discussions with Quebec about such matters in December 1964.*

3. In the Quebec Government, a committee under the Department of Education had been assigned responsibility for assistance to underdeveloped countries, and an interministerial committee has been set up to deal with "foreign relations."

In April 1967 Daniel Johnson's government replaced this committee with a new Department of Intergovernmental Affairs. The Minister has the right to sign "with any Government or body outside Quebec, any agreement he deems consistent with the interests and rights of Quebec." Theoretically, "any government or body" may mean not only Ottawa or the Province of Ontario, but an African country or a UN agency. However, in international law, treaty-making, as distinct from signing agreements, is regarded as the prerogative of sovereign states rather than of provinces in a federation. Some

*It is interesting to note that procedures had been tidied up by November 1965, when Quebec signed a further accord with France. This time Canada had signed one a week earlier, and Mr. Martin's press release, on November 24, explained that he and the Ambassador of France had that day exchanged notes in which Canada concurred in Quebec's right to sign the agreement, which was being done in Quebec on this date.

commentators regard the new department as Quebec's "foreign office."

In addition to such formal channels, relations with the Francophone world have been multiplying at other levels. French-speaking Canadians belong as individuals or through organized groups to international academic and medical associations organized in French, and to similar associations of trade unionists, jurists, and journalists. AUPELF—*l'Association des Universités partiellement ou entièrement de la langue française*—was born at the University of Montreal, and Jean-Marc Léger, a well-known French-Canadian journalist, is secretary.

Such initiatives from Quebec may not seem to the outside observer very different from what other provinces have done. For example, Saskatchewan and Ontario have had representation in London for many years. So have all the other provinces except Manitoba. Manitoba, however, has its own policy of technical assistance and sent a delegation to Britain to recruit immigrants not long before the federal Minister of Manpower and Immigration went to France to encourage more French immigration. In 1965 B.C. Premier Bennett went off to Japan and arranged a multi-million dollar reciprocal trade agreement even though international trade, as some critics pointed out at the time, is clearly within the federal jurisdiction. Actions which may appear the same have different implications when they arise out of different contexts. What do Quebec's actions mean to French-speaking Canadians?

A Separate Foreign Policy For Quebec?

One of the most influential French Canadian spokesmen on international affairs, Jean-Marc Léger, claims that Que-bec has not only a *right* but a *need* to relate itself directly to other countries in the particular domains in which it claims domestic or internal jurisdiction.

The main lines of his argument have been expressed in *Le Devoir* in his editorial articles. Given the assumption that French Canadians are a "people" or a "nation," or a *"société globale"** —an assumption widely accepted by almost all shades of opinion within Quebec as well as by "indépendantistes"—then logic demands that French Canada should express itself not only within Canada but should project its image abroad, develop an international presence and handle its own relations with other countries, at least in the fields which it claims are constitutionally (at present or in future) within its jurisdiction: health, welfare, labour relations, cultural affairs, education, socioeconomic development. These are precisely the areas where international cooperation is most needed. Quebec therefore should seek close, helpful relations with the underdeveloped countries in general and with Francophone countries in particular. Perhaps it should even seek a special relationship with the international agencies concerned with these problems.

This is half the argument. The other half has been put in this way:

French Canadians are and will be more and more submitted to massive influence from the United States in every aspect of their life, their work, their thought. From this it follows that prompt and rapid development of close relationships with other French-speaking countries is an urgent necessity. . . .

---

*By this, Francophone social theorists mean a comprehensive society, including all the normal complex of social institutions.

It is no exaggeration to affirm that the entry of French Canada into the Francophone world has become a fundamental condition, a *sine qua non*, of survival. Yesterday, this could have been regarded simply as desirable or useful; today, it is necessary, it is vitally desirable.

. . . it is necessary also in order to revive our cultural heritage and to restore our language, and to open ourselves in French to the modern world. French Canadians should . . . discover that they belong to a great culture capable of expressing the whole contemporary world and its rapid progress. Planning, industrial development, technology, scientific progress, high-level administration, all this can be expressed, carried out, and lived, in French.

These quotations came from a working paper presented in Montreal in November 1966 at a conference of *Les Etats-Généraux*. This was an assembly of about 2,000 representatives sent by voluntary organizations or elected by special local committees, inside and outside Quebec, to consider policies for the survival and revitalization of French Canadian life.

The position paper recommended that Quebec should have a foreign policy of its own, and among the objectives should be:

1.   To become familiar with the cultural, scientific and technical resources of the Francophone world and to make them known in Canada.
2.   To make French Canadians aware of the world distribution of their language and to encourage an international outlook; to open their minds to the Orient and to Africa.
3.   To rediscover the true meaning of the French language and its spirit and to obtain assistance from the Francophone world in restoring the authentic language in French Canada.

Certain ways of pursuing this policy were advocated, including more agreements with France and other countries, more "délégations-générales," particularly to Black Africa, North Africa and the Near East.

The "Estates-general" conference passed no resolutions. The working paper was used simply as a basis of discussion. There was no vote to indicate how widely its recommendations might be accepted. But other voices in Quebec, inside and outside the Johnson and Lesage governments, have in almost the same words made the demand presented at les etats-généraux:

Quebec must possess the legal means of acting, that is the power to negotiate and apply agreements in all the domains of its present and eventual jurisdiction: education, culture, social security, employment, health, natural resources, civil law, and, in addition, the right to participate directly, even if as an associate member, in international organizations dealing with these areas such as UNESCO, WHO, FAO, etc.

To English Canada this may sound extreme but in Quebec today some observers claim it is closer to a minimum than to a maximum demand.

It is in this context that Quebec's interest in a French Commonwealth and its desire to lead the way must be understood.

Jean-Marc Léger, in an editorial in *Le Devoir*, put it this way:

For self-evident reasons, Quebec is vitally and directly interested in the project of a *Communauté francophone*: First, because it is a French-language country; next, because the natural domain of international cooperation among Francophone countries includes, as the very essence, the sectors which are exclusively or primarily under provincial jurisdiction; and finally, because in today's world . . . no people, certainly not a small people, can afford the luxury of isolation and indifference to international relations.

STORM AHEAD?

The position paper from which the foregoing quotations have been taken, and the editorials in *Le Devoir*, have received little circulation in English-speaking Canada if for no other reason than that they were of course published in French. Nor was the idea of a French Commonwealth seriously debated in English Canada immediately after Senghor's visit. His proposal aroused controversy mainly between Federal and Quebec French-speaking Liberals over which power should act first. It was a family quarrel, in a sense. It failed to rouse the English-speaking neighbours even if they were aware of the argument.

There have been some expressions of support for the proposed *Communauté* from English-speaking Canadians who would welcome Canadian participation as a practical expression of the bicultural nature of Canadian society. Canada would thereby present a dual personality abroad to match its bicultural character at home.

Canadians who see the British Commonwealth as the only natural association for Canada, and who might regard the French Commonwealth as a threat, may be heard from in future debate. They would make the case for a unilingual Canada and a foreign policy oriented to the English-speaking world.

Other Canadians may be willing to entertain the idea of participation in a French-speaking Commonwealth but may be troubled about how this would affect British Commonwealth commitments. After all, this latter association has evolved over a considerable period of time. Canada participates in its specialized agencies and takes part in regular and *ad hoc* consultations at various political and administrative levels. Would Canada as a member of two commonwealths be exposed to conflicting demands from outside? Would there be internal competition over the deployment of personnel and resources?

Mr. Martin has stated his view that *la francophonie* is "the business of Canada, particularly of French Canada, but really all of Canada." Spokesmen for Quebec declare that it is the business of Quebec. The main debate is likely to come not over whether Canada will participate but over how Canada will be represented. This is more than a question of what machinery is to be put into motion. It is a reminder that the present period is one of redefinition of the meaning of the Canadian Confederation and of dynamic change in the relations between Quebec and Ottawa. The outcome may be a new role for Canada abroad.

This possibility raises issues which might well be debated in English Canada as well as in French Canada. Canada has long been seen as the link and the interpreter between Britain and the United States: has the "golden hinge" become slightly tarnished? Would Canada now become a channel of communication between the new countries with a British heritage and those with a French past? Would participation in a French Commonwealth give Canada an "Atlantic" role of more flexibility and significance than the present commitment to NATO allows? Would it increase Canada's helpfulness in the third world where suspicions of French, British, American and Communist aid flare up so easily? The existence of two major cultural groups in Canada has been seen as an agonizing dilemma within the country: in our foreign relations it may turn out to be a major asset, another string to our bow, a new opportunity.

Jean Tainturier, ed., *De Gaulle au Québec* (Montreal: Editions du Jour, 1967), pp. 39-40. Reprinted by permission of Editions du Jour. President de Gaulle's speech in Montreal, July 24, 1967.

Vive le Québec Libre

A L'HÔTEL DE VILLE DE MONTRÉAL (À L'EXTÉRIEUR): «VIVE LE QUÉBEC LIBRE»

«C'est une immense émotion qui remplit mon coeur en voyant devant moi la ville de Montréal française. Au nom du vieux pays, au nom de la France, je vous salue de tout mon coeur.

»Je vais vous confier un secret que vous ne répéterez à personne. Ce soir, ici, et tout le long de ma route, je me suis trouvé dans une atmosphère du même genre que celle de la Libération.

»Et tout le long de ma route, outre cela, j'ai constaté quel immense effort de progrès, de développement et par conséquent d'affranchissement vous accomplissez ici, et c'est à Montréal qu'il faut que je le dise, parce que s'il y a eu au monde une ville exemplaire par ses réussites modernes, c'est la vôtre. Je dis: c'est la vôtre, et je me permets d'ajouter: c'est la nôtre.

»Si vous saviez quelle confiance la France, réveillée après d'immenses épreuves, porte maintenant vers vous! Si vous saviez quelle affection elle recommence à ressentir pour les Français du Canada! Et si vous saviez à quel point elle se sent obligée de concourir à votre marche en avant, à votre progrès! C'est pourquoi elle a conclu avec le gouvernement du Québec, avec celui de mon ami Johnson, des accords pour que les Français de part et d'autre de l'Atlantique travaillent ensemble à une même oeuvre française. Et d'ailleurs, le concours que la France va tous les jours un peu plus prêter ici, elle sait bien que vous le lui rendrez parce que vous êtes en train de vous constituer des élites, des usines, des entreprises, des laboratoires qui feront l'étonnement de tous et qui un jour—j'en suis sûr, vous permettront d'aider la France.

»Voilà ce que je suis venu vous dire ce soir, en ajoutant que j'emporte de cette réunion inouïe de Montréal un souvenir inoubliable. La France entière sait, voit, entend ce qui se passe ici et je puis vous dire qu'elle en vaudra mieux.

»Vive Montréal, vive le Québec, vive le Québec libre, vive le Canada français, vive la France!»

Hon. Mitchell Sharp, *Federalism and International Conferences on Education* (Ottawa: Queen's Printer, 1968). Reproduced with permission.

Quebec and External Affairs: the Ottawa View

The principles developed in connection with attendance at, and participation in, Commonwealth education meetings and international organizations such as UNESCO are also applicable, in the Government's view, to Canadian representation in *la Francophonie*. The establishment of specific procedures for federal-provincial co-operation in the latter field, particularly in respect of educational conferences, will require further consultation between the Federal Government and the provinces, but there can be no doubt that Canada's bilingual character entails a lasting interest on the part of all Canadians in close and harmonious relations with the French-speaking world.

Thus far, there have been no general conferences of all French-speaking states in respect of educational matters. However, for several years there have been meetings of the Conference of African and Malagasy Ministers of National Education which have brought together representatives from France and a number of French-speaking African states. These conferences are essentially regional in nature and deal with questions relating to educational exchanges between France and countries of the area. Thus, countries from outside the area which use French as an official or working language, for example in North Africa, Asia and Europe, are not participants. However, Quebec received an invitation to attend, and was present at, the session held in Libreville in February 1968 and was also present at the resumed session held in Paris in April 1968. Canada's attempts to obtain an invitation to these sessions, which would have allowed all of Canada to be represented, were not acted upon.

As will be seen below, the Federal Government has put forward certain proposals, of both a general and specific nature, concerning Canadian participation in intergovernmental meetings of *la Francophonie*. The Government considers that, although these proposals may require further elaboration, they provide in broad outline for procedures which take full account of the interests of Quebec, as the province in which the great majority of French-speaking Canadians live, as well as provinces with large French-speaking minorities such as New Brunswick and Ontario, and which at the same time respect the requirements of Canadian unity. . . .

In accordance with the Government's policy toward *la Francophonie*, and its desire to ensure that Canada should play a significant role in this movement, consultations were begun with the Province of Quebec in the late autumn of last year with a view to determining the nature of Canadian participation. Following initial indications that Quebec might be invited to attend the next session of the Conference of African and Malagasy Ministers of National Education, to be held early in 1968, and that a general conference of *la Francophonie* might be held later in the year, the Prime Minister wrote to the Prime Minister of Quebec on December 1, 1967, to suggest that arrangements be agreed upon between the two governments with respect to *la Francophonie* generally, which would allow for full Quebec participation in Canadian representation. The Government's proposals were based upon an extension of the principles underlying arrangements worked out between the Federal Government and the provinces for attendance at Commonwealth and UNESCO conferences on education. The Prime Minister's letter read as follows with respect to delegations to conferences of *la Francophonie*:

The composition of the Canadian delegation will, of course, be dependent on the subject matter of the meeting. If such a meeting, for instance, should deal with questions of a general character, or with external aid, it would then seem desirable for the Secretary of State for External Affairs to lead the Canadian delegation, which I would hope would also include strong representation from Quebec. If, on the other hand, the purpose of the conference was, for example, to deal exclusively with education, it would then be appropriate for the Minister of Education of Quebec to be a member of the Canadian delegation, if such was your wish. Needless to say, he should occupy within this delegation a place appropriate to his position, taking into account the nature of the conference. In certain cases, the Quebec Minister might well be the head of the Canadian delegation.

Discussions were subsequently arranged between senior federal officials—acting under the Prime Minister's instructions—and the Quebec authorities. During these discussions, the Federal Government proposed that the federal and Quebec governments should agree that the Quebec Minister of Education should head any Canadian delegation to the meeting of education ministers to be held in Libreville, Gabon, and that this arrangement should be communicated by the Canadian Government to the organizers of the conference with a view to an invitation being issued to Canada. The reaction of the Quebec authorities was non-committal, and no agreement was reached on the composition of a Canadian delegation.

The conference took place in Libreville from February 5 to 10, and was attended by France, Quebec and 15 independent *francophone* African states. Delegations were represented at the ministerial level. The Minister of Education of Quebec was accompanied by a delegation of three officials from the Quebec government.

Following the failure to reach agreement on the composition of a Canadian delegation to attend the Libreville conference, the Government again communicated with the Quebec authorities with a view to arriving at an understanding on future meetings. In a letter of March 8 to the Prime Minister of Quebec, Prime Minister Pearson re-emphasized that the Federal Government's purpose was to find arrangements which "would allow the Province of Quebec to make a full contribution to the development of *la Francophonie* and to be represented in discussions concerning various matters of interest to the French-speaking world in a manner which would be compatible with the continued existence of a sovereign and independent Canada".

With regard to education meetings, the Prime Minister summarized the Federal Government's position as follows:

I would envisage that at meetings of ministers of education held within the context of *la Francophonie*, the Minister of Education of Quebec would, as a general practice, represent Canada as chairman of the Canadian delegation, a possibility to which I referred in my earlier letter and which was followed up in subsequent discussions. At such times, I think it would be desirable and compatible with their responsibilities that ministers or officials from other provinces, particularly those with large French-speaking populations, should be added as appropriate to the delegation. I refer in particular to Ontario and New Brunswick. There would be occasions, no doubt, when it would be appropriate for a minister from another province to be chairman of the delegation. If there were advisers from the Federal Government on the Canadian delegation, they would not, of course, involve themselves with questions of education but rather with aspects of these conferences which relate to the federal responsibility for international relations.

In view of the effective role which the Council of Ministers of Education has played in providing provincial nominations for Canadian delegations to Commonwealth, UNESCO and IBE meetings, the Prime Minister also made the suggestion in the letter that one way to work out suitable arrangements in respect of *la Francophonie* would be to request the Council "to recommend the general composition of the delegation for each education conference".

The Prime Minister went on to underline the Government's conviction that:

we can find a way to work out among ourselves and without aid or interference of outside powers an acceptable method of representation in *la Francophonie* which would give your government and others concerned the opportunity of playing a full and active role without weakening the structure of Canada or its presence in the world.

He concluded by again emphasizing that Canada's structure and its presence abroad:

would certainly be weakened—and ultimately destroyed—if other countries invite Cana-

dian provinces to international conferences of states, if those provinces accept the invitation, and if the provincial delegates are treated formally as representatives of states while the Government of Canada is ignored.

A sovereign state—and Canada is one—must maintain responsibility for foreign policy, and for representation abroad, or it ceases to be sovereign. I know you do not wish this fragmentation of our country before the world to happen. That is why I am writing to you again on this matter and why I earnestly hope that discussions between our two governments may lead to arrangements in the conduct of international affairs which will be satisfactory to both.

As the Libreville ministerial meeting was soon to resume in Paris, and as no reply had yet been received to these letters, the Prime Minister, in view of the gravity and increasing urgency of the situation, wrote a further letter (dated April 5, 1968) to Prime Minister Johnson in order to emphasize to the Quebec authorities the importance of finding a mutually acceptable solution. Prime Minister Pearson suggested that the proposal put forward earlier, that Canada as a whole should be represented at *Francophonie* education conferences, would be particularly appropriate in the case of the Paris meeting. He continued as follows:

Other provinces, the population of which comprises a very large number of *francophones*, New Brunswick for example, would, I believe, be interested in participating, within a Canadian delegation, at conferences such as the one which is expected to take place in Paris. Would this not be an occasion to seek a solution which completely respects the internal jurisdiction of provinces while permitting Canada to be and remain a single country on the international plane? This problem other federations have had to solve and I cannot believe that it would be insoluble for us. I cannot, nevertheless, hide my extreme anxiety in seeing it being resolved gradually in a way which is hard to reconcile with the survival of our country as an international entity.

It seems to me essential, therefore, to establish a dialogue between us as soon as possible on this question as a matter of great importance. You will understand that my greatest wish is to avoid finding ourselves in a situation which would force the Canadian Government to react in a way which would cause a controversy which could do nobody any good. Indeed, it is evident that a new confrontation would have consequences which would be damaging to us all. I am writing you in the profound conviction that with goodwill we could find a solution which would be compatible with the interests and the responsibilities of our two governments.

During the period of consultation with the Province of Quebec, the Government was also in touch with the Province of New Brunswick regarding the development of cultural links with France and participation in meetings of *la Francophonie*. In recent statements the New Brunswick authorities have made clear that they hope to take full advantage of opportunities open to them in this field and to be represented in Canadian delegations to international conferences on education which are held by French-speaking states. The Province of Ontario has also expressed an interest in developing exchanges with France and discussions have been held between the federal and provincial authorities, and between Ontario and French officials, with this end in view.

On April 9, 1968, Prime Minister Johnson sent a personal letter to Prime Minister Pearson which constituted the only reply received to the three letters cited above. This reply was received the day before the Minister of Education of Quebec publicly announced his government's decision to attend the conference. The meeting was held from April 22 to April 26.

The Canadian Government was never officially informed of the status of the Quebec delegation at the Paris meeting. While there had been indications in connection with the earlier session at Libreville that the Quebec Minister of Education had been invited in a strictly personal capacity, it appears from the proceedings of the conference that he participated on the same basis as other delegates. In the case of the Paris session, the Quebec Minister stated after the conference that Quebec had participated on the same basis as other delegations.

Le Devoir, September 14, 1968 (as translated by Toronto *Globe and Mail*, September 16, 1968).

Canada, France and Quebec

Relations between Canada, France and Quebec these days are creating the most bizarre triangle imaginable.

While the two who really and spontaneously love each other don't miss an opportunity to get together, each of the two has to continue separate relations with a third who wishes to love, but whose insistence on a certain code of behavior does not always correspond to the new reality.

Though I find injudicious the attack which Mr. Trudeau made a few days ago on a French official who was visiting Canada, I must confess to no more than a feeble interest in the details of the matter.

Those who have closely followed the recent evolution of relations between France and Quebec know that, on either side, many lower-level civil servants and politicians have shown more zeal than the political leaders themselves. Several times —particularly during Expo—I had the experience of chatting with French visitors who, I felt, quite frankly, were going a little too far in the freedom with which they discussed the future of Quebec and of Canada. At first, this impertinence offended me a little. After a while I became used to it . . .

Among these who have been visiting us assiduously in the past few years, could there have infiltrated some "agents" of a secret information service, or for purposes of political contact? Is it possible that France engaged (as Peter Worthington of the Toronto Telegram thinks he discovered) in rather inelegant exercises of clandestine information-gathering?

Anyone who knows anything about the reality of politics would not find it in the slightest unlikely. I am not saying that such activities have taken place. I simply say that, if they had taken place, they would be rather typical of the kind of surveillance with which the more important countries honor each other behind a facade of friendship and collaboration, and that they should in no way bring into question the fundamental collaboration between the two countries. . . .

What stands out for me in Mr. Trudeau's action is not the activity of Mr. Rossillon or of any other excessively zealous civil servant, be he French, Quebecois or Canadian. It is rather the inanity of any step tending, consciously or unconsciously, to restore the climate of suspicion which was born last winter around the Gabon conference, and which was very harmful not only for a properly understood national unity, but also for the development of relations between France, Canada and Quebec.

The federal government's thesis on this subject is classic and well-known. There can and must be relations between France and Quebec, but they must exist and develop under the umbrella of the more general agreements between Ottawa and the Quai d'Orsay.

Now we felt yesterday, and we still feel today, that there cannot be normal relations between Ottawa and Paris unless there are at the same time, and parallel to these, close and free relations between Quebec and Paris.

This special type of relation between Quebec and France meets, for the state of Quebec, an urgent need of Quebec's own mission in North America and in Canada. The Government of Quebec, because of the composition of its population and the very history of the last century, has a very particular responsibility for the flowering of French life in North America. Bearing exclusive responsibilities in areas as vital as education, welfare, labor relations, justice, economic and social development, the Government of Quebec experiences spontaneously, as soon as it wishes to breath, the need to have relations with the country that above all incarnates French life. It wishes to be able to communicate directly with that country.

It is loath to have to submit, in developing these relations, to the jealous supervision of a mother-in-law, no matter how benevolent she may be.

France, for her part, reacted spontaneously to this desire of Quebec. Not only did she understand and recognize it. She wished to follow up on it effectively. She also understood, no doubt, that it was to her own interest to collaborate with Quebec. Why draw the conclusion that France is pursuing here, under the veil of Franco-Quebec cooperation, the promotion of separatism or the undermining of the American Anglo-Saxon empire, and making more difficult the already difficult goal of world peace? Why not admit that Franco-Quebec cooperation is first and foremost a fact of life and that as such it deserves respect rather than distrust? . . .

Franco-Quebec cooperation, though it corresponds to spontaneous aspiration of French-Canadians, also awakens in them age-old distrust as soon as it takes extreme forms. The French-Canadian loves France, and knows, in the depth of his being, that he needs her. He also remembers, however, a stiffness and a certain attitude of superiority which individual Frenchmen have often betrayed in their relations with French Canadians. He can applaud De Gaulle today, and just as easily be brought tomorrow to boo the French. Is it desirable, just when Quebeckers are beginning to overcome their old distrust of the French, to awaken this feeling because of specific events which arise out of individual excesses rather than an overall policy?

Then, too, there is the even deeper distrust which still exists in English Canada toward France, and more particularly toward General de Gaulle. We saw at the time of the General's visit to Quebec and of the Gabon conference to what verbal extremes, to what unfairness this closed distrust could lead English-speaking Canada. Here again one has to ask whether the undue seizing upon certain isolated aberrations which might have taken place is really likely to facilitate an understanding and the development of friendship.

Relations between Canada, Quebec and France have in the last few years taken forms which are not spelled out on paper. Between these three poles, the most travelled route is now that which goes directly from Quebec to Paris, and vice versa.

We think it is a wholesome development. It is only by starting from a positive and loyal acceptance of this fact that we can build normal and cordial relations between Canada and France . . .

Part VI

The Future of Canadian Foreign Policy

Where do we go from here? The pace of change is accelerating every day and today's technology increasingly makes yesterday's policy obsolescent. Still there are not very many potential courses open for Canada. One might be to continue on the course we have pursued for a generation—to be a good ally of the Americans, generally filling our commitments and generally—if with occasional grumbling—accepting the direction pointed to by Washington. This is not an exciting option, but it unquestionably seems the safest. In addition, experience seems to indicate that other options can be explored from underneath the shade of the American umbrella. But what are the costs involved, not least the psychic costs? Much more challenging for Canadians would be to strike out in new directions, to concentrate on alternatives to the arms race and the cold war. A third possible course might be to recognize reality, to abandon the myth of independence and to succumb to the seductive lures of the American way of life and death. If rape is inevitable, the old saw goes, lie back and enjoy it.

These are the options that are discussed in this section. Escott Reid, a former Deputy Undersecretary of State for External Affairs, High Commissioner to India and Principal of Glendon College, calls for the bold course. Canada should seek out new directions, Reid says, concentrating on developmental aid to the third world and creating in Canada a genuine expertise about China. John Holmes would certainly not rule out these initiatives, but in his essay he stresses the characteristics that permitted Canada to achieve positions of influence in the past. Now the Director General of the prestigious Canadian Institute of International Affairs, Holmes implicitly calls for more of the same, for more "middle-powermanship". Dalton Camp, a former President of the Progressive Conservative Party, is the first politician to be represented in this section. In his address at the Montmorency Conference of 1968, Camp looked forward to the day when Canada would be free of alliances and able to concentrate on aid. This was not a new concept, certainly, but Camp was the first major political figure to go so far in a public statement.

Significantly, Camp's call for a new policy led directly to a review of foreign policy by the Department of External Affairs. And when Pierre Elliott Trudeau became Prime Minister in 1968 the review was extended and broadened. One of its first products was Trudeau's statement on April 3, 1969 when he announced the government's intention to proceed with a planned and phased reduction of Canadian troops in Europe. Another product of the review process was the gaudy six-pack of pamphlets, *Foreign Policy for Canadians*, released at the end of June, 1970. Very few specifics were sketched out, but the review was quite explicit in setting up priorities for the future. The Department of National Defence was also undergoing the same review process, and in the late summer of 1971 its white paper, *Defence in the 70s*, was released. To at least one observer, J. L. Granatstein of York University, the white paper was ominous in its intentions, particularly as they affected the question of aid to the civil power, an important topic since the Quebec crisis of October 1970. Finally, in the autumn of 1972, Mitchell Sharp, the Secretary of State for External Affairs, rectified the major omission in *Foreign Policy for Canadians* when he published a statement on Canada's relations with the Americans. Again the options were sketched out and tentative suggestions advanced for a Canadian course.

But had the long review process changed anything very much? Was it more than met the eye? Or was it the same old policy with a new gloss and with one or two new wrinkles? At this time it is still too early to tell for certain. But what seems clear is that foreign policy has largely ceased to be an issue in the early 1970s. The public seems unconcerned with diplomacy, and while that is not necessarily wrong it leaves a great deal in the hands of the government of the day. This is particularly true of relations with the United States, a subject that was scarcely mentioned in the 1972 election campaign. But the question of Canada's role in North America—independence or satellite?—was a real one still, and only a rash man would predict in which direction either the government or the people of Canada would move.

Escott Reid, "Canadian Foreign Policy, 1967-1977: A Second Golden Decade?", *International Journal*, XXII (Spring, 1967), pp. 171-181. Reprinted by permission of The Canadian Institute of International Affairs and the Author.

A Second Golden Age?

I believe that Canada could undertake during the next ten years two crucially important creative tasks in world affairs. I believe that if Canada were to undertake these tasks the next ten years could become a golden decade in Canadian foreign policy, comparable to the great decade of 1941 to 1951. . . .

Why and how were we able to play such an important role in the decade from 1941 to 1951? It was, I suggest, because of two things. First, a gap had been created in the Western World. Second, we organized ourselves so that we could move into that gap.

In the war years, virtually the whole of Western Europe was in the hands of the enemy. In the immediate post-war years, the European governments were so weakened by war and occupation, so heavily involved in reconstruction, so dependent on the United States, that they were not able to take their traditional place in the concert of powers.

The second reason we were able to play the role we did was the intellectual and emotional drive of a relatively small group of cabinet ministers and senior officials. Intellectual ability of a high order. Hard creative work. A sustained determination that Canada should do all that it could to help create a great galaxy of international institutions which might make depression and war less likely.

If there is a moral to be drawn from the golden decade of Canadian foreign policy, the moral is surely this. Where there is a gap and where we in Canada have prepared ourselves to act and act wisely, we can play an important role in world affairs.

What is the biggest gap today in the defences of civilization? Is it the kind of gap which Canada can move into?

I submit that there can be no doubt about the answer. The most serious gap in the defences of civilization is the gap between what the rich developed nations of the world should be doing to help the poor countries speed up their economic development and what they are, in fact, doing. It is a gap which Canada can move into.

Here, may I make three points very clear.

The first is that without greatly increased foreign aid and without greatly increased opportunities to build up their export trade the poor countries of the world cannot lift themselves out of their poverty. Greater aid and greater trade are essential. But by themselves they are not enough. All they can do is to supplement what the poor countries do for themselves.

Out of their poverty, out of their very scarce resources of materials and skills, the poor countries must squeeze a greater proportion for economic development. If prestige projects such as big dams, steel plants, nuclear power plants, international air lines, new capital cities, yield a low real rate of economic return, they must be willing to postpone them indefinitely. They must concentrate on projects which give a quick and high yield. Most of them must concentrate for the next ten years or more on increasing their production of food and on decreasing their production of children.

The second point I want to emphasize is this. Increased resources for foreign aid mean sacrifices by the peoples of rich countries, not sacrifices in our present standards of living but a giving up of a part of those future increases in our standards of living which we can reasonably look forward to. Increased foreign aid means for Canadians levels of taxation higher than they otherwise would be, unless we were to finance the increased aid by increasing our imports of capital from abroad. I assume we do not want to do that.

The third point is that the amounts of foreign aid I shall talk about either for Canada or for the whole of the Western World are relatively very small.

The value of the present net long term official aid provided every year by all the rich countries of the Western World to all the poor countries of the world is just about the same as what one nation of the Western World, the United States, spends every year on space research. If the Western World had last year increased its aid by just one-tenth of last year's increase in its income, the flow of aid from the West to the poor countries would have doubled. In recent years, Canada has been raising the level of its foreign aid by $50 million each year. This is less than two per cent. of the annual increase in our national income.

In the past six years, the rich countries of the non-communist world have got a great deal richer. Their combined gross national products have been increasing at about $50 billion a year and have reached a level about $300 billion a year higher than the level of six years ago. The rich countries have not shared any of this vast new wealth with the poor countries. Their aid has remained constant for the past six years. If we of the Western World persist in our present policies on aid to poor countries, we will have earned the contempt of our children and our grandchildren. They will have every right to blame us for the kind of world we will have bequeathed to them. They will not easily forgive us for our short-sighted and ignoble policies on foreign aid.

Here is the most serious gap which exists today in the defences of civilization. Here is an opportunity for Canada to play a creative role in world affairs.

If Canada were to spend another $700 million a year on defence, this would increase the defence expenditures of the NATO countries by less than one per cent. If Canada were to give another $700 million of aid to poor underdeveloped countries to help them speed up their economic development, this would increase the net flow of long term official aid from the NATO countries to poor countries by about twelve per cent.

Canada has, during the past few years, been setting an example in foreign aid by the steady annual increases in the amount of our foreign aid and by the intellectual leadership which Canadian cabinet ministers and civil servants have been giving in the international aid effort. We started from a low level but we have been increasing our aid effort by $50 million a year until it has now reached a level of $300 million a year. The Government has announced that it intends to continue to increase our aid effort until we reach a level of one per cent. of our annual production of goods and services.

What I plead for is that the voluntary organizations in Canada concerned with public affairs organize public support behind this courageous decision of the Government and that the voluntary organizations say to the Government: "We congratulate you on what you have done. We want you to go further and faster. We will do everything we can to enlist public support behind a much larger aid effort. We want you to move at a faster rate. We want the goal not to be one per cent. of goods and services but a billion dollars a year. We hope you can reach this goal in five or six years. We want a substantial part of the increased aid to go to the International Development Association, the World Bank's agency for granting soft loans for hard projects in deserving poor countries. We will make clear to the Canadian people that increased foreign aid on this scale means that the Government would, through taxation, have to divert real resources from use in Canada to projects which add substantially to the income of developing countries."

More is, of course, needed than larger appropriations for foreign aid. The moral of the golden decade of Canadian foreign policy is that you fill gaps in the defences of civilization not only with money but also with sustained, creative, crusading, tough, intellectual activity by the Government.

Canada is in a peculiarly good position to undertake this catalytic task. There is no country in the world which has so many men in its cabinet and in the senior ranks of its public service who have worked on the problems of international economic development for the last twenty years or more. Canada has some of the best of the younger experts in the world. The Canadian Government service is small enough for these people to know each other.

Many of them are now working hard on the problems of the economic development of poor countries. They are, indeed, working too hard. Far too heavy a burden is being laid on far too few people. It is encouraging that their ranks have recently been strengthened by the appointment of Maurice Strong to head the Canadian External Aid Office. But if we are to take the place we can take in the forefront of the battle against world poverty, we need to strengthen very greatly the ability of the Canadian Government both in Ottawa and abroad to develop policy on foreign aid and to administer it. We need to recruit many more of the ablest social scientists, engineers and administrators in Canada, men who are driven by a passionate concern for the welfare of the poor peoples of the world, men of intelligence, industry, zeal and integrity.

We need to strengthen the ranks of the government services so that men of this kind, who are now in the public service, may be relieved of all or a substantial part of their ordinary duties and thus be enabled to devote time to the task of studying how the whole international effort to help poor countries speed up their economic development can be made more effective.

What is needed is a mobilization by the Canadian Government of the intellectual resources required and the assignment of clearly defined tasks. . . .

Canada would thus be making a most significant contribution to the war against world poverty if it strengthened its corps of experts on this problem in the public service and if this corps of experts were instructed to examine in turn each of the international agencies to which Canada belongs which is concerned directly or indirectly with the economic development of

poor countries and to draw up recommendations on what steps should be taken
to make each of them more effective, by
changes in their practices or management,
by increasing their resources, if necessary
by changes in their constitutions. The
recommendations of the Canadian experts
would constitute a basis for discussions
with other countries. Gradually, a consensus might emerge.

Thus, by contributing more money,
more brains, more crusading zeal, Canada could do much to fill the most serious
gap in the defences of civilization, a gap
which constitutes a clear and present
danger to the security and welfare of the
people of Canada.

II

Where is the next biggest gap in
the defences of civilization? Is it not in
knowledge and understanding, particularly
on this continent, of what is happening
in a quarter of the world, China? . . .

It is now eighteen years since the
United States and Canada withdrew their
embassies from China. The embassies
were a valuable source of current information. What is more important, they were
training grounds for foreign service officers
to become experts on China. The result
of the closing down of the embassies is
that there is an ever-diminishing amount
of expert, recent, first-hand knowledge
and understanding of China in the Department of External Affairs in Ottawa
and in the State Department in Washington. . . .

Suppose that within the next two
years Canada were able to work out an
agreement with China for the establishment of a Canadian embassy in Peking.
Suppose Canada were to maintain at that
embassy four of our most brilliant foreign

service officers for periods of two years.
Suppose that this period of service in
China had been preceded by two years or
so of concentrated study at a first class
institute for the study of contemporary
China and were followed by further work
on China. What would be the result ten
years from now? The result would be that
we would have built up a group of sixteen
or so officers in the Canadian foreign
service with considerable knowledge and
understanding of China. . . .

. . . I should like to see the Canadian
Embassy in Peking in the 1970s be a
forcing ground for talent on China which
could serve well the whole of the Western
World.

If Canada is to make the largest contribution it is capable of to the long
laborious task of reaching a *modus vivendi*
between the rest of the world and China,
more is, of course, required of Canada
than the training in the Canadian foreign
service of experts on China.

The Toronto *Globe and Mail* has
been making a significant contribution to
a better understanding of China by maintaining a full-time correspondent in China.
I very much hope that it will be possible
for a number of other Canadian newspapers and agencies to follow the *Globe's*
example. There are only four full-time
Western press representatives in China.
The other three are representatives of
news agencies, British, French, German.
The Toronto *Globe* is the only newspaper
in the whole of the Western World with
a full-time correspondent in China. Canada can be proud of the example the
Globe has set.

Voluntary associations in Canada can
intensify their efforts to get in touch with
Chinese scholars, professional men, administrators.

Above all the universities of Canada
should co-operate in establishing a first-

rate institute in Canada for the study of contemporary China. It is a national disgrace that there is no such institute in Canada today. Such an institute could become one of the great centres in the world for the study of China. To it our foreign service officers would go for two or three years before they were posted to China. To it they would return to make reports and to continue their studies when they came back from China. To it would go newspapermen, businessmen, scholars, for training. To it newspapermen, businessmen, scholars, who had lived in China, would return to study and teach and write.

To encourage such an institute of Chinese studies, the federal government should inform the universities of Canada that it is prepared, through the Canada Council or in some other appropriate way, to make not only a generous capital grant but also an annual operating grant. It should also provide every year, say, twelve scholarships of $5,000 a year tenable for three years at the institute by brilliant young Canadian university graduates. This expenditure of $180,000 a year on scholarships to the Canadian Institute of Chinese Studies might turn out to be the best investment Canada has ever made.

*   *   *

In the next ten years as in the past hundred years, we in Canada will be beset by many harassing problems in foreign affairs. A country of Canada's size has only limited resources of wealth and manpower to devote to foreign affairs. If it is to make the maximum impact it must select areas where it is likely to make the best contribution, the contribution most likely to serve the welfare of the people of Canada.

The two great problems of the last third of the twentieth century are the economic development of poor countries and the relations between China and the rest of the world. We must speed up greatly the rate of economic advance of poor countries. We must move quickly to narrow the gap between China and the rest of the world. Otherwise, the prospects for our children's children are bleak indeed.

Canada can by its actions and its example make a substantial contribution to the solution of these two problems, a contribution much more substantial than its mere size and wealth would warrant. Here is a task worthy of Canada as it enters the second century of its existence. By taking up this task we, the people of Canada, can make the first ten years of that century a second golden decade of Canadian foreign policy.

John W. Holmes, "Is There a Future for Middlepowermanship?", *in* J. King Gordon, ed., *Canada's Role as a Middle Power* (Toronto: CIIA, 1966), pp. 22-28. Reprinted by permission of The Canadian Institute of International Affairs and the Author.

A Future for a Middle Power?

First of all it may be useful to try to list those factors which, it seems to me, have enabled Canada in the past to play, both successfully and unsuccessfully, the role of a middle power—a concept which I have recognized as nebulous but nevertheless useful when seen in its context.

1. First of all I would place our relative security. I say *relative* security because if we had continued to think we lived in "a fireproof house" we would not have been spurred to action and initiative. We know that we have a stake in an orderly world. Even those Canadians who argue for neutralism do so not because they believe we could thereby escape involvement in war, but because they think such a status would make our preventive diplomacy more effective. We owe our feeling of security to NATO, to the overwhelming power of our neighbour, and to the precarious safety provided by nuclear deterrence. Our soil is protected not by American generosity but by American self-interest, which is more dependable. We are fortunate, however, that our powerful protector recognizes our right to a considerable latitude of independence in foreign relations. The Americans need not fear our own hostility, but they would not tolerate our connivance with their antagonists. On our own we are too weak to threaten them. Knowing on which side of the Cold War our own interests lie, we are not disposed to press our independence farther than would be allowed. We can tell our neighbour when we think he is wrong, but we know that in the end we will, in our own interests, side with our neighbour right or wrong. Because of this security, we are able to play our own game more confidently than our more distant allies. They must be more careful not to offend. Unlike us, they lack the assurance of American military or economic support whether or not the United States is pleased with what they do. Canada is not the No. 1 satellite, as is often assumed because of our geographical situation. If we are a satellite we are about No. 10. There are limits to our freewheeling. In our own interests we do not want to take action which might adversely affect the power and prestige of the country whose strength is of decisive consequence for us. Our concern is more economic than strategic. We want to keep Washington sweetly disposed towards our commercial and financial affairs. We do also, of course, out of concern for our sovereignty, want to avoid their being tempted to move in and take over our defences to protect themselves.

The question for the future, however, is whether the critical nature of the world-wide confrontation in which the United States is involved will reduce American tolerance and also affect our own calculation of how far out of step we want to get. Furthermore, the supercession of aircraft by missiles is reducing the military importance to the United States of Canadian soil and of our collaboration in continental defence. They may feel freer in the future to ignore us. Will this trend give us more freedom of action within a looser military alliance, or merely reduce our influence and bargaining position, small though it may be, vis-à-vis Washington?

2. The second factor has been our capacity to produce the goods. We are one of the best-equipped military powers among those of secondary rank. Without such an establishment we could not respond to requests for military training from Ghana and Tanzania. Our expertise, experience, and diversity have been major factors in qualifying us for international peace-keeping—even when our alignment and the colour of our skins might have disqualified us. Participation in peace-keeping operations is by no means the only outlet for middle powers, but it has become a badge of middlepowermanship, and the willingness to contribute and pay has given Canada a valuable reputation for responsibility. It has also, as in Cyprus or Indo-China, given us a right and also the firsthand knowledge to play a part in the diplomacy of the area and to have our voice heard. The extent of that influence cannot be measured by the obvious fact that it has not been decisive; who do we think we are, even at our best? Our record in economic aid and development is less good, but especially in such large projects as the Canada-India reactor or the Warsak Dam in Pakistan, it has been of sufficient consequence to be noted.

There seems no serious difficulty in our continuing to produce the goods, and the policy adumbrated on the Defence White Paper suggests increased attention to our capacity for peace-keeping. This, however, is not the issue. The questions about peace-keeping are whether there will continue to be conflicts for which this technique is applicable and whether Canadians will be wanted. We do not know whether the U.N., after the present crisis, will be able to mount new operations. Our close alignment with the United States in the present Vietnam crisis may disqualify us for any further assignment in that area and damage our reputation for independent thinking. This kind of work may be taken over by regional bodies such as the Organization of American States or the Organization of African Unity or the Arab League to which we do not belong. On the other hand, since we first began wondering at the time of the Congo operation whether we would ever be wanted again, we have been asked to serve in Yemen, West Irian, and Cyprus, in fact in every U.N. operation that has been set up. These obligations and opportunities never have been predictable and never will be, but the law of averages may be commencing to work, and that law suggests we should count on getting further work.

3. Our alignment has been a factor of strength and also, of course, a handicap. Membership in NATO has rarely in fact bound us to support the causes of our colonialist allies. Because it is complemented by our Commonwealth ties to the anti-colonialists, we have been induced to work for compromise and settlement. The positions we have taken on South Africa, Rhodesia, or the Portuguese colonies, issues which could make or break our middle reputation, are determined not so much by our alliance as by our mixed pragmatic and idealistic approach to such questions. They reflect recognition from our own experience that colonialism and self-government are complex issues. Our embarrassment in colonial issues affecting our allies has persuaded us also to keep

our mouths shut, to avoid denouncing either side, and this kind of discretion has been one of our soundest qualifications for an intermediary role. Alliance with the great Western powers has given us influence where the great decisions are made—not much perhaps, but more at least than most middle powers can command. There is reason to believe that the nonaligned have taken us more seriously, because we are a country which they think has the ear of Washington and London, than they would have done if we floated free. On the other hand, there is no doubt that we had to fight against suspicion of our independence over Suez and the Congo, and we must constantly prove ourselves by giving evidence of independent thought and action. Our possession of nuclear weapons, regardless of fancy arrangements about keys, does affect our reputation in middle-power diplomacy. On the other hand, there is no evidence that it has been decisive. The factor of alignment ought not to be regarded too categorically.

4. Our NATO alliance has always been counterbalanced by our other associations, especially the Commonwealth. We have never considered ourselves at the U.N. as fixed members of any bloc, and have tried to pay due regard to our loyalties to both NATO and Commonwealth associations. This has been a risky game for a country which needs to make friends to influence events, but we have done reasonably well and honed our diplomacy in the process. Our role in the transformation and maintenance of the new Commonwealth has abetted our reputation, provided us with close and influential friends, and given us intimate relationships with the major nations of Asia and Africa. Our special role is nowhere better illustrated than by the military training mission

we have sent to Ghana and Tanzania.

This association with different camps can continue so long as the camps maintain their liberality of outlook. It would be threatened on the one hand by an increasingly formalized Atlantic Community or on the other hand, a more likely prospect, by the intensification of racial antagonism over Rhodesia and South Africa, a split in the Commonwealth, or the replacement of the present African leaders by fanatical racialists or Communist stooges.

There are many other factors in middlepowermanship, of course. I have mentioned in detail those which seem to me basic and are too often ignored in our calculation. We concentrate a little too much on the purity of our souls, our freedom from the blight of imperialism—whatever that is, and our genius for compromise. I do not want to be cynical. There is something in all these claims. At the very least, our hypocrisy sets for us standards of conduct to aim at. Let us not forget, however, that we and our reputation are getting a bit tarnished after twenty years of the kind of active diplomacy that rarely satisfied anyone. We are no longer looked upon as a fresh young force come out of the North. We have left a lot of people with grudges against us, and we dare not act as if we are still universally lovable. We passed the test of not being old-fashioned imperialists, but we may not be as free of the test of neo-imperialism as our financial and industrial enterprises spread through the globe and Canadians come to be tangible figures instead of fairy princes in faraway places. As for our genius for compromise, I have no doubt that our successful existence as a bi-tribal state has not only tempered our international political awareness, it has also been a source of inspiration to new countries struggling against much greater odds to establish multi-tribal states. I have no doubt also that a stronger assertion of the French fact in Canada would strengthen our diplomatic hand. However, we are now getting a reputation abroad for intolerance rather than compromise, and internal tensions may inhibit the vigour of our foreign policy.

In conclusion I would like to say that I think we must look at the future of our foreign policy with hard realism, but without cynicism. We cannot live by old slogans. Every nation's foreign policy must undergo constant re-examination in the light of changing world circumstances. If the old ways no longer fit the circumstances we must cast them off. We must, however, find something to take their place. It is easy to be ironical about the phrases we have clung to—like the term "middle power" itself; it is so contradictory it provokes sarcasm. Its achievements have inevitably been so far short of its pretensions that it can be made to sound flatulent. I recognize, furthermore,

that it prescribes a sophisticated and perhaps too professional approach to be generally understandable or acceptable. An impatient public has frequently demanded more tangible proof of success. Our young idealists are frustrated by what seems to them moral deviousness. We must, however, have some conception of our role in the world if we are to be an independent state at all. This we cannot avoid. Even an acceptance of satellite status is a logical conception, however unattractive. If our conception is to be realistic, adapted to our size and the shape we are in, it seems to me that it is bound to be complex in nature, sensitive to equilibrium and opportunity and, for the most part, discreet. At the same time, we must be able to wrap it in an acceptable formula, oversimplified of course, but honest, to give Canadians some kind of guide to go by and an idea to be proud of. Canadians being what they are, I think that the danger of delusion of grandeur is less to be feared than the danger of paralyzing abnegation.

"Address by Dalton K. Camp," in *Progressive Conservative Party, Report on the Montmorency Conference, August 7-10, 1967*, (Ottawa, 1967). Reprinted by permission of the Progressive Conservative Party Headquarters.

A New Foreign Policy

In the immediate future foreign policy will be of greater significance to the nation and, therefore, of greater importance to a political party than it has been in the last decade. I do not mean to say that it has been unimportant, but one's experience would testify to the fact that, of all the areas of national policy which parties give their study to, foreign policy has been, in the past few years, a neglected area.

Canadians are as at least concerned in the vital issues of war and peace as any other people save those, of course, who are immediately involved in conflict. Canadians are also concerned about the uncertain question of their sovereignty. I am not speaking of sovereignty in the historic, classic sense, because most of us accept the view that technology, geography, economics and history all have played their part in rendering what was a rather more simple concept meaningless. What Canadians mean—or many of them—when they express concern over their sovereignty is their growing awareness that they do not seem to have any clearly defined initiatives of their own, and they must have doubts as to efficacy of their present international commitments.

It has been argued that those who are anxious for security can best find it by being hived in larger and more powerful units. The consequence, however, so far as a nation such as Canada is concerned, is that one becomes lost in bigger and more powerful units, and in our case, it means singular absorption in one powerful unit—the United States.

What we should be doing in the months ahead is to give some expression to the growing concern of Canadians who are anxious to know what is to replace the familiar external relations they have known, but which are now in the throes of change; what, if any, the alternatives are; and what are the responsibilities, and the consequences which might flow from pursuing these alternatives.

This would apply to our vested interest in peace-keeping, to our role in NATO and in NORAD, to our apparent awakening interest in foreign aid, and to our continuing, evolutionary relationships with the United States, Great Britain and, I am happy to say, France. . . .

I will have to begin by hypothesizing. Let us consider NATO, and make some assumptions. The United States is withdrawing some 35,000 of its NATO personnel this year. General Gavin, among others, has testified that it could reduce its personnel by half and still retain the same capability. One could assume a continuing displacement of personnel by technology and, as well, by the demands for conventional forces elsewhere.

We need to know whether or not the implications of the present Canadian military policy mean, as they seem to suggest, the withdrawal of the Canadian brigade to Canada, and a change in its present role from a nuclear to a conventional one. Are we likely to have a conventional force stationed in Canada with the alleged capability of being committed to NATO, in appropriate circumstances, by airlift, by the C5's now on order? What are the alternatives? They can only be a continued Canadian presence in Western Europe, in either a new conventional role or a new nuclear one.

Of these three alternatives, the most realistic in terms of the present and potential concerns in Europe, at least as far as I found them to be, was the continuance of a Canadian presence in Europe as a psychological buttress—for want of a better phrase—against the subtly mounting fears of a renascent German nationalism, feeling shared by Germans as well as by their European neighbours, and the Middle and Eastern Europeans as well. Presumably it is not essential that a "psychological" force have a nuclear role, a conclusion already arrived at by NATO partners of comparable status and power.

For a nation such as ours, the purpose of our Armed Forces is not to fight, and our only real defence is peace. This leads one to the consideration of yet other possibilities, and my only argument now is that we have the temper, and take the time, to consider them.

Every politician, or public man, is a prisoner of his advisers. He can only be liberated by his values. The advice one gets from some quarters is persistent enough to be considered, which is to accept the fact that the solutions of Europe's problems are going to be found by Europeans. And they will to a lessening degree be influenced by the United States, and to a negligible degree by Canada.

If this is so, should we not inquire into the future validity of our relatively substantial commitment to NATO in terms of cost, and should we not examine closely the plausibility of our 100,000-man conventional force being employed for engaging in a conventional war on short notice?

I do not have too many old-fashioned concepts to cling to. One of them is, however, that one's military policy flows logically from the commitments that are in the direct inheritance of one's foreign policy. What we are in the process of doing is to develop a military policy after which, presumably, we are to develop a foreign policy that suits it. Supposing, instead, we were to develop a foreign policy that suited our needs for nationhood—in Laurier's words, ". . . the supreme issue . . . all else is subordinate." . . .

I am sometimes warned not to get into NORAD. This is not difficult for one who would like to get out of it. Here again, we live with the open secret of obsolescence. Arguments are made that as technology advances, it may advance to the point where the manned bombers will be reintroduced, and the Bomarc will then have its long-sought respectibility. Following this to its logical conclusion, we should be making bows and arrows.

Further, it does not appear credible to me that this nation could be persuaded to undertake a multi-billion dollar commitment to the age of the Anti-Ballistic Missile. I do not like homilies, but there comes a time when the cost of defending against the indefensible, literally and morally, is greater than the risks taken in not doing so. One should consider, more seriously, the worthiness of the risk for Canada of a posture of nuclear detachment. At the same time, admitting to the fact we share a continent with others. We need not begrudge our friends the reasonable advantage of our geography. Whatever else we might do, it would seem both decent and provident to maintain the DEW Line, and extend fly-over rights to our most powerful friend and ally, and to participate in any other sensible policy that is within our means, but within the terms of reference of our new policy. No matter how you allocate and reallocate the not quite limitless resources of Canada, within the reasonable boundaries of common sense and judgement, you can not arrive at a policy which promises national security through military means. I am not denying its benefits—the blessings it distributes in the economy, the prerequisites it may bestow in diplomacy and the rank and station it allows in certain powerful alliances. But I do question its ultimate credibility. . . .

Anyone who was close to the political events during the 1963 Bomarc crisis in Canada will realize that our American friends can be extremely aggressive in their persuasiveness. In addition to pure propaganda, there were possibilities of economic reprisals that are sometimes stronger than suggestion. However, those events of 1963 were really not an ideal example of anything, much less diplomacy. And those who were the chief protagonists were seen at their worst, not their best. The point is that if, indeed, we do not have freedom of reasonable choice, then we do not have any decisions to make in these vital matters. Decisions as to whether we sell uranium to France, or divest ourselves of any nuclear arrangements, or recognize Communist China, or vote our national concern and interest at the United Nations rather than abstain in some other interest, are questions that cannot be determined in the exclusivity

of pure Canadian content. But they can be determined as a result of the prime consideration of the national self-interest, and with a confident sense of our right to do so. Few Canadians would want a policy that was noisily critical, or hostile, or turbulent, in regard to the area of Canadian-American relations. In the reappraisal of Canadian policy, we have to consider our mutual interests—but the emphasis in that phrase is on the word *mutual*.

If, for example, we were to conclude that the most appropriate and meaningful contribution Canada can make towards the improvement of world conditions would be through a substantially increased aid program, and if this meant a reallocation of our resources and a contracting of our military role, we should seek new associations for that program. Among these could be participation in the Organization of American States, in a role hopefully of a determined non-military nature. I believe there is a role for Canada in the Organization which could be, in the years to come, of genuine significance to the future trading relationships of Canada, and, as well, genuinely helpful to the United States, already overburdened by obligations throughout the world in regard to aid and technical assistance. At the same time, one would be reluctant to assume, in such a relationship, anything of the character of a military obligation.

Then, this is not an argument for a Canada that is non-aligned, but for a Canada re-aligned in terms of new obligations, commitments and responsibilities. Would we have any less a voice among our traditional allies, since those relationships are secured not only by history, but in the reality of the present? Of all the nations in the world, we do have, if we choose, the possibility of other roles and a greater flexibility.

Our policy could become a mere accessory to the growing folly of deterrence, overkill and limited wars. We have now reached a junction in the course of human affairs. The grave decisions to be made will be taken by those to whom the nation has assigned political responsibility. It cannot reasonably have confidence in that judgment unless it has first learned more of the nature of things as they now are, understood implications of decisions now being made, and has before it the options and alternatives it might enjoy. This ought to be the function of the political party and it ought to be the duty of those in the party system.

In summary, then, I believe Canada can create a sense of itself through the creation of a foreign policy that is a demonstrable expression of its uniqueness. The basic pillars of that policy are not NATO, NORAD and the United Nations. They are disarmament, non-proliferation and the development of a special role in foreign aid and assistance, related both to our unique capacity and our special interests.

Put in its crudest, simplistic form, I would hope that ten years from now this nation would be without the encumbrance of any nuclear association, whether one key or two. That our commitment to foreign aid would be maximum, and our obligations to military alliances and a military establishment would be minimal.

I have said before that Canadians can become the first citizens of the world, that we can best serve the higher purposes of American foreign policy not being imprisoned in their tactical considerations, but by remaining free to complement their strategic objectives, about which I have no doubts as to their worthiness.

I am well aware there is another point of view—and it has all the attractiveness of comfort and convenience. But there are alternatives that suggest, to some at least, a more challenging role to befit a country that would be a great nation. I conclude by saying that both as Canadians and Conservatives, it will be to our sorrow if we do not at least consider them.

No Future at all

Canada, I have long believed, is fighting a rearguard action against the inevitable. Living next to our nation, with a population ten times as large as theirs and a gross national product fourteen times as great, the Canadians recognize their need for United States' capital; but at the same time they are determined to maintain their economic and political independence. Their position is understandable, and the desire to maintain their national integrity is a worthwhile objective. But the Canadians pay heavily for it and, over the years, I do not believe they will succeed in reconciling the intrinsic contradictions of their position. I wonder, for example, if the Canadian people will be prepared indefinitely to accept for the psychic satisfaction of maintaining a separate national and political identity, a per capita income less than three-fourths of ours. The struggle is bound to be a difficult one—and I suspect, over the years, a losing one. . . .

Thus while I can understand the motivating assumptions of the Canadian position, I cannot predict a long life expectancy for her present policies. The great land mass to the south exerts an enormous gravitational attraction while at the same time tending to repel, and even without the divisive element of a second culture in Quebec, the resultant strains and pressures are hard to endure. Sooner or later, commercial imperatives will bring about free movement of all goods back and forth across our long border; and when that occurs, or even before it does, it will become unmistakably clear that countries with economies so inextricably intertwined must also have free movement of the other vital factors of production—capital, services and labour. The result will inevitably be substantial economic integration, which will require for its full realization a progressively expanding area of common political decision.

The Prime Minister's Statement of April 3, 1969, as printed in *The Globe and Mail*, April 4, 1969.

Trudeau's New Directions?

A Canadian defense policy, employing in an effective fashion the highly skilled and professional Canadian armed forces, will contribute to the maintenance of world peace. It will also add to our own sense of purpose as a nation and give renewed enthusiasm and a feeling of direction to the members of the armed forces.

It will provide the key to the flexible employment of Canadian forces in a way which will permit them to make their best contribution in accordance with Canada's particular needs and requirements.

The Government has rejected any suggestion that Canada assume a non-aligned or neutral role in world affairs. Such an option would have meant the withdrawal by Canada from its present alliances and the termination of all co-operative military arrangements with other countries.

We have decided in this fashion because we think it necessary and wise to continue to participate in an appropriate way in collective security arrangements with other states in the interests of Canada's national security and in defense of the values we share with our friends.

Canada requires armed forces within Canada in order to carry out a wide range of activities involving the defense of the country, also supplementing the civil authorities and contributing to national development.

Properly equipped and deployed, our forces will provide an effective multi-purpose maritime coastal shield and they will carry out operations necessary for the defense of North American airspace in co-operation with the United States. Abroad, our forces will be capable of playing important roles in collective security, and in peacekeeping activities.

The structure, equipment and training of our forces must be compatible with these roles and it is the intention of the Government that they shall be. Our eventual forces will be highly mobile and will be the best-equipped and best-trained forces of their kind in the world.

The precise military role which we shall endeavor to assume in these collective arrangements will be a matter for discussion and consultation with our allies and will depend in part on the role assigned to Canadian forces in the surveillance of our own territory and coast lines in the interests of protecting our own sovereignty.

As a responsible member of the international community, it is our desire to have forces available for peacekeeping roles as well as for participation in defensive alliances.

Canada is a partner in two collective defense arrangements which, though distinct, are complementary. These are the North Atlantic Treaty Organization and the North American Air Defence Command.

For 20 years NATO has contributed to the maintenance of world peace through its stabilizing influence in Europe.

NATO continues to contribute to peace by reducing the likelihood of a major conflict breaking out in Europe where, because the vital interests of the two major powers are involved, any outbreak of hostilities could easily escalate into a war of world proportions. At the same time it is the declared aim of NATO to foster improvements in East-West relations.

NATO itself is continuously reassessing the role it plays in the light of changing world conditions. Perhaps the major development affecting NATO in Europe since the organization was founded is the magnificent recovery of the economic strength of Western Europe.

There has been a very great change in the ability of European countries themselves to provide necessary conventional defense forces and armaments to be deployed by the alliance in Europe.

It was, therefore, in our view entirely appropriate for Canada to review and re-examine the necessity in present circumstances for maintaining Canadian forces in Western Europe.

Canadian forces now are committed to NATO until the end of the present year. The Canadian force commitment for deployment with NATO in Europe beyond this period will be discussed with our allies at the meeting of the defense planning committee of NATO in May.

The Canadian Government intends, in consultation with Canada's allies, to take early steps to bring about a planned and phased reduction of the size of the Canadian forces in Europe.

We intend as well to continue to co-operate effectively with the United States in the defense of North America.

We shall accordingly seek early occasions for detailed discussions with the United States Government of the whole range of problems involved in our mutual co-operation in defense matters in this continent.

To the extent that it is feasible we shall endeavor to have those activities within Canada which are essential to North American defense performed by Canadian forces.

In summary, Canada will continue to be a member of the North Atlantic Treaty Organization and to co-operate closely with the United States within NORAD and in other ways in defensive arrangements. We shall maintain appropriate defense forces which will be designed to undertake the following roles:

—The surveillance of our own territory and coast lines, i.e., the protection of our sovereignty.

—The defense of North America in co-operation with United States forces.

—The fulfilment of such NATO commitments as may be agreed upon.

—The performance of such international peacekeeping roles as we may, from time to time, assume.

The kind of forces and armaments most suitable for these roles now is being assessed in greater detail in preparation for discussions with our allies.

Foreign Policy for Canadians (Ottawa: Queen's Printer, 1970), pp. 10-39. Reprinted by permission of Information Canada.

Priorities for Policy

The ultimate interest of any Canadian Government must be the progressive development of the political, economic and social well-being of all Canadians now and in future. This proposition assumes that for most Canadians their "political" well-being can only be assured if Canada continues in being as an independent, democratic and sovereign state. Some Canadians might hold that Canada could have a higher standard of living by giving up its sovereign independence and joining the United States. Others might argue that Canadians would be better off with a lower standard of living but with fewer limiting commitments and a greater degree of freedom of action, both political and economic. For the majority, the aim appears to be to attain the highest level of prosperity consistent with Canada's political preservation as an independent state. In the light of today's economic interdependence, this seems to be a highly practical and sensible evaluation of national needs.

Basic National Aims

In developing policies to serve the national interests, the Government has set for itself basic national aims which, however described, embrace three essential ideas:

that Canada will continue secure as an independent political entity;

that Canada and all Canadians will enjoy enlarging prosperity in the widest possible sense;

that all Canadians will see in the life they have and the contribution they make to humanity something worthwhile preserving in identity and purpose.

These ideas encompass the main preoccupations of Canada and Canadians today: national sovereignty, unity and security; federalism, personal freedom and parliamentary democracy; national identity, bilingualism and multicultural expression; economic growth, financial stability, and balanced regional development; technological advance, social progress and environmental improvement; human values and humanitarian aspirations.

Pursuit of Canadian Aims

Much of Canada's effort internationally will be directed to bringing about the kinds of situation, development and relationship which will be most favourable to the furtherance of Canadian interests and values. As long as the international structure has the nation state as its basic unit, the Government will be pursuing its aims, to a substantial degree, in the context of its relationships with foreign governments. While Canada's interests might have to be pursued in competition or even in conflict with the interests of other nations, Canada must aim at the best attainable conditions, those in which Canadian interests and values can thrive and Canadian objectives be achieved.

Canada has less reason than most countries to anticipate conflicts between its national aims and those of the international community as a whole. Many Canadian policies can be directed toward the broad goals of that community without unfavourable reaction from the Canadian public. Peace in all its manifestations, economic and social progress, environmental control, the development of international law and institutions—these are international goals which fall squarely into that category. Other external objectives sought by Canada, very directly related to internal problems (agricultural surpluses, energy management, need for resource conservation), are frequently linked to the attainment of international accommodations (cereals agreements, safeguards for the peaceful uses of atomic energy, fisheries conventions) of general benefit to the world community. Canada's action to advance self-interest often coincides with the kind of worthwhile contribution to international affairs that most Canadians clearly favour.

Canada's foreign policy, like all national policy, derives its content and validity from the degree of relevance it has to national interests and basic aims. Objectives have to be set not in a vacuum but in the context in which they will be pursued, that is, on the basis of reasonable assumption of what the future holds. The task of the Government is to ensure that these alignments and interrelationships are kept up-to-date and in proper perspective. In no area of policy-making is this whole process more formidable than foreign policy . . . .

The world does not stand still while Canada shapes and sets in motion its foreign policy. The international scene shifts rapidly and sometimes radically, almost from day to day. Within one week an assassination in Cyprus, a decision about another country's import policy, a coup in Cambodia, an important top-level meeting of two German leaders, a dispute in Niamey—while not all such events affect Canadian interest, some have done so, others will.

It is much the same on the domestic scene. An oil-tanker foundering in Canadian territorial waters endangers marine life and underlines once again the need for international co-operation to deal effectively with pollution of the sea as regards both technical remedies and legal responsibilities. A wheat surplus in Western Canada poses very difficult domestic problems and externally requires action to get effective international co-operation in marketing and production policies. A criminal trial in Montreal is considered in a friendly country to have race undertones and causes concern for Canadians and for Canadian business firms there.

The scene shifts constantly, foreign and domestic factors interact in various ways at the same time; they appear quickly, often unexpectedly, as threats or challenges, opportunities or constraints, affecting the pursuit of Canadian national aims. National policies, whether to be applied internally or externally, are shaped by such factors. The trick is to recognize them for what they are and to act accordingly.

The problem is to produce a clear, complete picture from circumstances which are dynamic and ever-changing. It must be held in focus long enough to judge what is really essential to the issue under consideration, to enable the Government to act on it decisively and effectively. That picture gets its shape from information gathered from a variety of sources—public or official—and sifted and analyzed systematically. The correct focus can only be achieved if all the elements of a particular policy question can be looked at in a conceptual framework which represents the main lines of national policy at home and abroad.

The Framework

Broadly speaking, the totality of Canada's national policy seeks to:
foster economic growth
safeguard sovereignty and independence
work for peace and security
promote social justice
enhance the quality of life
ensure a harmonious natural environment.

These six main themes of national policy form as well the broad framework of foreign policy. They illustrate the point that foreign policy is the extension abroad of national policy. The shape of foreign policy at any given time will be determined by the pattern of emphasis which the Government gives to the six policy themes. It is shaped as well by the constraints of the prevailing situation, at home and abroad, and inevitably by the resources available to the Government at any given time.

Policy Themes

The principal ingredients of Canadian foreign policy are contained in the following descriptions of the six policy themes:

Fostering Economic Growth is primarily a matter of developing the Canadian economy, seeking to ensure its sustained and balanced growth. This theme embraces a wide range of economic, commercial and financial objectives in the foreign field, such as: promotion of exports; management of resources and energies; trade and tariff agreements; loans and investments; currency stabilization and convertibility; improved transportation, communications and technologies generally;

manpower and expertise through immigration; tourism. It involves varying degrees of co-operation in a group of international institutions—e.g., the International Monetary Fund (IMF), the General Agreement on Tariffs and Trade (GATT), the Organization for Economic Co-operation and Development (OECD), the Group of Ten—vital to the maintenance of a stable and prosperous economic community in the world.

Safeguarding Sovereignty and Independence is largely a matter of protecting Canada's territorial integrity, its constitutional authority, its national identity and freedom of action. Sovereignty and independence are challenged when foreign fishermen illegally intrude into Canadian territorial waters, when Canadian constitutional arrangements are not fully respected by other governments. They may be affected by external economic and social influences (mainly from the United States); or qualified by international agreement, when Canada in its own interest co-operates internationally in trade (GATT) or financial institutions (IMF), for example. Sovereignty may have to be reaffirmed from time to time, especially when territorial disputes or misunderstandings arise, and should be reinforced by insistence on compliance with Canadian laws and regulations and by employing adequate means of surveillance and control to deal with infringement. Above all, sovereignty should be used to protect vital Canadian interests and promote Canada's aims and objectives.

Working for Peace and Security means seeking to prevent war or at least to contain it. It includes identifying the kind of contribution which Canada can usefully make to the solution of the complex problems of maintaining peace, whether through defence arrangements, arms control, peacekeeping, the relaxation of tensions, international law, or improvement in bilateral relations. In essence, peace and security policies are designed to prevent, minimize or control violence in international relations, while permitting peaceful change.

Promoting Social Justice includes policies of a political, economic and social nature pursued in a broad area of international endeavour and principally today with international groupings (the United Nations, the Commonwealth, la Francophonie). It means, in the contemporary world, focusing attention on two major international issues—race conflict and development assistance. It is also related to international efforts: to develop international law, standards and codes of conduct; and to keep in effective working order a wide variety of international organizations—e.g., the UN Development Programme (UNDP), the UN Conference on Trade and Development (UNCTAD), the International Development Association (IDA), the Development Assistance Committee (DAC).

Enhancing the Quality of Life implies policies that add dimension to economic growth and social reform so as to produce richer life and human fulfilment for all Canadians. Many of these policies are internal by nature, but in the external field they involve such activities as cultural, technological and scientific exchanges which, while supporting other foreign objectives, are designed to yield a rewarding life for Canadians and to reflect clearly Canada's bilingual and multicultural character. Part of this reward lies in the satisfaction that Canada in its external activities is making a worthwhile contribution to human betterment.

Ensuring a Harmonious Natural Environment is closely linked with quality of life and includes policies to deal not only with the deterioration in the natural environment but with the risks of wasteful utilization of natural resources. Implicit are policies: to rationalize the management of Canada's resources and energies; to promote international scientific co-operation and research on all the problems of environment and modern society; to assist in the development of international measures to combat pollution in particular; to ensure Canadian access to scientific and technological information in other countries.

Interrelationships

The conceptual framework serves particularly well to emphasize the various interrelationships which enter into the consideration and conduct of Canada's foreign policy: These include, for example:

the relationship between domestic and foreign elements of policy designed to serve the same national objective (The utilization of energies and resources in Canada is related to international agreements on their export, both elements being pursued to promote economic growth.);

the relationship between basic national aims and intermediate objectives for furthering their attainment (National unity is related to the external expressions of Canada's bilingualism and multicultural composition.);

the relationship between activities designed to serve one set of objectives and those serving other national objectives (Cultural and information programmes are related to trade promotion activities.);

the relationship between and among the six main thrusts of policy (Ensuring the natural environment is related to enhancing the quality of life; both are related to the fostering of economic growth; which in turn relates to the promotion of social justice.)

Hard Choices

Most policy decisions—certainly the major ones—involve hard choices which require that a careful balance be struck in assessing the various interests, advantages and other policy factors in play. As in so many fields of human endeavour, trade-offs are involved. For example:

In striving to raise national income through economic growth, policies may be pursued which adversely affect the natural environment by increasing the hazards of pollution or by depleting resources too rapidly. Such policies might also cause infringement of social justice (because of inflation, for example) and impair the quality of life for individual Canadians.

In seeking social justice for developing nations, through trade policies which offer them concessions or preferences, the Government's policy may adversely affect the domestic market opportunities for certain Canadian industries, or it might involve parallel policies to curtail or re-orient their production.

Similarly, if international development assistance programmes require a substantial increase in Canadian resources allocated, the trade-off may be some reduction of resources allocated to other governmental activity, like the extension of Canadian welfare programmes or the attack on domestic pollution.

Reductions in military expenditure may lead to results difficult to gauge as regards Canada's capacity to ensure its security, to safeguard its sovereignty and independence, and to make a useful contribution to the maintenance of peace; though resources might thereby be freed for other activities.

The most difficult choices of the future may result from seeking to recapture and maintain a harmonious natural environment. Such policies may be essential to enhance the guality of life (if not ensure human survival) but they may well require some curtailment of economic growth and freedom of enterprise and a heavy allocation of resources from both public and private sources.

Criteria for Choosing Policy

How then is the choice to be made? *First:* The Government could arbitrarily decide that it wants to emphasize specific policy themes like Peace or Independence or the Quality of Life in order to create a certain political image at home and abroad. This choice would be based not on any particular forecast of future events, nor on an assessment of the contribution which specific policy themes would make to the attainment of national aims, but on the pursuit of political philosophy largely in a vacuum. Applied alone, this criterion could easily produce unrealistic results.

Second: The Government could base its policy emphasis solely on what Canada's essential needs might be in various situations forecast. This would be largely a matter of deciding which of the policy themes would best serve to attain national aims in such situations. This approach would produce a foreign policy largely reactive to external events, and more often than not to those which posed foreseeable threats to Canadian interests. If this criterion were allowed to dominate, it could be very restrictive on policy choices because forecasts would be more concerned with constraints than opportunities, hampering the Government's initiative and freedom of manœuvre.

Third: Taking some account of forecasts, and especially the very obvious constraints, the Government could seek to emphasize those foreign policy activities which Canada could do best in the light of all the resources available, and under whichever policy theme such action might most appropriately fall.

In practice, these criteria may have to be applied from time to time in some kind of combination. In specific situations this might produce the best balance of judgment. Nevertheless, the Government regards the three criteria as optional approaches to ranking and has selected the third one as a main determinant of its choice of policy emphasis. The Government's preference stems in part from the conclusion that, since forecasting in the field of external affairs is likely to be more reliable in the shorter term, it will be desirable to assign more weight to forecasts when considering relatively short-term programmes rather than when setting the broad lines of policy. The Government is firmly convinced that Canada's most effective contribution to international affairs in future will derive from the judicious application abroad of talents and skills, knowledge and experience, in fields where Canadians excel or wish to excel (agriculture, atomic energy, commerce, communications, development assistance, geological survey, hydro-electricity, light-aircraft manufacture, peacekeeping, pollution control, for example). This reflects the Government's determination that Canada's available resources—money, manpower, ideas and expertise—will be deployed and used to the best advantage, so that Canada's impact on international relations and on world affairs generally will be commensurate with the distinctive contribution Canadians wish to make in the world.

Foreign policy can be shaped, and is shaped, mainly by the value judgments of the Government at any given time. But it is also shaped by the possibilities that are open to Canada at any given time— basically by the constraints or opportunities presented by the prevailing international situation. It is shaped too by domestic considerations, by the internal pressures exerted on the Government, by the amount of resources which the Government can afford to deploy . . . .

All government decisions on policy questions depend in some degree on the forecasting of events or situations likely to arise in future, whether short- or long-term. Forecasting in a field as vast and varied as foreign affairs is bound to be difficult, complicated and full of uncertainties. The variables of politics are in the broad arena of international affairs exaggerated, multiplied, diversified and often intensified in their impact. The risks of faulty or short-lived predictions run high and are compounded in an era of swiftly evolving events and technologies, even though some technological advances can be used to improve the process of forecasting. Forecasts for foreign policy purposes of necessity must be generalized. They rest on the facts and interpretations of international developments which are both subject to correction and change, and susceptible of widely differing deductions.

All this produces complex difficulties of targeting for any government wishing to set its objectives and assign priorities for policies intended to deal with specific issues arising, preferably before they become critical. The Canadian Government, moreover, must assess its various policy needs in the context of two inescapable realities, both crucial to Canada's continuing existence:

Internally, there is the multi-faceted problem of maintaining national unity, It is political, economic and social in nature; it is not confined to any one province, region or group of citizens; it has constitutional, financial and cultural implications. While most of its manifestations have a heavy bearing on Canada's external affairs—some have already had sharp repercussions on Canada's international relations—in essence they are questions whose answers are to be sought and found within Canada and by Canadians themselves.

Externally, there is the complex problem of living distinct from but in harmony with the world's most powerful and dynamic nation, the United States. The political, economic, social and cultural effects of being side by side, for thousands of miles of land, water and airspace, are clearly to be seen in the bilateral context. In addition the tightly mixed, often magnified and wide-ranging interests, both shared and conflicting, bring Canada into contact with the United States in many multilateral contexts. It is probably no exaggeration to suggest that Canada's relations almost anywhere in the world touch in one way or another on those of its large neighbour. This has both advantages and disadvantages for Canada.

The many dilemmas of the Canada-United States relationships, combined with—because they are linked in many ways—the no-less-complicated issues of national unity at home, have created for Canada a multi-dimensional problem of policy orientation and emphasis which few nations have faced in such an acute form. This many-sided problem raises some fundamental questions, for example:

What are the implications of sharing the North American continent with a superstate?

What kinds of policy should Canada pursue to safeguard its sovereignty, independence and distinct identity?

What policies will serve to strengthen Canada's economy without impairing political independence?

How can foreign policy reflect faithfully the diversities and particularities of the Canadian national character?

It was these questions and others in the same vein which ran like threads through the foreign policy review. They are reflected in a variety of ways in the policy conclusions now being presented to the Canadian people in this set of papers.

Power Relationships and Conflicts

Despite the trends toward a relaxation of East-West tensions, most of the available evidence suggests that Europe in the seventies will continue to be divided, with Germany split as two partly competing entities. This will be a source of strain and potential conflict, even though in Eastern Europe there is likely to be a slow evolution toward more liberal Communism, still under Soviet control however. Accordingly, security will remain one of the fundamental concerns of all European states and will affect almost every aspect of the continent's affairs. The relative stability of the past 20 years is likely to continue since the United States and the Soviet Union both seem convinced of the need to avoid nuclear war, whether by miscalculation or by escalation. The super-power competition in the development and deployment of offensive and defensive strategic weapons systems and nuclear warheads will continue but, if the bilateral U.S.A.–U.S.S.R. talks on strategic arms limitations were to succeed, the pace of the arms race would slacken, with proportionate reductions in risks and tensions. Some of these potential benefits may be lost or misplaced through the proliferation of nuclear and conventional armaments, or through failure to find the political and economic accommodation needed to allay perceived threats to vital security interests on both sides.

In any event, the Soviet Union will continue to be preoccupied by its relations with China and the Soviet interest in accommodations with other countries may reflect the degree to which the Chinese threat is considered to be credible to the Soviet Union. Any fighting between these two powers will probably be confined to frontier clashes of limited duration and scale, though the strategic nuclear threat posed by China will require a regular assessment of the strategic balance as regards China, the Soviet Union and the United States. Security in Asia may largely depend on the future attitudes and actions of China, whose place in the world power picture is not likely to be fully clarified until China emerges from its isolation, at least partly self-imposed. Its triangular relationship with India and Pakistan, together with their unresolved disputes, provides a source of potential instability. However, United States disengagement from the conflict in Vietnam, plus serious efforts at reconciliation, could bring about better relations between China and the United States. The eventual participation of China in world affairs—in disarmament talks and at the United Nations, for example—will reflect more accurately the world power balance and, at the same time, produce new problems.

There are likely to be significant adjustments in global relationships attributable to the emergence of new great powers, notably Japan and Germany. The success of the European communities—the European Economic Community (EEC), the European Coal and Steel Community (ECSC) and the European Atomic Energy Community (EURATOM)—has given the countries of Western Europe increased stability and prosperity and enhanced their international influence.

Because it is in the vital interests of the super-powers to contain sources of conflict there, Europe is likely to remain for some time an area of relative peace and stability. In other geographical areas the general situation is very fluid and political instability will continue to be widespread, though to some extent localized and separate as to cause and effect. There could be prolonged difficulty in reaching an early and satisfactory settlement in Vietnam, for example, and the possibility of subversive activities, communal strife and perhaps guerilla warfare in other Southeast Asian countries. The Middle East situation shows no promise of early solution, and could even deteriorate. In Latin America, more political coups, and perhaps limited conflicts between states, are probable. In southern Africa, racial tension is likely to aggravate in the form of terrorism and sabotage since the remaining white regimes seem determined to persist in their racist policies.

Canada cannot expect to exercise alone decisive influence on the kinds of international conflict implicit in these forecasts, especially those involving larger powers. Nevertheless, there is plenty of room for international co-operation and a continuing Canadian contribution to bringing about a relaxation of tensions, encouraging arms control and disarmament, improving East-West relations, maintaining stable deterrence. There could be further international demands for Canadian participation in peacekeeping operations—especially in regional conflicts. The Government is determined that this special brand of Canadian expertise will not be dispersed or wasted on ill-conceived operations but employed judiciously where the peacekeeping operation and the Canadian contribution to it seem likely to improve the chances for lasting settlement.

American Impact on Canada's Economy and other Economic Developments

On the assumption that reasonable civil order is preserved in the United States and that such international involvements as the Vietnam war are scaled down and avoided in future, the economic and technological ascendancy of the United States will undoubtedly continue during the next decade, although it will be tempered by the economic integration of Europe and the industrial growth of Japan. This ascendancy will continue to have heavy impact on Canada, with political, economic and social implications. The dependence of Canadian private industry and some government programmes on United States techinques and equipment (not to mention capital) will continue to be a fact of life. United States markets for Canadian energy resources and more advanced manufacturing goods will be of growing significance to the Canadian economy. Increasingly, the Canada-United States economic relationship will be affected by agreements between governments and arrangements by multinational corporations and trade unions.

While such developments should be beneficial for Canada's economic growth, the constant danger that sovereignty, in-

dependence and cultural identity may be impaired will require a conscious effort on Canada's part to keep the whole situation under control. Active pursuit of trade diversification and technological cooperation with European and other developed countries will be needed to provide countervailing factors. Improvements in United States relations with the Soviet Union and China—which would seem quite possible within the decade—would enhance Canada's peace and security but would also reduce trading advantages which Canada now enjoys with Eastern Europe and China. In general, United States developments and policies are bound to have profound effects on Canada's position during the seventies, even though there is no reason to believe that the United States Government would consider intervening directly in Canadian affairs.

National incomes will continue to increase at a constant and rapid rate in developed countries. However, there could be disturbances in the inter-related fields of finance, trade and economic activity generally. Individually, countries will probably experience balance-of-payments and other crises. There is a continuing temptation to autarkic policies which could be very unsettling to the varying patterns of trade.

Technological advances can be expected to produce rapidly-changing evolution in the world economic situation. The internationalization of industry, largely in the form of multinational corporations, appears to be a firm feature of the future economic scene and one which governments generally may have to grapple with more consciously and more frequently in future. The international machinery and internal arrangements within the major industrial countries should be able to prevent a major economic crisis from occurring, but developments of sufficient magnitude and duration to disturb Canada seriously could take place. The Canadian Government has a clear interest in sustaining the effectiveness of the international agencies concerned, and in maintaining close relations with governments in the key countries with a view to encouraging the right kinds of policy.

Canada must earn its living in a tough and complicated world. Perhaps the hardest choice in this area of policy—one which arises frequently out of today's economic realities—will be to maintain a proper balance of interest and advantage between Canada's essential needs in ensuring health and growth in its economy and Canada's determination to safeguard its sovereignty and independence. Nor are these necessarily in conflict at all points, for economic growth is essential to sovereignty and independence.

In developing the complex of vital relationships between Canada and the United States, Canadians must choose carefully if they are to resolve satisfactorily the conflicts which do arise between maintaining their high standard of living and preserving their political independence. They can have both. In an era of heavy demand for energy and other resources, the cards are by no means stacked in one hand.

The Rich-Poor Nation Imbalance

The frustration of developing countries during the next decade will increase as they feel more acutely the limitations on their own technological and material progress, compared with that of industrialized countries. Their sense of impotenec to gain quickly and effectively a more equitable distribution of needed resources will become more bitter if the signs of flagging interest and disillusionment on the part of more-developed countries are not reversed. The frustration is likely to manifest itself in various ways. Developing countries will increasingly set aside their political differences to form regional blocs that will urge and put pressure on developed countries to adopt policies that will accommodate the needs of developing countries. If these efforts fail, or do not succeed as quickly as the developing countries hope, recriminations, racial tension and, in some cases, political and economic reprisals against the governments, private investors and nationals of the more-developed countries are likely to increase in magnitude.

The emphasis of development efforts during the coming decade will probably be on human development, including education, social change and control of population. These in turn will lead to a greater awareness of the outside world and a greater appetite for quick change. In addition, a shift of emphasis can be expected from direct development assistance to a range of more sophisticated methods of effecting resource transfers to developing countries and of increasing their export earnings. Industrialized states will be called upon to take meaningful steps to facilitate the access to their markets of products from developing countries, and such other measures as financing unexpected shortfalls in the foreign exchange receipts of developing countries. There is likely to be growing pressure to recognize that a long-term solution to the growing disparity between rich and poor will entail a more rational international division of labour. This in turn would entail developed countries agreeing to make structural changes in their economies that would allow them to absorb the products that developing countries can produce most competitively.

Canada has been contributing to development assistance programmes as long as they have been in existence and increasingly as new nations emerged, in the United Nations, the Commonwealth and la Francophonie. The Government regards development assistance as the major element in its pursuit of Social Justice policies for the benefit of nations less fortunate than Canada. The alternatives in this field are not whether development assistance should be continued on an increasing scale but how and in what amount. Because of their importance, these and other questions are the subject of a separate policy paper in this series. Development assistance is clearly an integral part of Canada's foreign policy and increasingly is being co-ordinated with trade, financial and political policies. It enhances the quality of life not only in receiving countries but in Canada as well, as Canadians gain knowledge, experience and understanding of other people and find opportunities abroad to apply Canadian knowledge and experience to the solution of development problems which rank foremost in the priorities of the world today.

Technological Progress and Environmental Problems

The impact of science and technology in international affairs is becoming increasingly significant and varied as new advances are made. It will be important for Canada to be assured of access to scientific development abroad and to participate in multinational co-operation in scientific undertakings, co-operation which is expanding in scope and complexity. The direct impact of science and technology will bear significantly on such fields as transportation and mass communica-

tions, automation and the industrial process, the increasing internationalization of industry, and life in the developing countries (some of which may not be able to make the necessary adjustments with the speed required, widening the gulf between them and the developed countries). The problem of harnessing science and technology to serve human objectives, rather than allowing autonomous scientific and technological advances to dictate the accommodations to be made by man, may prove to be the major challenge of coming decades.

Already modern technology has produced serious social and environmental problems in developed nations and will continue to do so unless remedial measures are taken. This is an argument in favour of vigorous co-ordinated research, an institutionalized sharing of experience in various fields, and co-operative action in sectors of international responsibility. The principal changes in the everyday life of Canadians during the next decade are likely to be caused by scientific and technological changes, and by the social and political consequences which flow from them. There will be increasing demands for action to deal with such consequences by mobilizing science and technology to serve social ends. Legal structures, domestic and international, will have to be developed in tune with those demands.

It is already apparent that the existence of pollution presents complex problems which require effective action at all international and national levels. It is equally apparent that some remedial measures will be costly, complicated and perhaps disrupting to development and will affect the competitiveness of growing national economies. But even the existing threats of ecological imbalance may be among the most dangerous and imminent which the world faces. With about 7 per cent of the world population, North America is consuming about 50 per cent of the world's resources. The rising aspirations of expanding populations will demand that progressively more attention be paid to achieving the optimum economy in the consumption of non-renewable resources. Anti-pollution and resource conservation measures will of necessity have to be linked with others of a social nature designed to deal with acute problems of many kinds arising in the whole human environment—problems of urbanization, industrialization, rural rehabilitation, of improving the quality of life for all age-groups in the population. The problems and their remedies will continue to spill across national boundaries.

Governments at all levels in Canada, Canadians generally both as corporate and individual citizens, are clearly required to act vigorously and effectively in order to deal with a whole range of environmental problems, headed by pollution. There is no question about the high priorities which attach to these urgent problems. They lie squarely within the closely-related policy themes Quality of Life and Harmonious Natural Environment. The real alternatives which the Government is considering and will have to face increasingly, relate to finding the most effective methods. The international ramifications are obvious, especially in Canada-United States relations, and just as obvious is the need for solid international co-operation.

Social Unrest

Many ideologies will continue in the seventies to exert an influence, perhaps in new forms, but more likely as variants of the contemporary ones. Some of these

may become mixed with Canada's internal differences. The most profound effects for the Canadian people could be caused by the continued and widespread questioning of Western value systems— particularly the revolt against the mass-consumption society of North America with its lack of humanism. Powerful influences will undoubtedly come from the United States, but developments in Europe, Latin America and within the Communist group of nations could also have a bearing on the evolution of Canadian society. The implications for foreign policy are varied and not very precise. There might, for example, be some public sentiment in favour of restricting immigration or imposing other controls to ensure national security. Bitter experience of past decades has demonstrated rather conclusively, however, that ideological threats cannot be contained merely by throwing up barriers, military or otherwise. The alternative— and this the Government favours and is pursuing—is to seek as far as possible to pursue policies at home and abroad which convince all Canadians that the Canada they have is the kind of country they want.

The Conduct of Foreign Policy

"One world" is not likely to be achieved in the next decade or so. As suggested earlier, United States relations with either or both the Soviet Union and China could improve, making possible real progress toward more effective instruments for international co-operation, but generally speaking progress in that direction is likely to be slow.

There will probably be a continuing world-wide trend toward regionalism in one form or another. In Western Europe the growth of a sense of shared European identity has expressed itself in a movement toward greater integration, as exemplified by the EEC, which will undoubtedly be carried forward in spite of formidable obstacles. Elsewhere, loose regionalism, ranging from the Association of South-East Asian Nations (ASEAN) in the Pacific to the Organization of American States (OAS) and the Organization of African Unity (OAU), now seems to be an accepted type of grouping for many states but a number of more tightly-knit functional or sub-regional groupings have been growing (Caribbean Free Trade Area (CARIFTA), the regional development banks, or l'Agence de Coopération culturelle et technique for *francophone* countries) adding to earlier international bodies composed of countries with common interests (NATO, Warsaw Pact Organization, OECD and many others).

Nevertheless, international organizations, more or less world-wide in composition or representation, will continue particularly under the United Nations aegis. The role of those international organizations should gain more substance as there is a greater multilateralization of the policy-formulating process in such fields as communications, outer space, the seabed, anti-pollution, arms control, aid co-ordination, and rationalization of agricultural production. In some fields this need will require new institutional machinery, whereas in others existing institutions can satisfy the requirements, though they will regularly require strengthening or reorientation.

Membership in international organizations is not an end in itself and Canada's effort at all times will be directed to ensuring that those organizations continue to serve a useful purpose to the full extent of their capacity to do

so. The trend toward regionalism, on the other hand, poses problems for Canada because its geographical region is dominated by the United States; and because excessive regionalism in other geographical areas complicates Canada's effort to establish effective counterweights to the United States. Nevertheless, the Government sees no alternative to finding such countervailing influences, and this will be reflected in the new policy emphasis on geographical diversification of Canada's interests—more attention to the Pacific and to Latin America, for example—while taking fully into account new multilateral arrangements in Europe.

Challenges Close to Home

If there are no unpleasant political and military surprises on a grand scale, it may not be unrealistic to assume that for the next decade or so the real external challenges to essential Canadian interests could be:

trade protectionism in the policies of foreign governments or regional groupings which would impair the multilateral trade and payments system developed since the Second World War;

other developments abroad, including excessive inflation or deflation seriously affecting Canada's economy;

a sharpening of ideological conflict with a further upsetting influence on Western value systems (the effect of the Vietnam war has been massive in this regard); and/or deteriorating conditions (poverty, race discrimination, archaic institutions) leading to violent disturbances (including civil wars, riots, student demonstrations), which are not only important in themselves but can also be detrimental to trade and investment abroad and to unity and security at home;

the erosive effect on separate identity and

independence of international activities and influences, mainly under American inspiration and direction, in the economic field (multinational corporations, international trade unions). Such activities and influences have yielded many practical benefits, but the degree of restriction they impose on national freedom of action must be constantly and carefully gauged if sovereignty, national unity and separate identity are to be safeguarded.

Coupled with these challenges and also involving international co-operation will be the need to consult closely on the utilization of natural resources, the drive to sustain economic growth and the advances in science and technology, so that they serve to improve rather than impair the quality of life for all Canadians . . . .

From this whole review a pattern of policy for the seventies emerges. None of the six themes—Sovereignty and Independence, Peace and Security, Social Justice, Quality of Life, Harmonious Natural Environment or Economic Growth—can be neglected. In the light of current forecasts, domestic and international, there is every reason to give a higher priority than in the past to the themes of Harmonious Natural Environment and Quality of Life. Canadians have become more and more aware of a pressing need to take positive action to ward off threats to the physical attractions of Canada, and to safeguard the social conditions and human values which signify Canada's distinct identity. They are increasingly concerned about minimizing the abrasions of rapidly-evolving technologies, conserving natural resources, reducing disparities regional and otherwise, dealing with pollution, improving urban and rural living conditions, protecting consumers, cultural enrichment, im-

proving methods of communication and transportation, expanding research and development in many fields. All of these concerns have international ramifications. To enlarge external activities in these fields and to meet ongoing commitments such as development assistance (Social Justice), disarmament negotiations, the promotion of *détente* and peacekeeping (Peace and Security), it will be essential to maintain the strength of Canada's economy (Economic Growth).

Policy Patterns

To achieve the desired results, various mixes of policy are possible. For example, priorities could be set as follows: In response to popular sentiment, which is concerned with the threats of poverty and pollution and the challenge to national unity, the themes could be ranked beginning with (i) Social Justice, (ii) Quality of Life, (iii) Sovereignty and Independence.

OR

In order to meet growing environmental problems the emphasis could be (i) Harmonious Natural Environment; (ii) Quality of Life; (iii) Social Justice.

OR

In order to deal with economic crises the policy emphasis could be: (i) Economic Growth; (ii) Social Justice.

After considering these and other alternatives, and having in mind its determination to emphasize what Canada can do best in order to promote its objectives abroad, the Government is of the view that the foreign policy pattern for the seventies should be based on a ranking of the six policy themes which gives highest priorities to Economic Growth, Social Justice and Quality of Life policies. In making this decision, the Government is fully aware that giving this kind of emphasis to those themes of policy does not mean that other policies and activities would, or indeed could be neglected. Policies related to other themes (Peace and Security, Sovereignty and Independence) would merely be placed in a new pattern of emphasis. Emphasis on sovereignty and independence, in any event, primarily depends on the extent to which they are challenged or have to be used at any given time to safeguard national interests. Peace and Security depend mainly on external developments. On the other hand, the survival of Canada as a nation is being challenged internally by divisive forces. This underlines further the need for new emphasis on policies, domestic and external, that promote economic growth, social justice and an enhanced quality of life for all Canadians.

Inevitably, sudden developments, unanticipated and perhaps irrational, could require the Government to make urgent and radical readjustments of its policy positions and priorities, at least as long as the emergency might last. Flexibility is essential but so too is a sense of direction and purpose, so that Canada's foreign policy is not over-reactive but is oriented positively in the direction of national aims. This is one of the main conclusions of the policy review.

Emerging Policy

While the review was going on, while the conceptual framework was taking shape, the Government has been taking decisions and initiating action which reflect a changing emphasis of policy and Canada's changing outlook on the world:

The Government's intention to seek diplomatic relations with the People's Republic of China was announced in May 1968. After reviewing the alternatives for achieving that end, the Government decided the details of how and where to proceed, and did so. That action was linked with the Government's desire to give more emphasis to Pacific affairs generally.

At the same time the Government announced that it would give speedy and favourable consideration to the creation of the International Development Research Centre in Canada. Appropriate legislative action has been taken to establish this institute, which will seek to apply the latest advances in science and technology to the problems of international development. This signifies the Government's growing concern, both nationally and internationally, with policies relating to social justice and environmental problems.

The decision on Canada's future military contribution to NATO was taken after a very exhaustive examination of factors and trends in Europe (discussed in the sector paper on Europe), attitudes in Canada, and alternatives ranging from non-alignment or neutrality in world power relationships to increased involvement in the collective defence arrangements. The decision was based on the Government's belief that in years to come there would be better uses for the Canadian forces and better political means of pursuing foreign policy objectives than through continued military presence in Europe of the then-existing size. It was part of an emerging view that the Government must seek to make the best use of Canada's available resources, which were recognized as being not unlimited.

Other decisions, some taken more recently, reflected increasingly the shift of policy emphasis toward the policy pattern which has now been established.

The increased interest and activity in *francophone* countries is not only reflected in the extension of Canada's development assistance programmes but also demonstrates a desire to give full expression to bilingualism and to the technological and cultural achievements of Canada.

The decisions to block the proposed sale of Denison Mines stock and to establish the Canadian Radio and Television Commission reflected the Government's awareness of the ever-present need to safeguard Canada's independence and identity, while pursuing policies of economic growth and cultural development. Discussions about a Canada Development Corporation had similar objectives. In the same vein were decisions to proceed with legislation on Arctic waters pollution, on territorial sea and fishing zones. Such steps are taken not to advance jingoistic claims nor to demonstrate independence needlessly, but to promote national objectives and to protect national interests.

The pattern has now been set, the policy is in motion. The broad implications for the future are becoming apparent. If the seventies do present Canada with anything like the challenges and conditions foreshadowed in Chapter IV, prime importance will attach to internal conditions in the country and steps taken by the Government—at home and abroad —to improve those conditions. Sound domestic policies are basic to effective foreign relations. The most appropriate foreign policy for the immediate future will be the one:

which strengthens and extends sound domestic policies dealing with key national issues, including economic and social well-being for all Canadians, language and cultural distinctions, rational utilization of natural resources, environmental problems of all kinds;

which gives Canadians satisfaction and self-respect about their distinct identity, about the values their country stands for, about shouldering their share of international responsibility, about the quality of life in Canada; and,

which helps Canada to compete effectively in earning its living and making its own way with the least possible dependence on any outside power.

The salient features of policy in future can be seen in the summary descriptions that follow under the theme headings.

Economic Growth

The Government's choices, as reflected in this paper and the accompanying sector studies, underscore the priority which attaches to the network of policies, at home and abroad, designed to ensure that the growth of the national economy is balanced and sustained. Obviously, in the foreign field this means keeping up-to-date on such key matters as discoveries in science and technology, management of energies and resources, significant trends in world trade and finance, policies of major trading countries and blocs, activities of multinational corporations. It calls for constant efforts to expand world trade, bilaterally and multilaterally, through commercial, tariff and financial agreements; to enlarge and diversify markets for established Canadian exports. It requires intensive research and development studies in depth and on a regular basis, to discover and devise: new patterns of trade and investment, innovations in goods and services offered, new relationships with individual trading partners and with economic groupings. It also requires a sound framework of international co-operation.

Emphasis on economic growth assumes, as well, the continuation of immigration policies and programmes designed to ensure that the manpower requirements of a dynamic economy are fully met. It calls for an intensification and co-ordination of cultural, information and other diplomatic activity to make Canada fully known and respected abroad as a land of high-quality products, whether cultural or commercial, and as an attractive place for investors, traders, tourists and the kind of immigrant Canada needs. Increasingly these policies involve consultations with the provinces about relevant matters and co-operation with them in foreign countries. To resolve constitutional issues is not enough; to provide a better service abroad for all parts of Canada is necessary if Canadians are to be fully convinced of the advantages in Canada's federal system. Of necessity too, if Canada's external economic policies are to be fully successful, there must be closer contact between Canadian citizens —businessmen in particular—operating abroad and all departments and agencies in the foreign field, so that there may be a full awareness by both sides of all the possibilities for promoting—most effectively and economically—essential Canadian interests in countries and areas concerned.

Social Justice

Development assistance—which now implies trade and aid—is fully recognized as an expanding area of the Government's external activity, which has substantial benefit of an international significance transcending the relatively modest national costs incurred. Development assistance provides a special opportunity for a significant and distinctive Canadian contribution in the contemporary world.

It is, moreover, a principal manifestation of Canada's continuing willingness to accept its share of international responsibility, a self-imposed duty to help improve the human condition.

At the same time, the Government realizes that development programmes alone will not solve all the problems of stability in the Third World. Tensions exist there because of ancient animosities, stratified societies resting on large depressed classes, wide dissemination of armaments from Western and Communist sources. To be optimized, therefore, development assistance programmes will have to be correlated with policies relating to a set of very difficult international issues bearing such labels as the peaceful settlement of disputes, promotion of human rights and freedom, race conflict (which backlashes in a variety of ways in many countries), control of arms export, and military training programmes. Most of these issues arise in one form or another in the United Nations and Commonwealth contexts, where they tend to magnify the divergent interests of members. They can pose policy choices of great complexity if competing national objectives, very closely balanced as to importance, are involved (total rejection of race discrimination and continuing trade with white regimes in southern Africa, for example).

Quality of Life

There is a close link between environmental ills and the quality of life. The current emphasis on policies and measures to give all Canadians the advantages they have a right to expect as citizens ranks high in the Government's domestic priorities. In the international context, exchanges of all kinds—for purposes of education, science, culture, sport

—are multiplying with government encouragement and assistance. But Canada and the world community have yet to deal effectively with some urgent problems closely related to quality of life—hijacking and terrorism in the air when the airbus is here and supersonic aircraft are being tested; the alarming dimensions of the drug traffic today; internal security problems, not only based on legitimate domestic grievances but aggravated by outside agitation; organized crime across frontiers and trials with international implications; consumer protection against possible abuses by internationalized business activity. These are a few items on a much longer list. It is not that nothing is being done among countries but that much more must be done to bring such problems under control.

Most of the matters mentioned in this chapter will continue to have importance in international affairs, but they may have to give place, in terms of priority, to other problems which are pressing hard on the international community. These are the problems of the human environment. Anti-pollution programmes can be envisaged which eventually will open opportunities for creative international activity. Even now there is plenty of scope for institutionalized exchanges and for more concrete co-operative action. Canada has begun to take steps at home for dealing with the wide variety of environmental problems which a big industrialized country on the North American model is bound to face. The expertise resulting from domestic research and experience will be applied internationally to similar problems, just as foreign knowledge and experience can be tapped for the benefit of Canada. Like development aid, such programmes, and especially those involving effective anti-

pollution remedies, are likely to prove costly in future, the more so because crash action may be required if measures are to be made effective in time to check the present pace of deterioration. The job to be done assumes a healthy, expanding economy and concentration of resources on key problems.

It may call for a degree of intergovernmental co-operation not yet envisaged or practicable in existing international organizations. Whatever the difficulties and complications, the Government attaches high priority to environmental problems and intends to see that this priority is reflected in its national policies, at home and abroad.

Peace and Security

The policies and activities dealt with so far in this chapter manifest the Government's broad desire to do something effective to advance the cause of international stability and human betterment. They are not the only ways whereby Canada seeks to fulfil that desire. Participating in negotiations on arms control and on *détente*, seeking closer relations with individual countries in Eastern Europe, establishing diplomatic relations with China, joining in programmes for disaster and refugee relief, co-operating to promote trade expansion and to stabilize international finance, promoting progressive development of international law and standards in a variety of fields, seeking to improve peaceful methods (particularly peacekeeping) and to strengthen world order generally—all these are continuing external activities of Canada, and form part of the Government's ongoing foreign policy, not as matters of routine but as sectors of a broad front on which to probe systematically for openings toward solid progress.

Those activities are all important because they are broadly aimed at removing the obstacles to improvement in the international situation; clearly, as well, they serve Canada's self-interest, to the extent that they contribute to its national security and well-being. The Government is very conscious of its duty to ensure that national security is safeguarded in all respects. Defence arrangements must be maintained at a level sufficient to ensure respect for Canada's sovereignity and territorial integrity, and also to sustain the confidence of the United States and other allies. A compelling consideration in this regard is the Government's determination ot help prevent war between the super-powers, by sharing in the responsibility for maintaining stable nuclear deterrence and by participating in NATO policy-making in both political and military fields. The Government has no illusions about the limitations on its capacity to exert decisive or even weighty influence in consultations or negotiations involving the larger powers. But it is determined that Canada's ideas will be advanced, that Canada's voice will be heard, when questions vital to world peace and security are being discussed.

Canada has gained some special knowledge and experience in the broad area of "peace" talks—disarmament and arms control, *détente* and peacekeeping. It has more experience than many other countries when it comes to action in the peacekeeping field. The Government has no intention of relegating that know-how and experience to the national archives while the possibility remains that Canadian participation may be needed—in the sense that it is both essential and feasible in Canada's own judgment—to resolve a crisis or to ensure the successful outcome of a negotiation. In the whole area of peace activity, especially at the present time, it seems wise for Canada to hold something in reserve to meet emergency situations when a Canadian contribution can be solidly helpful. In the meantime, the Government will continue to give priority to its participation in arms-control talks and, as a minimum preparation for responding to other peace demands which may arise, the Government will keep its policy research and development on relevant subjects fully up-to-date. It will try to ensure, in any negotiations under way (arms control in Geneva, peacekeeping in New York), that Canadian interests and ideas are adequately taken into account.

Sovereignty and Independence

Seeing itself as a North American state, Canada has had to take a hard look across the oceans which surround it, and at the western hemisphere as a whole. In spite of the continuing and complex interdependence in today's world, Canada's particular situation requires a certain degree of self-reliance and self-expression if this country is to thrive as an independent state in a world of rapidly-shifting power structures and relationships. This special requirement has a very direct bearing on how the Government should: Manage its complex relations with the United States, especially as regards trade and finance, energies and resources, continental defence. The key to Canada's continuing freedom to develop according to its own perceptions will be the judicious use of Canadian sovereignty whenever Canada's aims and interests are placed in jeopardy—whether in relation to territorial claims, foreign ownership, cultural distinction, or energy and resource management.

Develop future relations with other countries in the western hemisphere, and with countries in other geographical regions. The predominance of transatlantic ties—with Britain, France and Western Europe generally (and new links with the Common Market)—will be adjusted to reflect a more evenly distributed policy emphasis, which envisages expanding activities in the Pacific basin and Latin America.

Deploy its limited human resources, the wealth which Canadians can generate, its science and technology, to promote a durable and balanced prosperity in the broadest socio-economic sense. There are limitations on what a nation of little more than 20 million can hope to accomplish in a world in which much larger powers have a dominant role.

Seek to sustain Canada's distinct identity, including particularities of language, culture, custom and institution. The Canadian contribution, to be most effective and distinctive, will have to be concentrated both as to kind and place.

Defence in the 70s: The White Paper on Defence (Ottawa: Information Canada, 1971), pp. 3-16. Reproduced by permission of Information Canada.

Defence in the 1970s

DEFENCE AS PART OF NATIONAL POLICY

Defence policy cannot be developed in isolation. It must reflect and serve national interests, and must be closely related to foreign policy, which the Government reviewed concurrently with defence. In the course of these reviews the principle that defence policy must be in phase with the broader eternal projection of national interests was underlined. In addition, internal aspects of national defence were also considered; these included aid of the civil power and assistance to the civil authorities in the furtherance of national aims.

National Aims: In the foreign policy review general national aims were defined as follows:

—that Canada will continue secure as an independent political entity;

—that Canada and all Canadians will enjoy enlarging prosperity in the widest possible sense;

—that all Canadians will see in the life they have and the contribution they make to humanity something worthwhile preserving in identity and purpose.

Policy Themes: To achieve these aims, the themes of Canada's national policy were more specifically defined as seeking to:

—foster economic growth,

—safeguard sovereignty and independence,

—work for peace and security,

—promote social justice,

—enhance the quality of life,

—ensure a harmonious natural environment.

The first concern of defence policy is the national aim of ensuring that Canada should continue secure as an independent political entity—an objective basic to the attainment of the other two national aims. In the policy themes flowing from the national aims, the Canadian Forces have a major part to play in the search for peace and security and also have an important and growing role in safeguarding sovereignty and independence. Accordingly it is to these two themes of national policy that the activities of the Canadian Forces are most closely related. However, defence policy can and should also be relevant to the other policy themes, and the contribution of the Department of National Defence to national development will be examined in this context.

PEACE AND SECURITY

The Changing Scene: One of the most important changes in international affairs in recent years has been the increase in stability in nuclear deterrence, and the emergence of what is, in effect, nuclear parity between the United States and the Soviet Union. Each side now has sufficient nuclear strength to assure devastating retaliation in the event of a surprise attack by the other, and thus neither could rationally consider launching a deliberate attack. There have also been qualitative changes in the composition of the nuclear balance. Of particular importance to Canada is the fact that bombers, and . . . bomber defences, have declined in relative importance in the strategic equation.

Greater stability in the last few years has been accompanied by an increased willingness to attempt to resolve East-West issues by negotiation, although it is still too early to judge the prospects for success. Formal and informal discussions are in progress between the U.S. and the U.S.S.R. on a long list of subjects, involving problems around the globe. Of overriding importance are the current Strategic Arms Limitation Talks (SALT) where signs of agreement are emerging. Other negotiations of major importance are the Four Power Talks on Berlin in which the U.S. and U.S.S.R. are joined by Britain and France in an effort to resolve one of the main issues still outstanding from Second World War. The Federal Republic of Germany has initiated a series of negotiations fundamental to the future prospects for East-West relations, which have already yielded important agreements with the U.S.S.R. and Poland. In addition, the Government hopes it will be possible to open negotiations on Mutual and Balanced Force Reductions (MBFR) in Europe in the near future.

At the same time the nations of Western Europe are growing more prosperous and are co-operating more closely, and the likelihood has increased that the European Economic Community will be enlarged. The European members of the North Atlantic Treaty Organization (NATO) are now able to assume a greater share of the collective Alliance defence, particularly with respect to their own continent. The North Atlantic Alliance remains firm but within it there is now a more even balance between North America and Europe.

Change has been even more rapid in the Pacific area where Japan's phenomenal economic growth continues and where China's military and political power is substantially increasing. Primarily as a result of these developments in Europe and Asia, but also as a consequence of change in other parts of the world, there has been a return to a form of multipolarity in the international system. Although the U.S. and the U.S.S.R. continue to have overwhelming military power, and in particular nuclear power, the relative ability of these two countries to influence events in the rest of the world has declined in recent years.

One other development in the international field of particular importance to Canada should be noted. In 1964 there was considerable optimism in this country concerning the scope for peacekeeping. In the intervening years the United Nations Emergency Force was compelled to leave the Middle East. Little progress has been made towards agreement on satisfactory means of international financing of peacekeeping forces. And amidst the tragedy of the Vietnam conflict, the effectiveness of the International Commission for Supervision and Control in Indo-China has further diminished. Additional observer missions were created and operated for a short time on the borders of West Pakistan and India following the border clash of 1965 and in Nigeria in 1969, but no substantial peacekeeping operation has been authorized since 1964 when the UN Force in Cyprus was established. For many reasons the scope for useful and effective peacekeeping activities now appears more modest than it did earlier, despite the persistence of widespread violence in many parts of the world.

Continuing Factors: A catastrophic war between the super powers constitutes the only major military threat to Canada. It is highly unlikely Canada would be attacked by a foreign power other than as a result of a strategic nuclear strike directed at the U.S. Our involvement would be largely a consequence of geography; Canada would not be singled out for separate attack. There is, unfortunately, not much Canada herself can do by way of effective direct defence that is of relevance against massive nuclear attack, given the present state of weapons technology, and the economic restraints on a middle power such as Canada.

Canada's overriding defence objective must therefore be the prevention of nuclear war by promoting political reconciliation to ease the underlying causes of tension, by working for arms control and disarmament agreements, and by contributing to the system of stable mutual deterrence.

Deterrence can be described in general terms as discouraging attack by demonstrating such a capability to retaliate— even after absorbing a massive surprise attack—that the possible gains of aggression would be outweighed by the losses the aggressor would sustain. The fearsome logic of mutual deterrence is clearly not a satisfactory long-term solution to the problem of preventing world conflict. But pending the establishment of a better system of security, it is the dominant factor in world politics today. Because of Canada's obvious inability to deter major nuclear war unilaterally, the Government's policy is to contribute to peace by participating in collective security arrangements. These arrangements have as their purpose the prevention or containment of conflict.

Canada's military role in North American defence involves contributing to the stability of deterrence by assisting the U.S. in operating a comprehensive system of warning, and providing some active defence against bombers and maritime forces. Canada's military role in the part of the NATO area which extends beyond the immediate North American area also constitutes a contribution to deterrence. It helps to minimize the danger of world war arising from conflict in the sensitive European and North Atlantic areas, where the super powers' interests are involved and thus the overall balance is at stake.

Canada's military role in international peacekeeping helps to prevent the outbreak or spread of hostilities in other areas of tension, so that underlying political problems can be settled through negotiation or a process of accommodation, and so that the possibility of great power involvement is minimized.

It is in Canada's interest that war should be prevented, but if unavoidable that it should be halted before it can escalate into a broader conflict which could affect the security of Canada. The Government intends therefore to maintain within feasible limits a general purpose combat capability of high professional standard within the Armed Forces, and to keep available the widest possible choice of options for responding to unforeseen international developments.

The Department of National Defence maintains a program in arms control research to support the Department of External Affairs. This has contributed to Canada's ability to make an effective contribution to the consultations held over the last two years at NATO to prepare for SALT, and to the preparations by NATO for negotiations on MBFR. It has also contributed to various other arms control proposals being discussed at the

Geneva disarmament conference, on such subjects as chemical and biological warfare and a proposed comprehensive test ban treaty. Canada also played a role in the negotiations surrounding the Non-Proliferation Treaty, and the treaties banning weapons of mass destruction from outer space and the seabed.

It should be stressed that a constant criterion for evaluating all aspects of policy is the determination to avoid any suggestion of the offensive use of Canadian Forces to commit aggression, or to contribute to such action by another state. Such a possibility would be unthinkable and unacceptable. With a view to ensuring the protection of Canada and contributing to the maintenance of stable mutual deterrence, Canada's resources, its territory, and its Armed Forces will be used solely for purposes which are defensive in the judgment of the Government of Canada.

SOVEREIGNTY AND INDEPENDENCE

Canada's sovereignty and independence depend ultimately on security from armed attack. In this sense, the contribution of the Canadian Forces to the prevention of war is a vital and direct contribution to safeguarding our sovereignty and independence. Defence policy must, however, also take into account the possibility that other challenges to Canada's sovereignty and independence, mainly non-military in character, may be more likely to arise during the 1970s. They could come both from outside and from within the country, and to deal with them may in some ways be more difficult. While deterring war is not an objective Canada alone can achieve, and is therefore one which must be pursued through collective security arrangements, the other challenges to sovereignty and independ-

ence must be met exclusively by Canada. The provision of adequate Canadian defence resources for this purpose must therefore be a matter of first priority.

External Challenges: By assuming the general responsibility for surveillance and control over Canadian territory, waters and airspace, in conjunction with civil agencies, the Canadian Forces help safeguard sovereignty and independence. Challenges could occur through actions by foreign agencies or their nationals involving territorial violations or infringements of Canadian laws governing access to and activity within these areas. This is not a new role for the Canadian Forces, but its dimensions are changing.

The North, in a sense the last frontier of Canada, has a unique physical environment presenting special problems of administration and control. Modern industrial technology has in recent years stimulated a growth of commercial interest in the resource potential of the area, and contributed to a major increase in oil and gas exploration in the Territories, especially on the Arctic Islands. These activities, in which foreign as well as Canadian companies are involved, have brought with them a need to ensure that exploitation of the resources is carried out in accordance with Canada's long-term national interests. There is a danger that this increased activity with its inherent danger of oil or other pollution might disturb the finely balanced ecology of the region. The Government therefore decided to take special measures to ensure the environmental preservation of this uniquely vulnerable area, and to ensure that these measures are fully respected. Strict regulations governing land use and mineral exploration and exploitation are being brought into effect. Legislation provides for the exercise of pollution control jurisdiction in an area extending generally 100 miles from the mainland and islands of the Canadian Arctic.

Canada is a three-ocean maritime nation with one of the longest coastlines in the world, and a large portion of the trade vital to our economic strength goes by sea. The Government is concerned that Canada's many and varied interests in the waters close to our shores, on the seabed extending from our coasts, and on the high seas beyond, be protected.

The Government has taken decisions with respect to the limits of Canada's territorial sea and fishing zones off the East and West coasts. Modern fishing techniques have resulted in a concern for the conservation of fishing resources in these areas. Legislation has extended Canada's territorial sea from three to twelve miles, and the former nine-mile contiguous fishing zone has been incorporated within the extended territorial sea. At the same time, new and extensive Canadian-controlled fishing zones have been created in areas of the sea adjacent to the coast. An order-in-council has been promulgated establishing such fishing zones in Queen Charlotte Sound, Dixon Entrance and Hecate Strait on the West Coast, and the Gulf of St. Lawrence and the Bay of Fundy on the East Coast, a total area of 80,000 square miles. Against the possibility of potentially disastrous oil spills, pollution control is also to be exercised in these areas.

Exploration and exploitation of the resources of the continental shelf are regulated under the Oil and Gas Production and Conservation Act. This area extends to the limits of exploitability, which Canada interprets as comprising the submerged continental margin. Although less extensive off the West Coast, it extends hundreds of miles off the East Coast, and encompasses large areas off the Arctic mainland and islands. In recent years there has been a tremendous increase in technological capability for exploitation of this resource potential.

Departmental Responsibilities and Relationships: The Government's objective is to continue effective occupation of Canadian territory, and to have a surveillance and control capability to the extent necessary to safeguard national interests in all Canadian territory, and all airspace and waters over which Canada exercises sovereignty or jurisdiction. This involves a complex judgment on the challenges which could occur and on the surveillance and control capability required in the circumstances.

The Canadian Forces do not have sole responsibility for ensuring respect for relevant Canadian legislation but they do have a general responsibility for surveillance and control over land, sea and airspace under Canadian jurisdiction. In peacetime this role of the Forces is in many respects complementary to that of the civil authorities. The requirement for military assistance is generally greater, however, in more sparsely settled regions until a stage of economic and social development has been reached, justifying an expansion of civil agencies and resources. Similarly, where the Canadian Forces have the capability to meet a shortage in civil resources for the policing of waters off the coasts, their role can be expanded.

The area to be covered is vast. In certain regions facilities are limited and weather conditions are often adverse. The problem would perhaps be simpler if it were restricted to the more traditional security threat of direct military attack from a predictable enemy. Instead, challenges could arise in more ambiguous circumstances from private entities as well as foreign government agencies. Incidents may involve, for instance, a fishing vessel, an oil tanker or a private aircraft. But the principle involved is well established. By creating a capability for surveillance and control which is effective and visible, the intention is to discourage such challenges.

Other departments of government already have specific responsibilities in many instances for regulating activity in Canadian territory, and these lead to requirements for carrying out surveillance and exercising control. National Defence has, however, ultimate responsibility to ensure that overall an adequate Canadian surveillance and control capability exists for the protection of Canadian sovereignty and security. Consequently the Government intends to establish Canadian Forces' operations centres on the East and West coasts which will work closely with the civil departments to co-ordinate surveillance and control activities. Where required by potential challenges to our interests the Canadian Forces will carry out surveillance and exercise control in those areas not covered by the civil departments, or in which the latter require assistance in discharging their responsibilities. Close consultation between National Defence and the civil departments concerned will be maintained on a continuing basis to ensure that surveillance and control is being exercised when, where, and to the extent necessary to satisfy the Government's requirements in the most economical way.

Internal Security: The Canadian experience over the last two years clearly indicates the necessity of being able to cope effectively with any future resort to disruption, intimidation and violence as weapons of political action. The three prime instances in which the Forces were used recently in this role were during the Montreal police strike, the political kidnapping crisis of last October and the Kingston Penitentiary riots. While civil disorder should normally be contained by the civil authorities, and the strength of municipal, provincial and federal police forces should be maintained at levels sufficient for the purpose, we must nevertheless anticipate the possibility that emergencies will again arise which will necessitate the Canadian Forces coming to the aid of the civil power. It is important that the latter should be able to rely upon timely assistance from the Forces. The Forces' role in such situations is important and could be crucial.

In addition to the possibility of future crises arising in Canada, there is also the possibility that violent events elsewhere could stimulate outbreaks in Canada. This problem is therefore one with clear international ramifications. Indeed, it appears that much of the world has already moved into an era which will see established order increasingly challenged by organized violence. These are times of confrontation when growing numbers of people appear to be prepared to resort to violence with a view to destroying the democratic process.

NATIONAL DEVELOPMENT

Although maintained primarily for purposes of sovereignty and security, the Department of National Defence provides an important reservoir of skills and capabilities which in the past has been drawn upon, and which in the future can be increasingly drawn upon, to contribute to the social and economic development of Canada. By their service and devotion to duty the members of the Armed Forces, and the civilians who support them, have made a significant contribution to preserving a democratic society in Canada against the threat of external challenges.

The Armed Forces make an important contribution to Canada's unity and identity in a number of ways. They bring together Canadians from all parts of the country, from all walks of life, from the two major linguistic groups and other origins, into an activity that is truly national in scope and in purpose. They are distinctively Canadian and this is symbolized by their new uniform. A career in the Armed Forces has enabled many Canadians to advance their education and skills, whether in university, in technical specialties or in a trade. The influence of the Forces is extended to young people through cadet and militia programs, and through the work of many individual members in youth organizations. The Department continues to view its support of such activities as a vital contribution to the well-being of the youth of our country.

The inherent characteristics of the Armed Forces combine effective command and organization, high mobility, great flexibility and a range of skills and specialties broader than that of any other national organization. These provide Canada with a resource which may be used to carry out essentially non-military projects of high priority and importance to national development. The objective will be to use the Forces primarily on projects which relate to their capabilities to respond efficiently and promptly to their basic defence roles.

The Forces will be called upon, therefore, in conjunction with other governmental departments, to assist development in the civil sector, especially in the remote regions where disciplined task forces with wide experience in adapting to unusual or challenging circumstances are required. Where possible, the Reserves will also be used in this role. A further objective of this policy will be to promote greater involvement of the military in the community, and to ensure that the community is aware of the ways in which the military sector contributes to achieving national aims and priorities. . . .

The Forces will make a major contribution to the preservation of an unspoiled environment and an improved quality of life by supporting the civil agencies in exercising pollution control in the North and off Canada's coasts. The Forces and the Canada Emergency Measures Organization will continue to play an important part in providing relief and assistance in the event of natural disasters or other civil emergencies, including those resulting from oil spills or other forms of pollution. . . .

The Forces can also give further support to foreign policy objectives through increased assistance in economic aid programs. National Defence has capabilities to assist in such fields as engineering and construction, logistics policies, trades and technical training, advisory services, project analysis and air transport. The Department will work with the Canadian International Development Agency and the Department of External Affairs to study the possible use of military capabilities in support of specific aid programs or projects as the need arises. . . .

To fulfill their assigned roles, the Armed Forces need highly sophisticated and costly equipment. Our experience in 1959 with the cancellation of the Arrow interceptor aircraft firmly established that, because of the costs and the small quantities involved, such development cannot be economically undertaken by

Canada acting alone. Because of costs and complexity, and the need for relatively long production runs, most countries have now accepted the need for co-operative efforts in producing their major equipment needs.

A significant portion of the capital equipment budget is thus spent abroad, largely in the United States. To ensure that Canada obtains equivalent economic, industrial and technological benefits for these expenditures, and in order to main-tain a domestic defence industrial base, arrangements have been made with our allies for Canadian industry either to share in the production of equipment or to export a like value of defence products to our allies. Co-operation with the United States and other countries in development and production-sharing programs has been a significant factor in allowing the Canadian Armed Forces to purchase the best equipment at the most advantageous prices.

J. L. Granatstein, "Defence in the 70s: Comments on the White Paper," in *Behind the Headlines* XXX (October, 1971), pp. 11-12.

Defence Against What?

On the surface *Defence in the 70s* seems to be little more than a reaffirmation of the *status quo post* Hellyer. At first glance, nothing of consequence seems to have been altered, and in this area as in others the government seems never to do by quarters what it can do by eighths or avoid altogether.

Take NATO, for example. The first paragraph in the section devoted to the alliance begins with the belabouring of the obvious—"Canada is one of only two partners in the NATO Alliance which station forces outside of their own continent"—and then proceeds to establish briefly quite a credible case for withdrawing the remaining Canadian troops from Europe by attacking "a widespread misconception that only the stationing of Canadian Forces in Western Europe constitutes a contribution to NATO's collective defence." But having ventured that far the government quickly retreats and pledges to maintain its European contingent and even to provide a new tank to replace the twenty-year-old Centurion. The commitment goes on, and about all the paper does is to delicately further the process of preparing the way for the eventual departure of the legions. Still, when the political costs of a pullback are minimal, it now seems clear, there can be

little doubt that the Canadian government will happily decamp.

The same reasoning seems to apply in the sections on NORAD. The only justification for the air defence scheme today is to prevent the Soviet bomber fleet from having a free ride. There is a rationale for this, but it is not particularly convincing, and if the Russians are shrewd they will always keep one bomber prominently parked at the Moscow airport terminal, thus ensuring that NORAD will live forevermore. The political reasons for the air defence system clearly are far more important to Ottawa than the military ones, and the unstated implication in the white paper is that Ottawa would like to be out in 1973 if possible. The recent inspired leaks in the *New York Times* about a new Soviet bomber may have had as one of their subsidiary purposes the shooting down of that particular hope. If the military reasons for NORAD can be beefed up, Washington can count on Canadian hawks to create enough noise to ensure another five-year renewal.

From the Canadian point of view, of course, there are good reasons for basing defence policy on political and national purposes. As the white paper makes clear, the only threat to Canada is that of all-out nuclear war, a certain truism. There are no alien hordes at our borders, no tigers at our gates. There is no physical threat to our security, none at all.

But this having been said, the paper's emphasis on sovereignty and surveillance has to be seen for what it is. Except for those in NATO and NORAD, and on peacekeeping duties, the bulk of the armed forces is to have as its first charge the maintenance of sovereignty. But what does this mean? What can it mean? Will there be huge new bases on the tundra? Not if the much-touted new northern headquarters is any indication of future plans. With its strength of thirty-five officers and men, it might be able to administer a battalion or two but not much else. Will there be fleets of aircraft and ships patrolling the ice floes? Fat chance. None of our fighting ships has a northern capability, and if the air force brass have anything to say about it there will be the minimum number of hours "wasted" in the Arctic.

Sovereignty is a fraud, a patently phony defence priority. There is no physical threat to our sovereignty in the north. There is no enemy there against which our armed forces can operate. There is simply no justification whatsoever for using troops in this role that only political weapons, firm leadership, and united public opinion can handle. The public is being gulled in a very skilful fashion. Skilful, because sovereignty sounds good today, attuned as we are to the neo-nationalism of our press, academics, and young people. Mr. Trudeau has evidently decided that the Liberal party should appear to be as nationalist as the others, and the sovereignty priority helps here. It assists too in providing a rationale for withdrawing troops from NATO and NORAD, something that I expect the Prime Minister hopes to accomplish. Important as they may be, however, these are clearly subsidiary reasons.

The real reason, the only possible reason, for the emphasis on sovereignty is the justification it offers for keeping troops in Canada. As the government sees it, these troops have to be in Canada to maintain civil authority, to suppress terrorism, to crush the separatists, to maintain the political *status quo*. Why else raise the ceiling on defence expenditures and manpower when overseas commitments are being cut, when peacekeep-

ing seems increasingly unlikely, when NORAD is being limited in roles? The enemy of Ottawa is in Montreal, not Moscow.

None of this appears in the white paper whose three paragraphs on aid to the civil power are singularly uninformative. But the fact remains that "aid to the civil authority" has been "priority one" at defence headquarters for at least two years now, that units have been relocated around the country with this in mind, and that the Prime Minister and presumably the majority of the cabinet see this as the major—the only?—threat to the nation in the 1970s.

Certainly the Prime Minister has given ample indication in the past that his view was focussed more on domestic than on international troubles. In November 1968, for example, he told a Queen's University audience that "I am less worried about what is over the Berlin Wall than about Chicago and what might happen in our great cities in Canada." The FLQ incident in Montreal last fall would seem to indicate that the Prime Minister had made a self-fulfilling prophecy.

If the government had stated that the major role for its forces was to be that of a French-style *garde mobile* there would have been a public clamour. Defence traditionalists would have foamed (one can hardly bear to imagine what Brigadier Malone would have said in the *Winnipeg Free Press*), and civil libertarians would have been justifiably frightened. In Quebec, particularly, the reaction would have been very sharp and the still-forming Bloc québécois would have been the chief beneficiary. It was obviously far better to talk of sovereignty rather than suppression, of surveillance rather than street fighting.

The message of the white paper, then, is not to be found in its pallid pages. Our armed forces are now to have as their primary task the maintenance of public order—which can only mean the maintenance of the political *status quo*. On innumerable occasions the Prime Minister has talked about the need to alleviate the lot of the poor and underprivileged, of the necessity of dealing calmly with the not unjust demands of the deprived. Are the armed forces to be one of the major weapons to be used in this role? Better to have no armed forces at all; better even to have armed forces preparing at great expense to fight wars that will never come. The white paper marks a fateful turn in our history as a nation. But how awful that its issuance passed with scarcely a complaint.

Mitchell Sharp, "Canada-U.S. Relations: Options for the Future," *International Perspectives* (Autumn, 1972), pp. 13-23.

Continental Possibilities and Problems

THE OPTIONS

This is not the first time Canadians have asked themselves which way they should go. The factor of geography remains a constant element in the equation. The disproportion between Canada and the United States in terms of power has not changed all that much. The continental pull itself has historical antecedents. The pursuit of a distinctive identity runs through the process of Canadian nation-building.

But if the signposts are familiar, the landscape is undoubtedly different. Many of the old countervailing forces have disappeared. The links across the common border have increased in number, impact and complexity. New dimensions are being added to the Canada-U.S. relationship all the time. On both sides, there is now difficulty in looking upon the relationship as being wholly external in character.

The world trend is not helpful to Canada in resolving this dilemma. For the trend is discernibly in the direction of interdependence. In the economic realm, in science, in technology, that is the direction in which the logic of events is pointing. In Canada's case, inevitably, interdependence is likely to mean inter-

dependence mainly with the United States. This is a simple statement of the facts. It does not pretend to be a value judgment. In point of fact, the balance of benefits of such a trend for Canada may well be substantial.

But this evades the real question that looms ahead for Canada. And that is whether interdependence with a big, powerful, dynamic country like the United States is not bound, beyond a certain level of tolerance, to impose an unmanageable strain on the concept of a separate Canadian identity, if not on the elements of Canadian independence.

To pose these questions is simple enough. To propound answers to them is more difficult because any answer is likely to touch on the central ambiguity of our relationship with the United States. The temper of the times, nevertheless, suggests that Canadians are looking for answers. It is also apparent that many of the answers are in Canadian hands. This is because a few of the problems engendered by the relationship are, in fact, problems of deliberate creation on the U.S. side. They are problems arising out of contiguity and disparity in wealth and power and, not least, out of the many affinities that make it more difficult for Canadians to stake out an identity of their own.

Three courses

The real question facing Canadians is one of direction. In practice, three broad options are open to us:

(a) we can seek to maintain more or less our present relationship with the United States with a minimum of policy adjustments;

(b) we can move deliberately toward closer integration with the United States;

(c) we can pursue a comprehensive, long-term strategy to develop and strengthen the Canadian economy and other aspects of our national life and in the process to reduce the present Canadian vulnerability.

Such a statement of options may err on the side of oversimplification. The options are intended merely to delineate general directions of policy. Each option clearly covers a spectrum of possibilities and could be supported by a varied assortment of policy instruments. Nevertheless, the importance of the options notion is not to be discounted. For, in adopting one of the options, Canadians would be making a conscious choice of the continental environment that, in their view, was most likely to be responsive to their interests and aspirations over the next decade or two. Conversely, no single option is likely to prove tenable unless it commands a broad national concensus.

Seeking to maintain our present position with minimum policy changes

The first option would be to aim at maintaining more or less the present pattern of our economic and political relationship with the United States with a minimum of policy change either generally or in the Canada-United States context.

The formulation notwithstanding, this is not an option meaning no change. In the present climate, any option that did not provide for change would clearly be unrealistic. The realities of power in the world are changing. Some of the international systems that have provided the context for our monetary and trading relations in the postwar period are in the process of reshaping. The United States is embarked on a basic reappraisal of its position and policies. The Canadian situation is itself changing and new perceptions are being brought to bear on the Canada-U.S. relationship. All this suggests that some adjustments in Canadian policy are unavoidable.

The first option would neither discount the fact of change nor deny the need to accommodate to it. But it would imply a judgment that, at least on the present evidence, the changes that have occurred or are foreseeable are not of a nature or magnitude to call for a basic reorientation of Canadian policies, particularly as they relate to the United States.

In practical terms, this would mean maintaining the general thrust of our trade and industrial policies, including a large degree of *laissez faire* in economic policy, a multilateral, most-favoured-nation approach as the guiding principle of our trade policy, emphasis on securing improved access to the U.S. market, the vigorous export of commodities and semi-processed goods, and continuing efforts to industrialize domestically by rationalizing production, in large part for export. Presumably, little or no change would be made in the present way of handling matters at issue with the United States, which is one of dealing with each problem as it arises and seeking to maintain something of a "special relationship".

New constraints

But there is another side to the coin. The changes that are taking place on both sides of the border point to new opportunities and new constraints emerging for Canada. We would aim at seizing the opportunities and managing the constraints to the best of our ability. In the process we would be concerned about the balance of benefits for Canada, but we would be less concerned about how any given transaction or act of policy fitted into some overall conception of our relationship with the United States.

Nevertheless, other things being equal, we would seek to avoid any further significant increase in our dependence on the United States and our vulnerability to the vicissitudes of the U.S. market and to changes in U.S. economic policy. An effort to diversify our export markets would not be incompatible with the first option; nor would a policy to take advantage of accelerating demand for our mineral and energy resources to secure more processing and employment in Canada and, generally, to reap greater benefits from this major national asset; nor would some further moderate Canadian action to achieve greater control over the domestic economic and cultural environment.

In sum, this is essentially a pragmatic option. It would not, by definition, involve radical policy departures. It would deal with issues as they arose on the basis of judgments made in relation to each issue. It is not a static option because it would address itself to the solution of problems generated by an environment which is itself dynamic. One of its main attractions is that, we trust, it would not foreclose other options.

The precise implications and costs of this option are difficult to predict because they would vary significantly depending on developments over the short and medium term. Accommodation of current U.S. preoccupations, however limited, would entail some costs and could involve an increase in our dependence on the United States. If U.S. difficulties proved more durable, and if significant improvements in access to other markets did not materialize, pressures might de-

velop in the United States and in Canada for further special bilateral arrangements. Alternatively, if protectionist attitudes in the United States were to find reflection in official policy, we might be forced to seek other markets on whatever terms we could and perhaps to make painful adjustments in order to reorient our industry to serve mainly the domestic market.

On more optimistic assumptions about the course of U.S. policy and the future of the international trading system, the first option might be followed for some time with ostensible success. The real question is whether it comes fully to grips with the basic Canadian situation or with the underlying continental pull. There is a risk that, in pursuing a purely pragmatic course, we may find ourselves drawn more closely into the U.S. orbit. At the end of the day, therefore, it may be difficult for the present position to be maintained, let alone improved, without more fundamental shifts in Canadian policy.

Closer integration with the United States

The second option is to accept that, in a world where economies of scale are dictating an increasing polarization of trade and in the face of intensified integrating pressures within North America, the continuation of the existing relationship, based on the economic separation of Canada and the United States, does not make good sense, and to proceed from that conclusion deliberately to prepare the ground for an arrangement with the United States involving closer economic ties.

The option spans a considerable range of possibilities. At the lower end of the scale, it might involve no more than the pursuit of sectoral or other limited arrangements with the United States based on an assessment of mutual interest. In effect, this would represent an extension of past practices except to the extent that such arrangements would be pursued more as a matter of deliberate policy. We might seek, for example, to adapt to other industries the approach reflected in the Automotive Products Agreement. The chemical industry is one such industry that could lend itself to rationalization on a North-South basis. The aerospace industry might well be another. We might also endeavour to negotiate a continental arrangement with the United States covering energy resources. Under such an arrangement, U.S. access to Canadian energy supplies might be traded in exchange for unimpeded access to the U.S. market for Canadian uranium, petroleum and petrochemical products (to be produced by a much expanded and developed industry within Canada).

This more limited form of integration has a certain logic to it and, indeed, warrants careful examination. It may be expected, however, to generate pressures for more and more continental arrangements of this kind that would be increasingly difficult to resist. Experience with the Automotive Products Agreement suggests that, in any such sectoral arrangements, there may be difficulty in maintaining an equal voice with the United States over time. Nor could we be sure that the concept of formal symmetry, on which the United States has lately insisted, is one that can easily be built into a sectoral arrangement without impairing the interests of the economically weaker partner. In the energy field, by dealing continentally with the United States, we would almost certainly limit our capacity to come to an arrangement with other potential purchasers, in Europe or Japan, quite apart from possibly impinging upon

future Canadian needs. In sum, we might well be driven to the conclusion that partial or sectoral arrangements are less likely to afford us the protection we seek than a more comprehensive regime of free trade.

A free-trade area or a customs union arrangement with the United States would, to all intents and purposes, be irreversible for Canada once embarked upon. It would, theoretically, protect us against future changes in U.S. trade policy towards the rest of the world, though not against changes in U.S. domestic economic policy. This option has been rejected in the past because it was judged to be inconsistent with Canada's desire to preserve a maximum degree of independence, not because it lacked economic sense in terms of Canadian living standards and the stability of the Canadian economy. . . .

Safeguards required

If we were to opt for integration, deliberate and coherent policies and programs would be required, both before and after an arrangement was achieved, to cope with the difficult adjustments that would be entailed for Canada. An adequate transitional period would be essential. Some safeguards for production and continued industrial growth in Canada would have to be negotiated. Agriculture might emerge as another problem sector. In practice, any safeguards would probably be limited largely to a transitional period and could not be expected to cushion the impact of integration for an indefinite future. A tendency for the centres of production—and population—to move south might, in the long run, be difficult to stem. But the more relaxed environment Canada has to offer and the lesser prominence of pressures in Canadian society might also, over time, exert a countervailing influence on any purely economic trend.

The probable economic costs and benefits of this option would require careful calculation. The more fundamental issues, however, are clearly political. In fact, it is a moot question whether this option, or any part of it, is politically tenable in the present or any foreseeable climate of Canadian public opinion.

Reactions and attitudes would no doubt differ across the country. The cleavage of interest between the central, industrialized region and the Western provinces on this issue has become apparent in recent years. Attitudes rooted in historical tradition could be expected to play their part in the Atlantic Provinces. The reaction in the French-speaking areas is more difficult to predict. On the one hand, they tend not to draw a very sharp distinction between the impact of economic control of local enterprise whether exercised from the United States or from elsewhere in Canada. But it is not unlikely that among many French-speaking Canadians the prospect of union with the United States would be viewed as risking their eventual submergence in a sea of some 200 million English-speaking North Americans and as a reversal of the efforts made in Canada over the last ten years to create a favourable climate for the survival and development of the French language and culture in North America.

There is a real question, therefore, whether the whole of Canada could be brought into union with the United States. Of course, full-fledged political union is not the basic intent of this option. But, to the extent that the logic of events may impel us in that direction, almost any form of closer integration with the United States may be expected to generate opposition in Canada. If it is true, moreover, as appears to be the case, that a more vigorous sense of identity has been taking root among Canadians in recent years, it is unlikely that opposition to this option would be confined to particular parts of the country.

A comprehensive strategy to strengthen the Canadian economy

The basic aim of the third option would be, over time, to lessen the vulnerability of the Canadian economy to external factors, including, in particular, the impact of the United States and, in the process, to strengthen our capacity to advance basic Canadian goals and develop a more confident sense of national identity. If it is to be successfully pursued, the approach implicit in this option would clearly have to be carried over into other areas of national endeavour and supported by appropriate policies. But the main thrust of the option would be towards the development of a balanced and efficient economy to be achieved by means of a deliberate, comprehensive and long-term strategy.

The accent of the option is on Canada. It tries to come to grips with one of the unanswered questions that runs through so much of the Canada-U.S. relationship, and which is what kind of Canada it is that Canadians actually want. It is thus in no sense an anti-American option. On the contrary, it is the one option of all those presented that recognizes that, in the final analysis, it may be for the Canadian physician to heal himself.

The option is subject to two qualifications. "Over time" recognizes that the full benefits will take time to materialize, but that a conscious and deliberate effort will be required to put and maintain the Canadian economy on such a course. "To lessen" acknowledges that there are limits to the process because it is unrealistic to think that any economy, however structured, let alone Canada's, can be made substantially immune to developments in the world around us in an era of growing interdependence.

The option is one that can have validity on most assumptions about the external environment. A basically multilateral environment, of course, in which trade is governed by the most-favoured-nation principle, would enhance its chances of success. But it would not be invalidated by other premises. That is because the option relates basically to the Canadian economy. Its purpose is to recast that economy in such a way as to make it more rational and more efficient as a basis for Canada's trade abroad.

The present may be an auspicious time for embarking on this option. Our trading position is strong. We are regarded as a stable and affluent country with a significant market and much to offer to our global customers in the way of resources and other products. Our balance of payments has been improving in relative terms. We are no longer as dependent on large capital inflows as we once were. A new round of comprehensive trade negotiations is in prospect during 1973. Above all, there is a greater sense of urgency within Canada and greater recognition abroad of Canada's right to chart its own economic course.

Keyed to exports

The option assumes that the basic nature of our economy will continue unchanged. That is to say that, given the existing ratio of resources to population, Canada will continue to have to depend for a large proportion of its national wealth on the ability to export goods and services to external markets on secure terms of access. The object is essentially to create a sounder, less vulnerable economic base for competing in the domestic and world markets and deliberately to broaden the spectrum of markets in which Canadians can and will compete.

In terms of policy, it would be necessary to encourage the specialization and rationalization of production and the emergence of strong Canadian-controlled firms. It is sometimes argued that a market of the size of Canada's may not provide an adequate base for the economies of scale that are a basic ingredient of international efficiency. The argument is valid only up to a point. The scale of efficiency is different for different industries and there is no reason why a market of 22 million people with relatively high incomes should prove inadequate for many industries which are not the most complex or capital-intensive.

The close co-operation of government, business and labour would be essential through all phases of the implementation of such an industrial strategy. So would government efforts to provide a climate conducive to the expansion of Canadian entrepreneurial activity. It may be desirable, and possible, in the process to foster the development of large, efficient multi-nationally-operating Canadian firms that could effectively compete in world markets. It may also be possible, as a consequence of greater efficiencies, for Canadian firms to meet a higher proportion of the domestic requirement for goods and services. But that would be a natural result of the enhanced level of competitiveness which the option is designed to promote; it is not in the spirit of the option to foster import substitution as an end in itself with all the risks that would entail of carrying us beyond the margins of efficiency.

The option has been variously described as involving a deliberate, comprehensive and long-term strategy. It is bound to be long-term because some substantial recasting of economic structures may be involved. It is comprehensive in the sense that it will entail the mutually-reinforcing use and adaptation of a wide variety of policy instruments. Fiscal policy, monetary policy, the tariff, the rules of competition, government procurement, foreign investment regulations, science policy may all have to be brought to bear on the objectives associated with this option. The choice and combination of policy instruments will depend on the precise goals to be attained. The implications, costs and benefits of the option will vary accordingly.

In saying that the strategy must be deliberate, it is accepted that it must involve some degree of planning, indicative or otherwise, and that there must be at least a modicum of consistency in applying it. One implication of the conception of deliberateness is that the strategy may have to entail a somewhat greater measure of government involvement than has been the case in the past. The whole issue of government involvement, however, needs to be kept in proper perspective. The Government is now and will continue to be involved in the operation of the economy in a substantial way. This is a function of the responsibility which the Canadian Government shares with other sovereign governments for ensuring the well-being and prosperity of its citizens in a context of social justice. A wide variety of policy instruments and incentives is already being deployed to that end, largely with the support and often at the instance of those who are more directly concerned with the running of different segments of the economy. It is not ex-pected that the pursuit of this particular option will radically alter the relation between Government and the business community, even if the Government were to concern itself more closely with the direction in which the economy was evolving.

Much the same considerations apply to the relationship between the federal and provincial jurisdictions. It is true that, in the diverse circumstances that are bound to prevail in a country like Canada, the task of aggregating the national interest is not always easy. There may be a problem, therefore, in achieving the kind of broad consensus on objectives, priorities and instrumentalities on which the successful pursuit of anything on the lines of the present option is likely to hinge. Part of the problem may derive from a divergent assessment of short-term interests. In terms of longer-range goals, it is much less apparent why federal and provincial interests should not be largely compatible or why the elaboration of this option should not enhance and enlarge the opportunities for co-operation with the provinces. Indeed, there are many areas, such as the upgrading of Canada's natural resource exports, where the implications of this option are likely to coincide closely with provincial objectives.

Impact on U.S.

What of the impact on the United States, which could be critical to the success of the option? There again, it is necessary to keep matters in perspective. There is no basic change envisaged in Canada's multilateral trade policy. On the contrary, we could expect to be working closely with the United States in promoting a more liberal world-trading environment. Nor does the option imply any intention artificially to distort our traditional trading patterns. The United States would almost certainly remain Canada's most important market and source of supply be a very considerable margin.

The fact remains, nevertheless, that the option is directed towards reducing Canada's vulnerability, particularly in relation to the United States. A good deal of this vulnerability derives from an underlying continental pull, which is inadvertent. To that extent, the risk of friction at the governmental level is lessened, although it would be unrealistic to discount it altogether. Much would depend on what policy instruments were selected in support of this option and how we deployed them. The state of the U.S. economy could be another factor determining U.S. reactions at any given time. On any reasonable assumptions, however, such impact as the option may unavoidably have on U.S. interests would be cushioned by the time-frame over which it is being projected and should be relatively easy to absorb in a period of general growth and prosperity. When all is said and done, the option aims at a relative decline in our dependence on the United States, not at a drastic change in our bilateral relationship. As such, it is not incompatible with the view, recently advanced by President Nixon in his address to the House of Commons, that "no self-respecting nation can or should accept the proposition that it should always be economically dependent upon any other nation"....

SUMMING UP

In looking into the perspectives for the Seventies, *Foreign Policy for Canadians* focuses on "the complex problem of living distinct from but in harmony with the world's most powerful and dynamic nation, the United States". The phrase is intended, presumably, not only to identify the problem but to define the parameters of the relationship. It is the requirement of both distinctness and harmony, therefore, that any option for the future of Canada-U.S. relations must be seen to satisfy, among others.

In essence, distinctness should be implicit in any relationship between two sovereign countries such as Canada and the United States. The very fact that it has to be singled out as an objective of foreign policy says something about the Canada-U.S. relationship. The relationship is characterized by an array of links that, given the disparity in power and population, impinge on the sense of Canadian identity. This might be a substantial challenge if evidence were not accumulating that the underlying trend in the Canada-U.S. relationship may be becoming less congenial to the conception of Canadian distinctness.

Distinctness has no autonomous virtue of its own. It is not an end in itself. In the process of nation-building, however, it is a substantial factor of cohesion. In the case of Canada, in particular, it is arguable that the perception of a distinct identity can make a real and discernible contribution to national unity.

The whole conception of distinctness is, of course, changing. There are challenges facing modern society that transcend national boundaries. There are areas of economic activity that can no longer be performed efficiently except on a scale that exceeds national dimensions. There is a whole host of linkages that lend cumulative substance to the reality of interdependence. This is a global trend from which Canada can neither claim nor expect to be exempt. It is a fact, nevertheless, that the Canadian situation in relation to the United States is unique in two respects: the linkages are probably more numerous and more pervasive than between any other two countries and the affinities between them are also such as to put particular strains on the definition of the Canadian identity. On both counts the problem of living distinct from the United States is only marginally related to the larger issue of global interdependence, which is a fact of life for all countries.

If Canadians say they want a distinct country, it is not because they think they are better than others. It is because they want to do the things they consider important and do them in their own way. And they want Canadian actions and life styles to reflect distinctly Canadian perspectives and a Canadian view of the world.

Against this yardstick the first option —seeking to maintain our present position with minimum policy changes—is not likely to represent much of an advance. On the contrary, if the continental pull is, in fact, becoming stronger, we may, like the proverbial squirrel, have to run harder simply to stay in place. In the final analysis, the first option is not really an option of strategy at all. Directed as it is toward preserving the present balance in the Canada-U.S. relationship in an external setting of predictable change, it would inevitably involve a substantially reactive posture on Canada's part.

Costs involved

The second option—closer integration with the United States—would involve costs in terms of the Canadian identity. Even if limited to a free-trade area, it would probably be unrealistic to assume that the momentum generated by this option could be confined to the economic and industrial sphere. The many common denominators, based on contiguity and affinity, that link Canada and the United States, would receive a strong

impetus. To resist them would require more deliberate effort and appear to make less sense because the second option implies a judgment that the effort to resist the continental pull is likely to be unavailing. To the extent that a real risk to Canada's distinctness as a political and cultural community was apprehended, recourse to the second option could involve a serious strain on the domestic consensus in Canada.

The third option—a comprehensive strategy to strengthen the Canadian economy and other aspects of our national life—assumes that the continental tide can be stemmed to some extent and contained within bounds that approximate more closely the wider, global thrust of interdependence. It sees, as did the recent foreign policy review, "the judicious use of Canadian sovereignty" as "the key to Canada's continuing freedom to develop accroding to its own perceptions". More specifically, it looks to the mutually-reinforcing use of various policy instruments as the proper strategy to achieve greater Canadian distinctness. It inevitably takes account of its own limitations. It does not seek to distort the realities of the Canada-United States relationship or the fundamental community of interest that lies at the root of it.

Distinctness is not the only criterion by which the options available to Canada in its conduct of the U.S. relationship should be judged. Independence is another. Distinctness and independence are clearly related, but they are not the same thing. In the broadest sense independence is related ultimately to the capacity of governments to formulate and conduct policy on the basis of national perceptions for the achievement of national objectives in the domestic and international environments. Distinctness, on the other hand, is an attribute that applies to a national society in all its various manifestations.

In trying to judge the constraints on Canadian independence arising out of the U.S. relationship, it is necessary to keep a proper sense of balance. In the first place, there is an all-too-natural tendency to think of such constraints as being deliberate manifestations of U.S. policy. This applies, in particular, to the integrating trend that is being apprehended on the Canadian side. In practice, there is no evidence to suggest that U.S. policy towards Canada is being conducted on other than pragmatic lines as distinct from some general conception of progressive integration that would have the effect of gradually extinguishing Canada's separate existence as a national entity. It is important to distinguish, therefore, between the impact on the Canadian scene of non-governmental U.S. actors (such as corporations, business groups, trade unions, and the media), on the one hand, and of policies and actions of the U.S. Government, on the other. As a general proposition, there is no real evidence that the U.S. Government does now pursue a concerted policy of continental integration in relation to Canada. Conversely, however, the U.S. Government should not be counted on to inhibit any integrating trend that may be emerging as a result of the separate actions or interests of various U.S. constituent communities.

Rewarding relationship

In the second place, the Canada-U.S. relationship, in whatever way we may look upon it, has been a rewarding and enriching relationship for Canada on most counts. In particular, of course, it has been instrumental in endowing Canadians with an industrial structure and the higher standard of living that goes with it in a shorter time span than might otherwise have been achievable on the strength even of Canada's substantial natural and human resources. This is something that cannot be left out of account in any judgment of the constraints the relationship may have placed on Canadian independence. Nor are Canadians disposed to make their reckoning without taking account of the many positive aspects of the relationship. This accounts for the element of ambivalence that has always been a feature of Canadian policy towards the United States. As the recent foreign policy review puts it, "for the majority of Canadians the aim appears to be to attain the highest level of prosperity consistent with Canada's political preservation as an independent state". The ambivalence has persisted, in essence, because policy choices at either end of the spectrum are likely to involve unacceptable costs to Canadians. To avoid such costs will presumably remain a primary objective of any policy option.

In the third place, it is difficult to make any pronouncement about the impact of the Canada-U.S. relationship on Canadian independence without at least a cursory look at the concept of the "special relationship". The term is not uniquely applied to Canada. Other countries, too, have intermittently used it to describe their relationships with the United States. This is presumably because it has been considered beneficial to enjoy a "special" relationship with the United States.

As far as Canada is concerned, there can be little doubt that the relationship with the United States has been and continues to be special in the sense that it is probably the most articulated relationship between any two countries in the world involving a unique level of mutual interaction, even if unequal in its impact. The intensity of the relationship and perceptions on either side of the border notwithstanding, it has been conducted, by and large, as a normal relationship between two sovereign states. On occasion, however, it has also involved transactions involving special ground rules that have not been extended evenly to other countries.

To the extent that the concept of the "special relationship" reflects an objective reality, it will continue to be valid. To the extent, on the other hand, that it denotes special arrangements between Canada and the United States, its currency is likely to diminish on both sides of the border. In the United States, the perception is gaining ground that the "special relationship" with Canada was an unbalanced relationship, that it involved accommodations in favour of Canada that are no longer tenable in the light of current economic and political realities, and that any restructuring of the "special relationship" would have to proceed on a basis of much more demonstrable equity of benefit to each country. On the Canadian side, there is a concurrent feeling that special arrangements with the United States, for all their acknowledged benefits, may in the end have curtailed our freedom of action, domestically as much as in the realm of foreign policy, and that the cumulative impact of such arrangements taken together carries the risk of locking Canada more firmly into a pattern of continental dependence. This probably does not rule out some special arrangements in future, arrived at selectively on a basis of mutual advantage, but the prospect under anything like the third option would be for a more normal nation-to-nation relationship.

Any discussion of the theme of Canadian independence would not be complete without some judgment as to the realistic parameters of such a discussion itself. It would obviously be absurd to proceed from the assumption that Canada is today substantially deficient in independence. In fact, Canada probably has much more independence than most countries in the modern world and more than many Canadians recognize. There is no denying, on the other hand, that the pervasive span of the linkages between Canada and the United States represents a set of potential constraints on the latitude Canada has in dealing with its national problems. Some of these linkages are immutable; others are susceptible to modification. The real question is to what extent we can look to any policy option to enhance the measure of independence Canadians now enjoy without involving unrealistic, unacceptable and unwarranted costs.

Diversifying interests

The foreign policy review brings the concept of countervailing factors into play. Among these, it instances the active pursuit of trade diversification and technical co-operation with countries other than the United States. The notion that Canada's interests are best served by policies that seek to diversify those interests on a global basis as one means of avoiding excessive reliance on the United States is, of course, not a new one. In one way or another, it has been an explicit assumption behind Canadian support for trade liberalization over the years. If trade liberalization has not contributed significantly, if at all, to our explicit objective of diversification, a less liberal world-trading environment would probably have led to even stronger links between the Canadian and U.S. markets. The fact remains that, with more than two-thirds of our total trade concentrated in the United States, Canada is unique among industrialized countries in having a trading pattern that, by the standard of diversification, is so unbalanced.

This suggests that we should be unrealistic to set our sights too high. There is clearly no possibility of our being able to surmount overnight Canada's heavy dependence on the United States for trade, investment and technology. But there is no reason why we should not aim, in the context of an expanding economy and expanding trade prospects, to achieve relative shifts that, over time, could make a difference in reducing Canada's dependence on a single market and, by extension, the vulnerability of Canada's economy as such. The stronger Canada that might be expected to emerge from the pursuit of such a policy is the objective of the third option. It is eminently clear, however, that for diversification to be achieved, even within the modest scale here suggested, trade policy will need to be harnessed to other policies—such as an industrial-growth strategy and a policy to deal with aspects of foreign ownership —that address themselves to the special factors at play in the North American situation.

There is one final point to be made about Canadian independence. There are those who believe that the growing trend toward regionalism in the world, coupled with the narrowing focus within which the United States may be induced to interpret its national interests in a period of retrenchment, will inevitably increase the continental pull exerted on Canada. Against this, however, it is arguable that, in the world foreshadowed by the Nixon Doctrine—a world in which power is likely to be more diffused and in which United States commitments may be tailored much more closely to resource capabilities and public attitudes in the United States—, the prospect of Canada's achieving its national objectives, domestically and internationally, will be enhanced rather than diminished.

Suggested Reading

There is a very large bibliography on the subject of Canadian foreign policy. The best place to begin is with the many publications of the Canadian Institute of International Affairs, particularly with its badly organized but still indispensable *A Reading Guide to Canada in World Affairs 1945-1971* (1972). The Institute's series, *Canada in World Affairs* has 12 volumes to date covering the years before the Second World War through to the mid-1960s. Additional volumes should be published soon. The CIIA's other main publications are *International Journal*, the best Canadian foreign affairs journal, *Behind the Headlines*, and a *Monthly Report on Canadian External Relations*. All are indispensable. Equally so for the period after 1960 is the *Canadian Annual Review's* section on External Affairs and Defence. Each year's long essay puts the news into perspective, making the *Review* a good beginning point for students.

The Canadian government, of course, publishes a good deal of material on foreign policy. The *Reports* of the Department of External Affairs should be looked at, as well as the series *Canada and the United Nations*. The Department's little newsletter, *External Affairs*, has died and been replaced by *International Perspectives*, a glossier and better publication. For historians, the Department has been publishing volumes in its series, *Documents on Canadian External Relations*, and the publications have now reached the outbreak of war in 1939. Publications of the Department of National Defence have largely stressed campaign histories, but there are white papers, annual reports, books and some monthly publications worthy of investigation. The Canadian Forces *Sentinel* is a monthly publication with occasional articles of interest. Students should also look into Hansard and into the minutes and reports of the House of Commons Standing Committee on External Affairs and Defence. The Senate's similar committee is also worth examination.

For the period before 1945, some good studies include P. E. Corbett and H. A. Smith, *Canada and World Politics* (Toronto, 1928); James Eayrs, *In Defence of Canada*, Vols. I and II (Toronto, 1964, 1965); G. P. de T. Glazebrook, *A History of Canadian External Relations* (Toronto, 1950); and R. A. MacKay and E. B. Rogers, *Canada Looks Abroad* (Toronto, 1938).

James Eayrs, *In Defence of Canada*, Vol. III (Toronto, 1972) must be looked at for the immediate postwar years. So should F. H. Soward and Edgar McInnis, *Canada and the United Nations* (New York, 1956) and J. M. Minifie, *Peacemaker or Powdermonkey* (Toronto, 1960). On Peacekeeping, see J. K. Gordon, ed., *Canada's Role as a Middle Power* (Toronto, 1966) and Alistair Taylor et. al., *Peacekeeping: International Challenge and Canadian Response* (Toronto, 1968). Other books that deserve reading are Andrew Brewin's *Stand on Guard* (Toronto, 1965); Eayrs' *Minutes of the Sixties* (Toronto, 1968) and his other volumes of collected newspaper pieces; Harald von Riekhoff's *NATO: Issues and Prospects* (Toronto, 1967) and R. W. Reford's *Canada and Three Crises* (Toronto, 1968).

Three books have thus far been published on the Trudeau foreign policy review and all are good. Bruce Thordarson's *Trudeau and Foreign Policy: A Study in Decision-Making* (Toronto, 1972) is probably the best, but Colin Gray, *Canadian Defence Priorities* (Toronto, 1972) and Peter Dobell, *Canada's Search for New Roles* (London and

245

Toronto, 1972) are also excellent.

Memoirs of diplomats and statesmen are few, but the late Lester Pearson's *Mike: The Memoirs of the Rt. Hon. Lester B. Pearson,* Vol. 1 (Toronto, 1972) is excellent. Arnold Heeney's *The Things that are Caesar's* (Toronto, 1972) is not much use, nor is Dana Wilgress, *Memoirs* (Toronto, 1967). There is good material in the *Mackenzie King Record,* Vols. I-IV, ed. by J. W. Pickersgill and D. Forster (Toronto, 1960-70); in Roger Graham, *Arthur Meighen,* Vols. I-III (Toronto, 1960-5); and in Henry Borden, ed., *Robert Laird Borden: His Memoirs* (Toronto, 1938).

Soldiers' memoirs are fewer still. General E. L. M. Burns' three books *Between Arab and Israeli* (Toronto, 1962), *Megamurder* (Toronto, 1966) and *A Seat at the Table* (Toronto, 1972) are all useful. Volume III of *McNaughton* by John Swettenham (Toronto, 1969) is also very informative.

There is still very little revisionist foreign policy writing. Two books should be mentioned: John Warnock, *Partner to Behemoth* (Toronto, 1970) and Stephen Clarkson, ed., *An Independent Foreign Policy for Canada?* (Toronto, 1968). The Clarkson collection is much more successful.

3 4 5 6 7 8 9   #131167   76 75 74 73